RAMAYAN
Soul of Indian Civilisation

About the Author

Prof. Ramchandra Mutatkar had his training in Anthropology at Dr. Harisingh Gour Vishwavidyalaya, Sagar, M.P., India, in 1959, as student of Prof. S.C. Dube and Dr. Leela Dube. He worked with Prof. Irawati Karve as Faculty, at the Deccan College Postgraduate and Research Institute, for ten years, till she passed away in 1970. He was the first Head of the Department of Anthropology, and first Director of the Interdisciplinary School of Health Sciences, Savitribai Phule Pune University, Pune. He chaired UGC Panel on Anthropology and Curriculum Development Committee to prepare Model curriculum for UGC in 2001.He has been Chairman of Indian National Confederation and Academy of Anthropologists (INCAA). He is Patron of United Indian Anthropology Forum and Society of Indian Medical Anthropology.

He established an academic institution, 'The Maharashtra Association of Anthropological Sciences' in 1976, and is Emeritus President. Prof. Mutatkar initiated research on social aspects of Leprosy at WHO, Geneva in 1981. He chaired the first working group on AYUSH in Public Health for the XI Five Year Plan. He chaired the first Scientific Behavioural Research Division at the ICMR. He has been a recipient of Tagore National Scholarship bestowed by Ministry of Culture (GoI), affiliated to Anthropological Survey of India.

Prof. Mutatkar has been honoured with 'International Gandhi Award for Leprosy' by Hon. Vice President of India as Chairman of International Jury Board, and 'Adivasi Sevak Puraskar' by Governor of Maharashtra.

His books "AYUSH in Public Health" (2 Volumes, 2016) , "Tribal Health and Malnutrition" (2018), "Sexuality and Sexual Behaviour—Social Science Perspectives" (2019), and "Anthropological Paradigm for Policy and Practice" (2020), have been published by Concept Publishing Co. Pvt. Ltd; New Delhi.

RAMAYAN
Soul of Indian Civilisation

Ramchandra Mutatkar

CONCEPT PUBLISHING COMPANY PVT. LTD.
NEW DELHI - 110059

ISBN: 978-93-5594-658-4 (HB)
ISBN: 978-93-5594-660-7 (PB)

First Published 2023

Published and Printed by

Concept Since 1974

Concept Publishing Company Pvt. Ltd.
A/15-16, Commercial Block, Mohan Garden
New Delhi-110059 (India)
T: +91-11-41101460
E: publishing@conceptpub.com, *W*: www.conceptpub.com

Cataloging in Publication--Courtesy: D.K. Agencies (P) Ltd. <docinfo@dkagencies.com>

Mutatkar, R. K. (Ramchandra Keshav), 1936- **author.**
Ramayan : soul of Indian civilisation / Ramchandra Mutatkar.
pages cm
Includes bibliographical references and index.
ISBN 9789355946584 (HB)
ISBN 9789355946607 (PB)

1. Vālmiki. Rāmāyana. 2. India--Civilization. 3. Hinduism and culture--India. I. Title.

LCC BL1139.26.M88 2023 | DDC 294.5922046 23

"Dedicated to the People of India,
who have kept Indian Civilisation throbbing and
vibrant on the Path of Satyamev Jayate"

Preface

I

This book, "Ramayan: Soul of Indian Civilisation" is not contemplated to merely narrate the biographical journey of Ramchandra, son of Dashrath and Kaushalya, or husband of Sita; the King of Ayodhya, who demolished the mighty Demon-King, Ravan, heralding the victory of *Dharma* over *Adharma*. This book is also not a scholarly treatise about Indian Philosophy, believed to be rooted in Vedas and Upanishads. As a student of Anthropology, this is an attempt to understand the eternal values, which people of India continue to cherish, by referring to Ramayan and enjoying it, as expressed in plural communication and visible forms. Anthropological theory and methods claim to look and understand life, from people's perspective, through their spectacles. The theories have largely evolved, based on the participatory studies of Cultures—ways of life, of geographically isolated communities, generally referred as pre-literate tribal communities. Their geographical domain is small, and history is known, through oral traditions. Being pre-literate, spoken dialects having no script, no written texts are available. The people have their own stories about their origin, about the universe, and about relationships with the living and non-living elements, which we may brand as myths, legends, folkways, expressed through rituals, dance, drama, music etc. Ramayan connects the river valley civilisation having well developed urban centres, with the forest dwelling simple people, who share the universal moral values of truth—Satya and righteous behaviour branded as *Dharma*, in the philosophical texts.

Ramayan is about an ideal human personality, deified subsequently as Divine, and idolized as the deity, being worshipped through the centuries. Sri Ramchandra is invariably referred as '*Maryada Purshottam*'. Ram as a prince, designated to be the king, had to pass through travails, with equanimity; not imaginable by the common people. Although victorious, he does not carry the baggage of tragedies on his mind. As the king, he sacrifices his family well-being, honoring the desires of the people. The masses get enlightenment and their ignorance dispelled, when the truth unfolds, through effective musical communication by the young bards; who happen to be Ramchandra-Sita's sons, neither known to the king, nor to the masses, nor to the children themselves. Some of the universally adored values, emerging from Ramayan, appear to be: *Tyag* (Sacrifice) for the common good; *Satya* (Truth) and *Dharma* (Righteous conduct), including *Raj-Dharma* (duties of the king).

Ramayan in Contemporary Media

Ramayan continues to be popular subject for presentation and discussion, on the visual and print media, also as oral presentations in public halls; besides as conventional *Bhajans*, *Kirtans* in temples. Ramayan written by Tulsidas, is read at the open public places; at the *Chaupal* ground, in several villages in the Hindi belt of India. Ramlila is enacted in almost all the villages. The digital media is also contributing to its dissemination.

The TV serial on Ramayan produced by Ramanad Sagar in Hindi, and projected on Government Television Channel, Doordarshan in 1987, was the highest viewed programme in the world, with 40 mn. viewers on a single day. The same serial recast during coronavirus lockdown period in 2020, on Doordarshan TV Channel, had a single day viewership of 77mn., on 16th April 2020. During this period, the other commercial TV channels were also telecasting the same Ramayan serial. How do we explain this phenomena? The story of Ramayan, about the sequence of events, is known to all the viewers. There is no element of surprise, as in the novels, or other serials and movies. We distinctly remember, the senior parliamentarians in 1987, making a formal request to the Speaker of the Parliament and the Government, to reschedule the timings of the sessions of Parliament, to facilitate to view the serials of Ramayan and Mahabharat, at their residence, if not in the hall of Parliament. Public roads had a deserted look during the period of TV show, as public-voluntary curfew. Usually, curfew is imposed by law enforcement authorities of the government, as an emergency, to control the riots. This public expression or public mind, needs to be explained and analysed, to understand the mass psychology, which sustains the civilisation. Folk songs about marriage ceremonies of Ram and Sita, continue to be very popular marriage songs in Bihar even today.

The natural curiosity is about the sway Ramayan continues to hold over the minds of millions of Indian people, through centuries, expressed and symbolized by way of temples; through art, dance, drama, music, paintings and literature. There are scores of movies and TV serials, in different languages, based on Ramayan. The folkways are linked with the textual writing, what in Anthropology is commonly discussed as 'Great-Little tradition interaction'. Ramayan covers the geographical area which largely coincides with the current territorial nationhood of India. There are thousands of temples with idols of Ram-Sita-Laxman and Hanuman in India; thousands of people bearing the name of Ram and Sita, or as Sitaram, or Ram as suffix or affix to their personal names; several place names of towns and localities, rivers-streams, hills, with the name of Ram. People greet each other with the name of Ram. Ramayan held sway over the saint-poets in India, during medieval times, which prompted them to write their own versions of *Ramayan* in poetic format, based on Valmiki Ramayan. The leaders in contemporary India, such as Swami Vivekananda, Rabindranath Tagore, Mahatma Gandhi, C. Rajgopalachari, S.

Radhakrishnan, have discussed Ramayan, in their discourses and in writings.

This book is an attempt to put together under one cover, Ramayan as history, '*Itihas*', which may have been presented in different forms, over a period of history, in different linguistic regions of India. History is not dead past. History is about the evolution and sustenance of cultural values, about the plural cultures, developing as civilisation. Civilisation is symbolized as the main trunk of Banyan tree, and varied cultures, as its hanging branches, gradually taking firm roots in the soil. The past evolves into the present, providing vision for the future. There may be ups and downs in the history, due to invasions or misrule, to unabashedly collect wealth for comfort. But the mythological leadership emerges like Sri Ram or Sri Krishna, or spiritual leadership like Mahavir, Buddha, Guru Nanak; historical leadership like Mauryan dynasty represented by a scholar-teacher, Chanakya, and warrior Chandragupta, by Ashok; and kings like Chhatrapati Shivaji; or social leaders, like Vivekananda, Gandhi, Tagore, scholar-politician like Tilak; and the saint-poets, who are deified by the people, for their commitment to uphold and reinstate the basic moral values. The universal absolute moral values of *Satya* (Truth) and *Dharma* (Righteous conduct, not religion), have been recognised as the Motto, '*Satyamev Jayate*' (Truth Alone Prevails), of the Republic of India, inscribed in Devnagari script, under the national emblem, an adaptation of the Lion Capital of Ashoka, from Sarnath.

In the process of writing the text of this book, multiple versions of Ramayan have been read. Several books about history of India and the writings of Vivekanada, Tagore, Gandhi, Rajagopalchari and Radhakrishnan, have been referred. But this book by no means is an academic research document. The book is meant for reflection by the common people, about the continuity of moral values, through the history of India, which provides a distinct identity to Indian Civilisation. Ramkatha, no doubt, very interesting, forms the bulk of the book, since people are familiar with the basic story, and keep on discussing the values as symbolized by personalities. They are ever willing and eager, to listen to other variations, and interpretations of the events, as detailed in different versions of Ramayan.

There has been tremendous curiosity among the academic peers, about Ramayan being presented by a student of Anthropology, who is expected to present an ethnographic monograph of a tribal or peasant community, following the traditions of the academic discipline. Ramayan as life history follows the anthropological methodological tool, to document the culture of a group or community. Anthropologists have been discussing Culture, presenting the ethnography of small and isolated communities. There is a conceptual difference between Culture and Civilisation. Anthropologists from the West, the pioneers, with their diverse academic backgrounds, focused on the study of 'other people', and developed meaningful theories. With the gradual waning of colonial intellectual impact, we are planning to discuss our own people, guided by philosophical texts, contributed by plural religious doctrines, sharing the universal absolute values, of humanity. The Indian Civilisation, has evolved and regenerated through history, through the medium of Ramayan, as common people believe it as faith. The soul of Ramayan, as immortal basic values of *Satya* and *Dharma*, has taken several rebirths, including the spiritual and practical guidelines in *Gita*, during Mahabharat. The *Bhakti* literature of the saint poets have contributed to the sustenance of Indian Civilisation.

Anthropology of Epics: Understanding Infrastructure of Indian Civilisation

Ramayan and Mahabharat are the great Indian Epics, branded also as Anthropology of literature. One of the well known classical Anthropologists, Prof. Irawati Karve who worked all her life at the prominent scholastic Deccan College Postgraduate Research Institute, Pune, Maharashtra, India, wrote a book on Mahabharat, titled, 'Yugant' (end of an era). She was honoured with the highest literary Sahitya Akademy Award in Marathi language, for the book, which got translated in several languages. Prof. Irawati Karve's anthropological book, '*Kinship Organisation in India*' is considered a classic on Indian kinship, whereby she has linked the kinship terms in contemporary India to the kinship terms in Ramayan and Mahabharat. She has presented the genealogies of Ayodhya and Janakpur dynasties and has pointed their kinship links. She departed from classical Euro-American anthropology, whereby an anthropologist wrote at least one field-based, ethnographic monograph on a tribal community and/or about a peasant village. Her research has been on the culture region, such as Maharashtra, or about the civilisation, such as about kinship patterns covering the whole country, since epic times, to the current practices.

'*Yugant*' is not merely a literary work, but projects anthropological interpretation of a predominant pastoral society in Mahabharat times. The presentation is of literary style, with occasional subjective feminist expressions.'*Yugant*' has presented Mahabharat by way of depicting the personalities in Mahabharat, such as Draupadi, Kunti, Gandhari, Karna, Vidur, Krishna, and their response to the events. Personalities have been discussed as historically living persons, devoid of any traces of divinity, including about Sri Krishna, not as divinity. Krishna is commonly identified as an incarnation of God Vishnu, after the incarnation as Ram, to establish *Dharma*. As friend-philosopher-guide to the Pandavas, he extricated them from death-traps and rescued Draupadi from public molestation in the presence of her five husbands, elders and King Dhritrashtra. Krishna is identified as the author-narrator of '*Gita*' which is considered as the most important holy treatise of Indian Philosophy, and widely referred internationally. *Gita* was the creation, out of dialogue on the battlefield, between a great warrior but crest-fallen, nervous Arjun, and his mentor Krishna, with an intention to motivate Arjun to fight the battle, to exterminate *Adharma* and establish *Dharma*.

According to Irawati Karve, both Mahabharat and Ramayan focussed around the women, Draupadi and Sita. Mahabharat presented the universal human weakness of greed for power and property. Ramayan presented the ideal values and behaviour, personified as Ram, and the sufferings of a woman, Sita, in a patriarchal kinship society. Ram has been projected as an ideal son, ideal brother, ideal king, ideal friend and an ideal husband, taking pains to fight with the powerful enemy for releasing Sita from captivity, and upholding monogamy, as an ideal marriage pattern, and joint family as an ideal primary kin group. Sita has also been projected as an ideal wife, manifesting as his shadow, caring for him, suffering to uphold the dignity of the husband's dynasty, without complaining about it; and as an ideal mother, rearing children as a single woman. She has also been projected as an empowered and strong woman, with great moral stature. She rejected the patriarchal mindset about the image of women, who would surrender to the opulent lifestyle, offered by those in power. Sita as one of the *Panchkanya*, has been presented as a role model for women, in a patriarchal society, whose resolve resulted in the crash of mighty empire of Ravan. The sway that Ramayan holds over the Indian people, is very widespread, across all sections of society.

II

I had at the back of mind an experience, before coming to Pune in 1960, as a faculty, under the supervision of Irawati Karve. I enrolled for Ph.D. with my teacher, Prof. S.C. Dube, to extend the work on 'Caste Dimensions in a Gwalior village', undertaken as Master's dissertation, at Sagar University in 1959. University Grants Commission (UGC) had just announced first Junior Research Fellowship (JRF) scheme for Ph.D. entrants. We were interviewed at Delhi by a committee chaired by Sir C.P. Ramaswamy Aiyer. Discussing about caste, he asked me about the caste of Ravan. Although familiar with the story of Ramayan, I did not know such details, at that young age. I said, I did not know his caste, but he was a Mahapandit (eminent scholar). He seemed satisfied with my answer, and asked me to start the Ph.D. work. I was selected as one of the 25 JRF fellows of the first batch of JRF of the UGC, across the country, representing all academic disciplines. There is considerable discussion about the Brahmin parentage of Ravan, particularly in Uttarkand of Valmiki Ramayan. There is contradiction about the personality of Ravan, as son of a Brahmin sage, belonging to Demon race, and constantly exhibiting the inflated ego, which caused his downfall.

I felt, that the kind of anthropological analysis of Mahabharat, undertaken by Irawati Karve, was not attempted about Ramayan. This book is an attempt in that direction.

The current book, '*Ramayan: Soul of Indian Civilisation*' has taken into account '*Valmiki Ramayan*' as the standard text, realizing that probably the stories about the origin of Ravan and his ancestors etc. as being told to Ram, in Uttarkand, appear to be appendices added at a later date. About the rejection of patriarchal values, seeking a woman to be always in the dock, and defend her 'purity' or loyalty to husband; Sita going back to Bhumata, Mother-earth, from where she came, we have accepted the version of *Bhavarth Ramayan* in Marathi, written by Sant Eknath. Essentially, we are acknowledging and honoring the continuing faith of common masses of India, about the story of Ramayan, expressing Ram and Sita as inseparable, as Siyaram or Sitaram. Siyavar Ramchandra refers Ramchandra, with his primary identity, as Sita's husband. Anthropological insights refer to the emic perspectives of people, as evolved and continued through historical times, amalgamating the folk literature, art, music, drama, myths and legends with connection to texts, shared by people in the various geographical areas, across the country, revered as sacred geography.

Summary of Chapters

Chapter 1 presents the relevance of Ramayan to be discussed from anthropological perspectives. It takes a broad review of what common people know about the epics and how do they interpret the characters. What do people know about the sacred geography connected with Ramayan and about the saint poets who have kept on writing about the epics. The folk and contemporary media in

India continue to present Ramayan which people seem to enjoy. The tribal connection of Ramayan is very important, culminating in the tribal army of King Sugreev helping Sri Ram in the war, with the use of 'pre-historic' stone tools. Contemporary leaders like Vivekanand, Gandhi, Tagore, and scholars like Radhakrishnan and Rajgopalchari have interpreted Ramayan.

Chapter 2 details the plural versions of *Ramayan* as written in regional languages in India and in the languages in south-east Asian countries. Vivekan and telling the story of Ramayan to Western audience has been presented. However, the essential principles, such as *Dharma* and *Satya* (Truth) are presented in all the versions.

Chapter 3 presents the detailed Ramkatha based on the text of *Valmiki Ramayan*, with some variations of interpretations, given in *Bhavartha Ramayan* written by Sant Eknath in Marathi. Some of the controversial issues like fire-test by Sita, and Ram abandoning her, have been discussed. Empowered Sita rejecting the patriarchal mindset about defilement of women, decided to rejoin her mother-earth, Bhumata.

Chapter 4 discusses the concepts of Soul and *Dharma*, as discussed mainly in *Gita*, and other stories from Upanishad. Culture and Civilisation as basic concepts in Anthropology have been analysed. The quotes have been provided from scholarly books.

Chapter 5 presents Indian Civilisation as analysed by scholars and leaders, giving a brief review of Indian history, and the contributions of religious leaders such as Buddha, Mahavir, Guru Nanak and their distinguished followers like Ashok. Islam taking roots in Indian history through Mughal rule and their contribution to refine Indian Civilisation need more scholastic interpretations. The contributions of Bhakti movement and dissemination of Indian Civilisation to South-East Asia have been briefly presented.

Chapter 6 provides the destination of the basic principles of *Dharma* and *Satya* (Truth) culminating the Indian civilisation, as the Nation, as the Republic of India, with national symbols such as the national flag and national emblem, with motto of *Satyamev Jayate*. The Preamble to the Constitution of India provides the basic values of nationhood, providing the road-map to usher in Ram-Rajya, as envisioned by Mahatma Gandhi.

Particularly, in chapters 5 and 6, long quotations, by way of compilations from the writings of respected leaders, such as Vivekanad, Gandhi, Radhakrishnan, and C. Rajagopalachari etc. have been given, to minimize the interpretations, by the author. Quotes have also been provided from the writings of well-known anthropologists, whose concepts, hypotheses and theories provide the base to the academic advancement of Anthropology.

There are certain tricky issues about the presentations of Indian phonemes in a book in English language. *Valmiki Ramayan* has been written in Sanskrit language. There are several words having a cultural meaning which could not be translated in the English lexicon, the meaning in the English dictionary being entirely different. The word *Dharma* means religion in English. However, in Sanskrit and Indian languages, it refers to righteous conduct, varying in time, space and social roles, played by people on various occasions. *Rajdharma* becomes a special category referring to the duties of those in-charge of governance, who would not show any discrimination or favour to even the nearest kin. Such words have been freely used, presented in italics, the meanings given in glossary. The spellings of certain words, or as they are used and pronounced, in different linguistic regions of India, such as *Yag, Yajnya* or *Yadnya* are varied. The English keyboards of the computers have different variations, such as Indian or American, which provide slightly varying spellings. Similarly, the personal names or designations used by different authors are also slightly different, such as Asok and Ashok. The Nishad king is referred Guha or Guhak. Ayodhya chief administrator or Minister is named Sumant. The spelling of Vashishta also varies, according to pronunciations in south, east and north India. In English language, invariably, the letter 'a' is added, such as, it is always 'Rama' or 'Laxmana', while the Indians pronounce in spoken expression as 'Ram' or 'Laxman'. In various chapters, there may appear minor repetitions, caused due to linking the context with the text. Vivekanand narrated the story of Ramayan to foreign audience in the year 1900. Luv-Kush sang Ramayan on the streets of Ayodhya and again in the Court of Sri Ramchandra in his presence. The style of narration and the focus of events had to be presented, albeit the narration being slightly repetitive. However, the readers would kindly ignore such minor variations and repetitions in the text. Even in one textual or literary language, there are several spoken dialects. *Ramcharitmanas* by Tulsidas is written in Avadhi dialect. Such issues form the subject matter of the science of Linguistics, which has been a sub-branch of Anthropology.

Similarly, the concepts such as Soul, *Dharma*, Truth, Sacrifice, which have been discussed in Vedas and Upanishads with illustration in Puranas, in Ramayan and Mahabharat, have been discussed by great social, political and spiritual leaders and thinkers, like Vivekanand, Gandhi, Tagore, Radhakrishnan, Rajagopalachari, in their writings. Concepts of Culture and Civilisation, particularly about Indian Civilisation, have been discussed by Indologist such as Basham, and other reputed anthropologists like Mandelbaum. It has been considered more appropriate to present the literature review by way of quotes from the writings of such luminaries, particularly, in Chapters 4 and 5, instead of paraphrasing their ideas in our words.

I express my affectionate gratitude to my son, Madhusudan, a senior Army Officer in the Indian Army, who pointed out that the principles of posting formations of battalions at the gates of Lanka, directed by *Senapati* (General) Ramchandra, heading Sugreev army, continue to be referred in contemporary conventional wars. His brief write-up about these principles have been presented in the section on *Yuddhakand*. Sri Ashok Mittal of Concept Publishing Co. (P) Ltd., New Delhi, discussed and encouraged me to write such a book, about three years back, and exercised patience over the delay of my presentation of the manuscript. I am deeply grateful to him. Smt. Sharvari Nisal helped me with computer applications in finalising the typescript for publication.

I feel indebted to the common people of India whose faith and respect for *Ramayan* has been evident as seen on the visual, print and social media. As a student of Anthropology, it becomes our bounden duty to grasp the spirit of their faith and feelings, which sustains Indian Civilisation. Sri Ramchandra had appreciated the minuscule contribution by a squirrel, made towards the construction of Ramsetu. It would be satisfying to be a squirrel, to contribute to reconstruct the march of Indian civilisation. The Ramayan motivates us to make an honest attempt to understand Indian Civilisation, in a holistic and integrative perspective, claiming to network the emic-etic approaches in Indian Anthropology.

Due to time constraint, and lack of secretarial assistance, the Hindi and Marathi translations to be attempted by the author, are getting delayed. One feels apologetic on that count, which would be rectified in the near future.

Ramchandra Mutatkar

Contents

Glossary

Arati: Waving a sacred lamp, around the face of a person, deity, or in veneration of sacred rivers like Ganga, Narmada; a plant, like holy basil, by way of worship.

Adharma: Violating the established social norms and values, amounting to committing a sin.

Adyakavi: The first poet in the world, referring to Sage Valmiki.

Agni: Fire, usually referred to as sacred fire.

Agnidivya: Ordeal equivalent to going through blazing fire.

Agnihotra: A ritual in honour of Sun-God, by way of a small *Homa* or *Yag*, by offering ghee and rice grains to fire, in a small copper pot, at household level, while chanting Vedic *Mantras*.

Agnipariksha: An allegory of purificatory test of gold undertaken by a goldsmith Alha and Udan.

Amatya: Refers to the position of Prime-minister of Magadh King, Dhananand, followed by Chandra Gupta period.

Amrit: Nectar of immortality.

Antratma: Inner voice, from the heart.

Apsara: Celestial nymph.

Aranyakand: Period in *Ramayan*, spent by Ram-Sita-Laxman in the forest.

Arthshastra: A book on political economy and governance, written by Chanakya.

Ashok-van/ vatika: Royal garden in Lanka where Sita was kept in captivity.

Ashram: Hermitage of sages.

Ashvamedh Yagnya/Yag: Ritual of horse sacrifice as a symbol of sovereignty by kings in ancient times.

Astra: Weapon, may be of divine origin, or sacred weapon.

Atharva Ved: One of the four Vedas, like Rigved, Yajurved and Samved.

Atma: Soul.

Avatar: Incarnation of God such as Vishnu as Krishna.

Baisakhi: Harvest festival in Punjab, Sikh new year day, usually on 13/14 April.

Bajrangbali and *Maruti*: Hanuman referred with these names also.

Bal Kaandam, Ayodhya Kaandam, Aranya Kaandam, Kishkindha Kaandam, Sundara Kaandam, Yuddha Kandam and Uttar Kaandam : Names of chapters in Valmiki Ramayan detailing the biographical period of Sri Ram.

Bhabhi: Kinship term to refer/address elder brother's wife.

Bhagwad-Gita: Commonly referred as 'Gita', referring to counselling dialogue between Lord Krishna and Arjun on the battlefield of Kurukshetra, during Mahabharat war.

Bhajan/Kirtan: Devotional songs.

Bhakti: Devotion as disciple of the divine.

Bharat-Bhet: Refers to memorable embrace of Sri Ram and brother Bharat discussing *Dharma* and *Rajdharma.*

Bharatratna: Highest Civilian Honour bestowed by Government of India.

Bhavarth Ramayan: Ramayan written by Sant Eknath in Marathi.

Bhumata/Bhumi-Mata : Mother-earth.

Brahmacharya/Brahmacharyashram : Period of celibacy in the life cycle of a Hindu.

Brahma-Rishi: Hindu Sage with highest moral stature.

Brahmastra: Most lethal weapon blessed by Lord Brahma.

Chakravyuha: A specific battle formation to trap the warriors in war used in Mahabharat war.

Chandala: A traditional term to refer to untouchable caste groups or individuals.

Chandan: Sandlewood.

Chandravansha: Of Lunar dynasty.

Chaupal: A common meeting place in a village for village meetings or meetings of caste groups in Hindi belt.

Chhatra: A decorated umbrella, held over the head as a mark of respect.

Chudamani: An ornamental hair clip of women.

Dakshina: A sacred gift in currency to the presiding priest, performing rituals.

Danav: Demon.

Dev: Celestial bodies referred to as gods or demi-gods.

Dandakaranya: Forest covering present-day forested area in Odisha, Chhattisgarh, Madhya Pradesh and North Maharashtra.

Darbar: Formal court of the Kings.

Darbha: Sacred grass used as offering to idols or during sacred rituals.

Dargah: A muslim shrine or tomb built over the grave of a respected person or saint, usually associated with Sufi. A muslim pilgrimage centre.

Daridranarayan: Mahatma Gandhi referred to poor or poverty-stricken people, as part of divinity, who needed to be served with compassion.

Dashanan: Ravan, with ten heads.

Dhanurvidya: Training about expert use of bow and arrow.

Dharma: Righteous conduct, as per cultural patterns and social norms.

Dharmashastra: Approved behaviour and customs as per texts about traditional law.

Doordarshan: Government of India Television Channel.

Dussera: Also known as Vijayadashmi, an auspicious Hindu festival connected with Mother Goddess, also linked with Mahabharat war. The effigies of Ravan, Kumbhakarna, and Meghnad are burned as public event.

Galit-kushta: An Ayurvedic term referring to leprosy.

Gandharva: Celestial musician.

Geet-Ramayan: Ramkatha lyrics composed by a Marathi Poet G.D. Madgulkar.

Ghar: A bird, Hawk.

Gitarahasya: A book in Marathi about critical commentary on *Gita* written by Bal Gangadhar Tilak.

Godbharai: A social ritual focusing on a pregnant woman with gifts of good food and other presents, promoting her physical and mental health.

Gram Swarajya or *Panchayati Raj:* A term used by Mahatma Gandhi for self rule by the villagers, now statutorily termed as Panchayati Raj.

Grihasthashram: Period of life as married householder, in the life cycle ; supporting children, parents and spiritual persons, not members of any family.

Guhak: Chieftain of *Kevats* (Boatmen) and *Nishad*, expert tribal hunting group.

Guru/ Gurudev/Guruji: Traditional term for teacher.

Gurdwaras: Sikh temple.

Gurukul Ashrams: Hermitage as schools, headed by a sage-teacher.

Hanuman Jayanti: Birthday of Hanuman.

Hanuman-Chalisa: Devotional hymns in veneration of Hanuman, written by Tulsidas.

Hanuvati: Lower jaw.

Hindu: Religious faith followed by majority of Indians.

Homa-Hava: Sacred fire ignited for performing rituals of worship.

Hutamta: Martyr.

Indra-astra: Divine weapon blessed by Indra.

Itihas: History.

Jai Ramjiki: Way of verbal salutation.

Jana: People. Refers to tribal people in Ramayan.

Janasthan: Habitation area of tribal communities, in Ramayan

Janjati: Term for tribal communities.

Jatak tales: Buddhist tales about the births of Buddha.

Jauhar-Mela : Pageantry with tableaus on a particular day, in memory of women in the royal fort of Chittorgarh in Rajasthan, who sacrificed their lives in historical times, to protect their dignity, from the invading enemy army by jumping in fire.

Jivatma: Soul of living being.

Jus ad bellum: Traditional regulations to govern the conduct of warfare, e.g. no war after sunset in *Ramayan* and *Mahabharat.*

Jyotirling: Shiva temple recognized for pilgrimage.

Kamandalu: A special pot made of metal or special wood carried by spiritual mendicants used for collecting food, given by people.

Kanya: Refers to girls usually in the pre-puberty stage.

Karkidakam: Name of month as per Malayalam calendar.

Karma: Duty as prescribed by social norm.

Karmayoga: Performimg duties as a sacred act.

Kathopanishad: One of the prime Upanishad.

Kavad: Two wooden or bamboo baskets hanging from a wooden stick, balanced on a shoulder.

Kheer: Rice gruel cooked in milk, also known as *Payasam.*

Krounch: Bird called as Crane.

Kshatriya: Belonging to the warrior class as per Indian Varna classification.

Kshatriya-dharma: Assigned traditional duties to protect country and people from enemies and punish the wrong doers.

Kul: Lineage, Dynasty.

Kumbh Mela: A sacred congregation of people at designated river sites, for a dip in the holy river, in celebration of elixir drops from a divine pot dropping and purifying the river waters.

Laxmanrekha: Protective line drawn by Laxman around the hut, for safety of Sita.

Lokpal: A governance position overseeing the welfare of people.

Mahapandit: Eminent scholar.

Maharshi: Senior sage.

Mahasati: A woman of great moral and spiritual strength.

Mantras: Sacred hymns.

Mantri: Minister in the government.

Maryada Purshottam: Ideal human being, not defiling the moral-ethical behavioural norms.

Ma-Mata: Mother.

Mauli: Mother, generally referring to motherhood of large number of people.

Maya: Illusion, Hallucination.

Moha: Intense affection.

Moksha: Merger with the soul of God, Freedom from the cycle of birth and rebirth.

Mudrika: A ring with personal, distinct identity.

Muhurta: An auspicious day and time to perform an important activity.

Mul Nakshtra: Refers to inauspicious planetary constellation at birth.

Nasika: Nose in Sanskrit language.

Paduka: Wooden footwear with distinct identity of a person.

Panchkanya: Five ideal women in Hindu mythology: Ahilya (Sage Gautam's wife), Tara (Harishchandra's wife), Sita (Ram's wife), Mandodari (Ravan's wife) and Draupadi (wife of five Pandavas).

Panchmahabhuta: Five natural elements of which the Universe is composed of.

Panchtantra: Indian folk stories of wisdom, used for training of young princes.

Parampara: Traditional customs, norms and behaviour.

Pariwar Dharma: Family norms and customs.

Parmatma: God, Supreme Spirit.

Patal-Lok: Underground world, usually the residence of evil spirits and demons.

Pati-dharma: Traditional patterns of behaviour and duties, as husband.

Paurânika: Referring to ancient past.

Prasad: Sacred gift from divinity, usually after prayers to God.

Potli: Objects tied in a piece of cloth, used as a bag.

Prabhu: Referring or addressing the God.

Praja: Citizens.

Pratyancha: Bow-string.

Prithvi: Earth.

Puranas: Stories of ancient legends about Gods. Deities and sages.

Purnima: Full moon day.

Purushartha: Four ends of life: *Dharma* (Righteousness), *Arth* (Livlihood), *Kama* (Sensuality), *Moksha* (Freedom from birth-rebirth).

Pushpak viman: Name of flying chariot-aircraft of Lanka.

Pushya naksatra: One of the 27 planetary constellations in Indian astronomy. Considered particularly auspicious if coinciding on Thursday.

Putrakameshti yagnya: A ritual performed with Homa-Havan, for begetting children.

Raghukul parampara: Traditions of Raghu dynasty.

Rajdharma: Duties of the King towards the citizens.

Raj-Guru: Spiritual head of the kingdom; Consultant to the King.

Raksha: To protect, defend the people.

Rakshas: Demons.

Rakshsini: Demoness.

Ram Nam Satya Hai, Satya Bolo Satya Hai: Ram represents, nothing but Truth. So speak the truth by repeating Ram's name.

Ram-Ban: Hundred per cent/sure-shot.

Ramcharitmanas: Name of the book on Ramayan written by Sant Tulsidas.

Ram-Dhun: Mahatma Gandhi's evening prayer.

Ramkatha: Biographical story of *Ramayan.*

Ramlila: Ramkatha dramatized at the local, village level, by local actors.

Ram-Mandir: Temple with idols of Sri Ram, Sita, Laxman and Hanuman.

Ram-nadi: A river or a stream in the name of Ram.

Ram-tekdi: A hill in the name of Ram.

Ram-navmi: The birth anniversary of Ram.

Ram-Rajya: An ideal or utopian governance of the kingdom.

Ramsetu: Name of the bridge constructed by Ram-Sugreev army connecting Dhanuskodi and Lanka.

Ravan-Dahan: Refers to burning the effigy of Ravan on Dusserah.

Rishi-Muni: Refer to Sage.
Sabala: Name of the powerful, sacred cow of Sage Vashishta.
Sadachar: Good behaviour.
Sadhus-Sanyasi: Spiritual Hindu god-men.
Sahitya: Literature.
Samavaya eva sadhuh: Refers to concord of religions that is meritorious.
Sanjeevani: Life saving herb.
Sankat-Vimochan: Hanuman is referred as remover of hurdles.
Sant: Saint.
Sanyas: Fourth stage in Hindu life cycle; total renunciation as Monk.
Sati: A pious, morally and spiritually strong woman.
Satva, Raja, Tama : Refer to attitude of mind. Also discussed in Ayurved as personality types, and with diet patterns. Even Varna and Caste personality chacteristics are linked.
Satya: Truth.
Satyam, Shivam, Sundaram: Refer to supreme values of Truth, Goodness and Beauty.
Satyamev Jayate: Truth Alone Prevails; The motto of Republic of India.
Satyanarayan Pooja: Worship of Vishnu, for getting rid of woes. Recommended ritual performance on full Moon day.
Sena: Army.
Senapati: Chief of Army.
Shabdbhedi: Hitting the target in the direction of sound.
Shakuntal: A literary play written by Kalidas about the legendary love story of Shakuntala and King Dushyant.
Shankhanad: Blowing the conch-shell.
Shapath: Oath.
Shāstras: Texts written by Sages on various subjects.
Shivling: Faceless symbol of Lord Shiva as an object of worship.
Shloka: A hymn set to the rhythmatic musical composition.
Shudra varna: Occupational groups supplementing and helping peasantry put in one category called as Varna.

Sita Mata ki jai, Siyavar Ramchandra ki jai: Hailing Mother Sita and Sita's husband Ramchandra.

Sita-ki-Rasoi: Sita's kitchen in Valmiki ashram where she cooked food.

Sita-Mai: Mother Sita.

Sita Ram/Siya Ram: Ram addressed as Sita's husband.

Suryavansha: Solar dynasty of kings.

Swadesh: An advocacy Hindi movie about returning back of non-resident Indian to serve the motherland.

Swaraj: Self Rule as a free and independent country.

Swayamvar: Ceremony whereby a bride publicly chooses her life partner.

Tantra: Technique.

Tantric: An expert technologist.

Tirdi: A kind of open coffin, made of bamboo, to carry the dead body, usually lifted by four persons on their shoulders.

Treta yug: Second divine era when Ram was born. Lord Krishna was born in Dwapar era.

Trilok: Refers to three habitation sites, Heaven for the celestials, Earth for the Humans and other living beings, and *Patal* underground for the devils.

Tyag: Sacrifice.

U, nou lake: Lake created as per legend, currently located on the border of Maharashtra and Gujarat.

U, Nou?: Shall I take bath?

Upnayan: The sacred thread ceremony for the three Varnas.

Upnishadas: Concluding philosophical texts concluding the Vedas

Vaidya: Ayurvedic Physician-Surgeon.

Vairagya, Virakti: Feeling and behaviour commensurate with renunciation.

Vaishya varna: Third Varna occupational group of merchants and traders.

Vajra: Fatal, powerful weapon of Indra.

Vak patutvam: Expert communicator.

Vanaprasthashram: Third stage in individual life cycle, denoting retirement from householder duties.

Vanwas: Refers to punishment to live in the forest, leading a hard life.

Varna-Caste: Socio-economic stratification in Indian social organisation.

Varnashram: Indian Social organization guiding the individual life cycle and social groups.

Varnashram Dharma: Assigned duties as per individual life cycle and social position.

Vastushant: Ritual house-warming as prayers to Divinity to protect the inmates of the house.

Vayu: Wind god.

Vedant: Pursuit of knowledge as in Vedas and Upanishads.

Veena: A sacred musical instrument, traditionally associated with Sarasvati, goddess of learning.

Yag, Yajnya or Yadnya: Terms used for Homa-Havan with ritual offerings of ghee and rice, while chanting sacred hymns.

Yaksha: Nature spirits, usually residing in trees, hills, lakes, rivers. Majority of them are benevolent.

Yama-Lok: Abode of Lord of Death.

Yatras or *Urus:* Fairs as regional or local sacred pilgrimage centres on specific days or weeks, visited by all religious groups in India.

Yoga-Vashistha: Text of philosophical orientation of Ram-Laxman by Sage Vashishta.

Yuvraj: Crown-Prince.

1
Introduction

Anthropology as an academic discipline is the 'Holistic and Integrated Science of Man', which in common parlance is known as an exclusive discipline of tribal studies. Anthropology is also considered as history, interested in unravelling the mystery of biological evolution of Man, the *Homo sapien*, and the resultant cultural evolution of human institutions. Human societies across the world manifest uniformities in human behaviour, expressed as 'psychic unity of mankind', as also plural cultures, expressed as bio-cultural diversities. The concepts of Culture and Civilisation have developed to analyse these phenomena.

In the University system in India, anthropology as a knowledge system is projected as originating from the studies of isolated communities with 'queer customs', initiated by the Western scholars. The anthropological thought of understanding Man and his philosophy, his works in a civilisation like that of India, has been in existence in the texts of antiquity. We have the discussions in '*Arthshastra*' by Chanakya. Charvak, Vatsayan's *Kamsutra*, Kalidas; Charak, Sushrut and Vagbhat and several others have discussed human behaviour, in varying contexts. During Golden Jubillee celebrations in 2011, 'Anthropological Society' discussed Vivekanand, Bankim Chandra Chatterjee, Tagore, Gandhi, Ambedkar and Jyotiba Phule as alternative voices in anthropology.

Gandhiji's attire from three piece suit in South Africa as a pleader, to loin cloth in India, and local living style in Sevagram *ashram* at Wardha, is how we identify ourselves, when we live in a tribal hut, with a tribal family and their cattle. We 'go native' to understand their perspectives, as Gandhiji tried to understand *Daridranarayan*, which culminated into his famous talisman about the philosophy of working for the people. (Mutatkar, 2020: 17-18).

How do we understand India, that is Bharat, in this context? What kinds of uniformities, pluralities and diversities are seen in India, and how have they evolved, sustained or have undergone change, over the centuries? Common people have a vague perception that we have to understand the *Vedas*, *Upanishads*, *Puranas*, *Bhagwad Gita*, and the epics like *Ramayan* and *Mahabharat*, to understand Indian Civilisation, as it has evolved, and continues its distinct identity. Common people find it difficult to understand the abstract thoughts and discussions, as given in the *Vedas* and *Upanishads*, as also given in the religious texts of other religions.

However, people have heard of the names of sages, and the legends associated with them. People also see and visit thousands of temples, across India and also in the eastern and south-eastern Asia, and are aware about the kings who constructed these architectural marvels, which reveal the knowledge of basic sciences and technology in ancient India. There are thousands of monuments, seen as forts or palaces, which appear desolate and abandoned, each having its own history. There is pan-Indian and local history about shrines, rivers, trees, hills, animals and birds, which continues through rituals, ceremonies and festivals. All the abstract knowledge in the ancient scriptures, and visible symbols, associated with history, spread over the geography of Indian sub-continent, together constitute Indian Civilisation. People live pursuing their customary cultural practices in various social groups, mostly common in different religious communities in India. They cherish similar attitudes and values which are expressed in life cycle rituals, pilgrimages; paying homage to their ancestors; to social and religious leaders from the historical past, who helped to construct and continue the national identity and self-esteem of India. There are academic disciplines in the Universities such as Anthropology, Archaeology, Linguistics, Indology, Ancient History, Literature, and several sub-disciplines, which try to unravel the evolution and continuation of Indian Civilisation.

Anthropological Understanding of Ramayan

The anthropological curiosity about Ramayan, is prompted by the ground reality, as to how and why the millions of people of India, are so much devoted to Ram. There are literally, thousands of temples in India, called as *Ram-Mandir*, which have the idols of Ram, Sita, Lakshman and Hanuman, as deities. The birth anniversary of Ram, known as *Ram-navmi* is celebrated as a national festival, with gaiety. At 12 noon, Ram as baby is put in a cradle, singing the lullabies. Thousands of people throng at the Ram temples to celebrate the birth ceremony.

In almost all cities and villages, *Ramlila* is dramatized for about ten days ending with burning the effigies of Ravan, Kumbhkarna and Meghnad on *Dussera*, a sacred day as per Hindu calendar. This day, Ravan was killed by Ram, ending the war, for liberation of Sita, from his captivity. Actually, Kumbhakarna as ferocious brother and Meghnad as devoted, warrior son, who had defeated Indra, had admonished King Ravan for kidnapping Sita by deceit, and counselled to send her back to Ram, with dignity. However, despite their advice being ignored by Ravan, they decided to fight the war, pledging loyalty to Ravan as King, and Ravan as head of the family. So, unlike Bibhishan, they tacitly became the accomplices on the side of *Adharm*. At several places now, particularly in small towns, only Ravan's effigy is burnt, which is termed as Ravan-*Dahan.*

At Delhi, there is *Ramlila* ground where *Ramlila* (*Ram Katha* enacted in a dramatic format) is played for ten days. Several times, the President, Vice-President and the Prime Minister of India or one of them, have been present on the last day of *Ramlila*, while the effigies of Ravan, Kumbhakarna and Meghnad are burnt, symbolising victory of truth over evil. The response of the national leaders, holding high office, to the public mind, is a testimony of acknowledging the faith of the people, about Sri Ram and his journey of life, that is, Ramayan. As commonly known, *Ramlila* is played in thousands of towns and villages, across the country, the local citizens acting the roles of Ramayan characters. This has been depicted nicely in a prominent Hindi movie, '*Swadesh*'.

There are hundreds of books on Ramayan in different languages, with slight variations in local or regional versions, without vitiating from the main story of Ram being exiled to forest, kidnapping of Sita, *Ram-setu*, Ram-Ravan war, with assistance of Sugreev army, and *Ram-Rajya*. There continue to be presentations and discussions about *Ram Katha* on various platforms about the various facets of Ramayan, by well-known god-men, *sadhus*, *sanyasis* and accomplished orators and authors, linking Ramayan events to contemporary issues, including to war strategies and diplomacy.

Valmiki Ramayan written in Sanskrit language is considered the standard version of Ramayan. Sage Valmiki not only documented the story of Sri Ram as an ideal personality, but became a participant in the life journey of Sri Ram, when Sita landed in his *Ashram* during her pregnancy. Sons, Luv and Kush were born in the *Ashram*, were trained by Valmiki in the art of living, and as expert warriors. They challenged the *Ashwamedh Yagnya* launched by Ram as a symbol of declaration of Ayodhya as the Sovereign Empire. Luv and Kush defeated Ram's army, and compelled King Ram to present himself, face-to-face with them, in battle format, in Valmiki *ashram*. They were aspiring to seek explanation from Sri Ram, as to why he abdicated his wife Sita, although he had liberated her, from the captivity of Ravan, after punishing him with death, in a great war. At young age, they became the seekers of truth. Luv-Kush had no knowledge then, that they were the sons of Ram-Sita.

Valmiki could reunite Ram, Sita and Luv-Kush, to complete Ram's family. He popularised the story of Ram, written in poetic format, which was set to music and sung by Luv-Kush, not only on the streets of Ayodhya, as young bards, but also in the Court of King Ram, as an entertainment event, associated with *Ashwamedh yagnya*.

This musical rendering of Ramayan by children, dispelled the gossip about 'defilement' of Sita in the captivity of Ravan, prevalent in Ayodhya, based on hearsay. In Maharashtra, a well-known poet, G.D. Madgulkar has written the lyrics in Marathi, as sung by Luv-Kush as "*Geet-Ramayan*". Another well-known music director and vocalist, Sudhir Phadke simultaneously rendered these lyrics into music, which has been very popular in Maharashtra. Hundreds of live performances of musical concerts by Sudhir Phadke were presented, in his life time, which are now continued by his singer son, to record audiences.

The bards singing mythological stories and philosophical messages, continue as the cultural practice by professional bards, who are recognized, respected and fed by the people in rural India. They are a part of rural social organisation. Nowadays, the rural bards also make trips to metropolitan area and sing the traditional compositions, on the streets, even in high profile suburbs. They are also visible in the railway trains singing traditional sacred compositions. They are not treated as beggars. People on their own give them donations/alms for their living.

Taking *Valmiki Ramayan* as the standard version, Ramayan has been retold by several authors in different Indian and foreign languages, with slight local variations and subjective interpretations, about Ram's abdication of Sita, after liberating her from Ravan's captivity. Winning a war against mighty Ravan has not been interpreted only as success of war craftsmanship, but indicated the success of moral values, against immoral evil designs, such as, to conquer the world, collect booty and molest women.

Ramayan reaffirms the age-old universal value that 'Truth shall always Prevail'. This universal value, constantly being referred from Ramayan, reinforced in *Mahabharat*, transmitting through history of India, has developed and sustained Indian Civilisation.

How do we reflect and interpret Ramayan which holds sway over the minds of Indians, through centuries? Despite criticism, mainly on the elite or feminist platforms, about Ram abandoning Sita, while she was pregnant, the masses of India do not separate

Ram and Sita, and the temples are invariably with the idols of Ram-Sita, Lakshman and Hanuman. Why? The common expression or victory slogan such as "*Siya-Ramchandra-ki-Jay*" or "*Siya-var-Ramchandra-ki-Jay*" refer to Sri Ram as *Sita Ram* or *Siya Ram*, as Sita's husband. Sri Ram is never referred as a single person, but always as *Siya Ram*. Sitaram is a common personal name of thousands of persons across the country.

Ramayan: Present Context

According to Jawaharlal Nehru:

"The two great epics of ancient India—The Ramayana and the *Mahabharat*—probably took shape in the course of several hundred years. . . . I do not know of any books anywhere which have exercised such a continuous and pervasive influence on the mass mind as these two. Dating back to a remote antiquity, they are still a living force in the life of the Indian people. . . . Most of the myths and stories are heroic in conception and teach adherence to truth and the pledged word, whatever the consequences, faithfulness unto death and even beyond, courage, good works and sacrifice for the common good." (1991: 99-101)

According to Vivekanand, "In fact, Ramayan and *Mahabharat* are the two great encyclopaedia of the ancient Aryan life and wisdom, portraying an ideal civilisation which humanity yet to aspire after." (Deshpande, Aruna, 2005: 74)

Ramayan

What about the epic, *Ramayan*, as a subject matter of Anthropology? People know that Ram, Sita and Lakshman lived in the tribal belt of Dandakaranya for 13 years during their exile, until Sita was abducted by Ravan from the present day Nashik town in Maharashtra, what was then a forest village, on the bank of Godavari river. It is widely believed that the name Nashik owes to the episode in Ramayan, whereby the nose (*nasika*) of Ravan's sister, Shurpankha was chopped off by Lakshman, when she attacked Sita. Nashik district continues to be the habitat of several tribal communities, and the city houses the head office of the Tribal Commissioner of Maharashtra State. Since anthropology is perceived in popular mind as an academic discipline prioritising the studies of tribal communities, living in geographical isolation, the issue is to introspect about Ramayan as a subject matter of Indian Anthropology.

Why do the common people in India dote upon Ramchandra as divinity, while he did not exhibit any miracles, but suffered whole life, while performing his duties as prince, as son, as husband, as king, and now branded as an ideal human being (*Maryada Purshottam*). The biographical journey of Ramchandra called as Ramayan, is variously referred as mythology, as history, as fiction, as poetry, and as an epic. Why Ramayan is enacted as a play, not in a theatre, but on open spaces in thousands of towns and villages in India, by the volunteered actors from the audience community?

As a student of Anthropology, focusing on India, why should there be an urge to delve into the great epic of Ramayan, which is also analysed as history, sacred geography or a combination of both? Ramayan is presented in paintings, dance, drama, sculpture, literature, movies, TV serials and all forms of visual and print media. There are thousands of temples with idols of Ram, Sita, Lakshman and Hanuman, across the country. There are Valmiki *ashrams*, at least, at five places where Ram-Sita's sons, Luv-Kush were believed to be born, and reared by Sita, under the patronage of sage Valmiki. There may be more than a million people having personal names from Ramayan, as Ramchandra, also with affix or suffix with Ram; names of females as Sita, Vaidehi, Mithila, Maithilee, Janaki; or as Lakshman, as Maruti etc. There are several towns and localities, named as Ramnagar, streams as *Ram-nadi,* hills as *Ram-tekdi* and so on, with the legends about connection with events in Ramayan.

Ramayan written in all Indian languages, as also in south-east Asian countries, have marginal regional variations about the details. Some of them have ended Ramayan with the killing of Ravan, and is interpreted as the end of Vishnu's incarnation as Ram, which was meant to destroy the cruelties of powerful demon-king Ravan.

However, Gurudev Tagore said that, "Divinity had not descended in the form of man, but in Ram, the man had risen to the level of divinity, by following and establishing the ideal human values".

Krishna in *Mahabharat* knew that he was an incarnation of Lord Vishnu, and had a distinct purpose to re-establish *Dharma,* which was too much vitiated, exemplified by such forces as Kamsa, Jarasandh, Duryodhan and Dushasan. The *adharm* (injustice) by Kauravas were tolerated by distinguished family elders like Bhisma and teachers like Dronacharya, for which they deserved to be vanquished, as advocated by Krishna to Arjun, what is generally referred as *Karmayog* in *Gita*. Kishna's biography exhibits miracles, since birth, associated with divine powers, unlike that of Rama.

In *Mahabharat*, the personality deified by the common people is that of Krishna, who was a mentor and kin of Pandavas, but did not take up the arms in the war. As the charioteer of Arjun, he gave guidance to boost up the morale of the Pandavas, who were brave, but could not match the machinations of Kauravas, conspired by their mother's brother, Shakuni.

In Ramayan, the kins are not involved, as in *Mahabharat*, save the palace politics of step mother, Kaikeyi, which heaped personal tragedies on Sri Ram and Sita. In fact, Bibhishan, a demon; Sugreev, referred as monkey, and Guhak, as Chieftain of *Kevats* (Boatmen) and *Nishad*, expert tribal hunting group, have been given the status of brother by Sri Ram. Hanuman, a monkey, is addressed as son by Sita. Basically, there is fight between the evil forces, practising *Adharma* and forces of justice, trying to punish the culprits, and establish *Dharma.*

Ramayan presents the ideal values, presenting Ram as an ideal son, ideal brother, ideal administrator, brave warrior, supporting the marginalised, irrespective of their social status in the prevailing *varna*—caste-based social structure. He has been portrayed as an ideal husband, as a protector of women, not showing any trace of sexual desires, beyond the natural instinct of biological reproduction. He must have been the monogamous king, when having multiple wives and concubines was an established norm for the ruling kings. His brothers also followed the value and practice of monogamy. In a patriarchal society, the citizens of Ayodhya, in Ramayan times, could never internalise monogamy as a moral value. Being loyal to a single woman, throughout life would be considered as masculine weakness, rather than a virtue. Such a person in patriarchal gossip could be taunted as a 'slave' of a woman, under her spell; as King Dashrath was branded, under the spell of Kaikeyi, by Ayodhya citizens. From the women's perspective, in patriarchal society, monogamy is a great virtue. Sita appreciated this virtue of Ram and respected him despite her abandonment. She accepted the tragedy of desertion with equanimity, imposed on her by the patriarchal and dominant male citizens of Ayodhya. She appreciated Ram's love for her, expressed in his refusal to replace Sita with another woman, as the Queen of Ayodhya. Ram as King sacrificed the mutual love of husband and wife, as individuals, to uphold the impersonal judgment against himself and Sita, while balancing it with rebutting a suggestion, to bring another woman in his life. The gossiping public of Ayodhya had anticipated remarriage by Ram, as a ritual requirement for performing *Ashwamedh Yagnya*. The priests supervising the religious rituals recommended King to have the Queen for the sacred rituals and for sharing the throne, as mother figure. Ram as a king could not summarily dismiss the widespread gossip about Sita's 'defilement' in Ravan's custody. But he firmly rejected proposals to have another wife for him. Issue of recommended ritual requirement as suggested by *Raj-Guru*, sage Vashisth, was met with a golden statue of Sita by his side, during religious rituals,

Lankan war has been interpreted in two ways. Kidnapping of Sita from the protective dwelling of the King, and his warrior brother, is a challenge to the kingdom and affront to the authority of the king. Sita was also the daughter of a great king like Janak. If King could not protect the Queen, in his house, or punish the enemy, how could he protect the women citizens, whose safety was his duty as the king? He performed his duty by punishing the wrong-doer and releasing Sita from the enemy custody. It has nothing to do with his affection for her, as per this argument. Another interpretation refers to his intense affection for her, which prompted him to enter into a diplomatic treaty of give and take with Sugreev, to help him to regain his kingship, in return of Sugreev helping him to locate Sita and be an ally in war. He would not have been ridiculed by public, if he had given up Sita, who was already 'defiled', due to kidnapping by an unknown devil, whose whereabouts were not known. An option left to a kidnapped woman, would be to concede the demand of the powerful, or to end her life. Sita was an empowered woman, blessed further by *Mahasati* Anusuya, to feel cool and strong during adversities. The practice of *Jauhar* referring to self-immolation in fire by Rajput queens and warrior's wives, to protect their chastity, from the cruelty by way of rape and molestation, by winning enemy army is eulogized, and remembered with the celebration of *Jauhar-Mela* at Chittorgarh in Rajasthan. The legend of Queen Padmavati committing *Jauhar* to protect her chastity from Alauddin Khilji is well-known and has been dramatised as a Hindi movie.

In contemporary India, deserting a wife, mostly for preferring another woman as wife, or for live-in-relationship, is not so uncommon. In present times, in urban India, women working on small wages in unorganized sector, admitted, that they tolerated an alcoholic husband, who occasionally indulged in domestic violence, since he protected their dignity, from other men, who had evil designs on them. The women confessed that if they chose to abandon their husbands and lived as single woman, with or without a kid or two, life would be totally insecure for them. Third option for them had been to revert back to their parents' or brother's house, referred as 'family of orientation' in anthropology, and live with them permanently. This was a common practice in case of child widows, as documented in literature about such practices in the 19th and early 20th century India.

We can see that the normal salutation in Hindi belt is Ram-Ram. When a person from a subordinate position greets a person from a higher position, he may say, '*Jai Ramjiki*'. When a dead body is carried on bamboo *'tirdi'* (a kind of open coffin, made of bamboo) on shoulders, in a funeral procession, the accompanied persons chant, "*Ram Nam Satya Hai, Satya Bolo Satya Hai*". (Ram represents, nothing but Truth. So speak the truth by repeating Ram's name). In armed forces, in India, the traditional salutation has been 'Ram-Ram', now being replaced voluntarily by some as 'Jai Hind'. Thousands of persons in India, both men and women, have their personal names, from Ramayan, such as Sitaram, Ramlal, Rameshwar, Ramaswami, Ramchandran, Rama Rao, or as Sita, Janaki, Vaidehi, Mithila, Sulochana, Sumitra, Urmila, Ramdulari etc.

Mahatma Gandhi was a great fan of Sri Ram, since his childhood, and started his evening prayers with '*Ram-Dhun*'. While he was shot by the assassin, the last words reportedly uttered by him were 'Hey Ram'. People commonly exclaim 'Hey Ram' or 'Hare Ram', if they face some grave problem, or do not get the expected result of their action. If a concept or an argument has to be disapproved, the colloquial expression is, "There is no Ram in it", that is, there is no worthwhile substance in it. If somebody wants to express the ultimate, hundred per cent effect of an action, the term used is '*Ram-Ban*', like a single arrow of Ram, which would not miss its target effectively. Good, effective medicine is referred as '*Ram-Ban*' medicine, or any lasting solution to a complex problem is referred as '*Ram-Ban*' (hundred per cent/sure-shot) solution. Many exasperated women also express their anguish by repeating what Sita had said, "Oh! *Bhumate*, please take me back into your womb." Swami Vivekanand has spoken about Sri Ram, and talked of Sita uniting with Ram, as an allegory of *Jivatma* trying to unite with *Parmatma*, which met with several hurdles.

We are aware about literally thousands of temples in India with idols of Ram, Sita, Lakshman and Hanuman, as one unit. Birthday of Ram, that is, Ramnavmi is a public holiday in India, with great celebrations in these temples. It is not unusual or rare for a senior Muslim musician, to sing *Bhajans* in a Ram temple at the birth-time of 12 noon, on Ramnavmi day. This has been personally witnessed in the Ram Temple at Gwalior. *Bharatratna* Bismillah Khan, *Shehnai* maestro from Varanasi reportedly played *Shehnai* whole day, in the *Sankatvimochan* temple of Hanuman, a day after the temple was attacked by terrorists. It was also reported that when he was asked as to why he did not repatriate to Pakistan, at the division of India, he said there was no Varanasi in Pakistan. Similarly, while he was recommended to shift his residence to the film city of Mumbai, he said, there was no river Ganga in Mumbai. These expressions symbolizes the secular spirit of Indian civilisation, originating with Ramayan.

In Orchha princely state (Tikamgarh) in Madhya Pradesh, Sri Ram is the King of the State. Every year, the marriage of Ram is celebrated as a public event, with marriage procession, music band etc. The entire population joins the marriage procession. Folk songs referring to Ram's marriage continue to be sung during the marriage ceremonies in Bihar, originating in Mithila. Sita is referred as 'Janaknandini'. Janakpur, where Sita was born as daughter of King Janak was probably in Mithila region of Bihar, which is now in Nepal. That is how, Sita is also called by the name Mithila, or Maithilee. The region ruled by King Janak, is also referred as Videha, and Sita referred as Vaidehi. There is a folk practice whereby the bridegroom's party coming to bride's place for marriage rituals and ceremonies, is showered with jocular taunts, by women, in songs. Such jocular folk-songs referring to wedding of Ram-Sita continue to be popular in Bihar, in marriage ceremonies, to the accompaniment of dances. Such pranks are possible only before the actual wedding, since after marriage, the son-in-law is traditionally treated with great respect, as a divine guest, throughout life, at least till the birth of a grandchild.

There is Jatayu temple near Bhadrachalam, which has been listed on the route of Ram towards Lanka. The largest bird sculpture in the world, is located in Kerala; given to the vulture-king Jatayu, friend of Dashrath, known as Jatayu Nature Park; is also known as Jatayu Earth Centre. It is believed that Jatayu fell somewhere in Kerala where the present sculpture has been made. The sculpture has only one wing, since Ravan had cut his wing with the sword, when Jatayu attacked him, while he was carrying kidnapped Sita in *Pushpak viman* to Lanka. There is a Malayalam month of *Karkidakam* in Kerala, noted for month-long prayers, fasts and austere lifestyle, when devotees recite *Ramayan* everyday, during this month.

In *Ram Katha*, Uttarkand is believed to have been an after thought, as an annexure. It is argued that Uttarkand documenting Sita giving birth to twin sons; *Ashwamedh Yagya*; Luv-Kush in a battle position with Ram, culminating in the family reunion, may not have been written by Valmiki, but by some other authors. However, there are at least five places in India and Nepal, identified as Valmiki *Ashram*, where Luv-Kush were supposed to have been born to abandoned Sita, while she was pregnant. These *ashrams* are tourist spots and are widely visited by people. Some of these exibit the details as to where Sita cooked food for her sons (*Sita-ki-Rasoi*) or where Valmiki gave them training in archery etc., what is referred as sacred geography in Anthropology.

The Uttarkand is represented by narrating the event of Luv-Kush rendering Ramayan in music, the reunion of Sita with Ram, and her rejoining the Mother Earth. There continue considerable feminist debates, projected even in movies, criticizing Ram and Ayodhya public, for unkind treatment to Sita, while she was pregnant, by abdicating her in the forest, or asking her to undergo '*Agniparikshá*' after liberating her from the custody of Ravan, from Ashokvan. In different versions of *Ramayan* in regional languages, these episodes have been treated differently. In this book, these episodes have been discussed in the chapter, *Ram Katha*, based on '*Bhavarth Ramayan*' in Marathi, written by Sant Eknath. He was a contemporary of Sant Tulsidas, author of '*Ramcharitmanas*', in the sixteenth century (1533-1599), during the reign of Emperor Akbar.

Saint Poets and Sacred Geography

Masses know about the saint poets from various regions, religious and language groups in India, such as Thyagraj, Mirabai, Kabir,

Surdas, Dnyaneshwar, Tukaram, Eknath, Namdeo etc. and the religious leaders like Shankaracharya. People know of Mahavir, Buddha, Guru Nanak, as founders of various religious groups, such as Jainism, Buddhism, Sikhism etc. People also know about the literary giants like Kalidas, Bhavbhuti and painting schools like Rajasthani or Madhubani art. Such information continues to be disseminated through films, fiction etc. at the national and regional levels. There are several TV channels in India, devoted to spirituality and dissemination of ancient knowledge. People do enjoy classical Hindustani music or Karnataki music, and several Indian dance forms. People know about marvels of temple architecture in various parts of India. Pilgrimage tourism has been commonly undertaken by all classes of people. People know about the ancient university of Taxila where Kautilya (Chanakya) and probably Buddha, Panini and Charak were students; and Nalanda, where students from China were getting trained in large numbers.

India is a land of temples, mosques, churches and *gurdwaras,* each of them having a story about its establishment, linked to local legends. Every Indian village and town has at least one temple, mosque, church, *gurdwara* and the like, depending upon the size of population of a religious group, in the locality. There are festivals, ceremonies, rituals, associated with every religious and social group, and with the life cycle, such as birth, marriage and death. These ceremonies and festivals are also celebrated with gusto by Indian diaspora all over the world. Public holidays are declared to facilitate people to celebrate birth anniversaries of Ram, Krishna, Jesus, Prophet Mohammad, Guru Nanak, Mahavir, Buddha, and some contemporary leaders like Gandhi and Ambedkar. Besides, in different geographical regions, there may be public holidays and celebrations, about birth anniversaries of historical leaders and eminent personalities, belonging to the respective regions. India has been and continues to be a secular country, respecting all religious faiths, and does not have, or profess any State religion. There are thousands of pilgrimage centres at the regional and national level, given to various religious faiths. Pilgrimage tourism is widespread in India, which take people to different parts of the country. People appreciate the architectural marvels like temples and carvings, mosques, churches, musical pillars, cave paintings. The rivers are sacred, and there are legends about the origin of rivers, legends connected with sacred trees, animals and birds, and mountains; people continuing to worship them. People know and use medicinal plants available in their vicinity, and know about the textual Ayurved, Unani, Siddha systems of medicine. People know about the role of Sushen Vaidya, Ravan's physician, and Hanuman procuring Himalayan herbs, to save the life of Lakshman, fatally injured in war.

There are largest human congregations of people on the face of the earth, by the side of sacred rivers, at Haridwar, Prayagraj, Ujjain and Nashik, known as *Kumbha Mela,* linking the legends about the fight between the demons and deities to capture the pot of *amrit* (nectar of immortality). The sustenance of faiths through rituals and pilgrimage tourism, such as to Tirupati Balaji, Shabarimala, Dwarka, Ajmer-sharif *Dargah,* Saint Francis Church in Goa and churches in other regions of India, Pandharpur, Badrinath, Amarnath Cave, Vaishnodevi, Jagannathpuri, Rameshwaram, Shirdi, Amritsar and Nanded, Varanasi-Sarnath, Bodh Gaya, ShRavanbelagola, and hundreds of them, provide common people, the feel of ancient Indian civilisation, and enhance their self-respect and distinct identity. People know about the geographical spread of the nation-state of India, coinciding with kinship connections of Ayodhya dynasty of Ram, and his geographical coverage on foot, through various places, starting with Ayodhya, through Chitrakoot, Nasik, towards Hampi and Rameshwaram to Lanka. There is a concept of Sacred Geography in Anthropology, linked with historical legends, which unravels Indian Civilisation. Sense of belongingness to pluralities, diversities and uniformities in a spirit of peace, tolerance and mutual respect, becomes the distinct character of Indian national personality. Over a period of centuries old history, turbulence occurred challenging the civilisational stability and basic values of humanity, due to greed shown by some in power, to usurp every single material comfort for their ephemeral pleasures. However, there arise some leaders with spiritual leanings, some of them being referred and respected as saints, who are successful in defeating such powers, and to re-establish and re-affirm the humanistic values and life patterns, facilitating the life of common man, in his small world, with satisfaction. In recent times, there have been social and spiritual leaders like Vivekanand, Tagore and Gandhi; and leaders like Ambedkar, who embraced Buddhism, continuing the spirit of Indian civilisation. These leaders are respected and adored at the level of divinity. There are several Spiritual Foundations and leaders, generally referred as God-men, who continue to interpret the ancient knowledge from *Veda, Upanishad* and *Puranas,* understandable to common people. These god-men are now international celebrities.

People internalize the universal values of humanity, by listening or reading the stories, as are told in the Epics and *Puranas,* or in the folk literature, such as *Panchtantra*, Aesop's fables. Arabian Nights, Gulliver's travels and multitudes of them in different parts of the world, with a limited or extensive geographical coverage. The textual or unwritten religious scriptures, through stories, hold the sway over the minds of the masses. The legends and the eternal values, are also presented in the form of art, dance, drama, music, movies, TV serials, Radio, TV knowledge and spiritual channels, painting, sculpture, proverbs, and through oral, written or visual media.

Mahabharat and Gita

Mahabharat gets philosophically crystallized as *Bhagwad-Gita*, referred internationally by people of all statures and calling, to find solutions to their complex and confusing problems, disturbing the mental peace. *Mahabharat* continues to be referred while discussing contemporary issues of politics, values, gender issues, kin quarrels, righteous conduct as *Dharma* and ultimate victory of *Dharma* over *Adharma*. Through dialogues of Krishna-Arjun, on the battle field, while the two armies were confronting each other in battle position, awaiting the signal to attack each other, the roles of persons and class-groups have been defined, which have to be followed as righteous conduct. Bal Gangadhar Tilak in his commentary of *Gita*, in '*Gitarahasya*', has professed *Karma-Yog*, with an argument, "What else but Karma, i. e. action, on the battlefield, when the armies are in battle formation confronting each other, awaiting war action?"

Bhagwad-Gita, has been interpreted, and commentaries written by sages like Dyaneshwar, Adya Shankaracharya, and by scholars of philosophy like Bal Gangadhar Tilak, S. Radhakrishnan, Aurobindo, or by public figures like Gandhiji and Vinoba Bhave. There are several new religious groups, like Chinmaya Mission, whose ordained leaders keep on interpreting *Gita* for their audience and readership. Several translations in English and other languages, as also commentaries on *Gita* have been tried. *Gita* probably has the largest readership after *Bible*, which is believed to be actively promoted by the Church organizations.

The moral value of *Dharma* has been pronounced by introspecting Bhisma on his death bed of arrows, when he admitted his mistake. He said, he tolerated blatant injustice and immoral behaviour, since he pledged his loyalty to the King, instead of to the Kingdom. Irawati Karve has discussed all these issues in '*Yugant*', about *Mahabharat*, from the perspectives of some personalities, as normal human beings, with their fads and foibles.

Chanakya seems to have taken a lesson from Bhisma's confession. He was successful in persuading the loyal prime-minister of deposed king of Magadh, Dhananand, to continue as the prime-minister (*Amatya*) of Chandragupta, the new king, in the interest of the nation. The administrative experience of *Amatya* was needed for the smooth functioning and solidarity of the nation, under a new Ruler.

Gandhiji and *Ramrajya*

Gandhiji popularised the term, and concept of *Ram Rajya*, which got translated as *Gram Swarajya* or *Panchayati Raj*, as a statutory mechanism of rural transformation, and decentralised democratic governance. Mahatma Gandhi, during the freedom struggle, modified his expression of Sri Ram into the concept of God, as a symbol of people, representing all religious faiths in India, not limiting him, as son of *Raja* Dashrath. He propagated Ram and Rahim as one, advocating secular leadership of Ram, protecting and promoting peace, prosperity and happiness to the people. There is no word 'Hindu' in *Valmiki Ramayan*. Gandhiji since his childhood was exposed to Ramayan as '*Ramcharitmanas*', written by Tulsidas, in sixteenth century, during the reign of Mughal Emperor Akbar, who professed a secular faith.

History of India

Common people vaguely know the history of India, as to who ruled India from Delhi, who invaded India and when? People know of some great kings, such as Chandragupta Maurya, Ashok, Vikramaditya, Prithiviraj Chauhan, Rana Pratap, Krishnadev Raya, Chhatrapati Shivaji, Ranjit Singh, and several others from different parts of India. People also know about the Mogul Emperors, such as Babur, Akbar, Jehangir, Shahjehan and Aurangzeb.

Everybody does not know the regional history, such as from the north-east, except probably the Ahom kingdom of Assam; or about Kashmir, Himachal Pradesh; or in the south such as in Tamil Nadu, Andhra, Karnataka and Kerala. There are temples in Himachal associated with the legends in Ramayan and *Mahabharat*. There is a Shiva temple on a hill near Srinagar called as a Shankarachrya temple. There is Amarnath Cave with Ice *Shiv-ling*, and Vaishnodevi temple in Jammu and Kashmir State, which are important pilgrimage centres. Bulk of the services to the Hindu pilgrims, are provided by the local Muslims.

We hardly know of the Indian political and cultural influence in the South-eastern countries, such as in Indonesia, Vietnam, Malaysia, Thailand, Laos and Cambodia, manifested as Hindu and Buddhist influence. South Indian empires, such as Chola, Pallava, Pandyan, extended their rule to south-east Asian countries and built huge Hindu and Buddhist temples. Bali islands as part of Indonesia, the largest Muslim nation in the world, continue to be Hindu. Angkor Wat temple complex in Cambodia, is the largest religious monument in the world, linked to Hindu and Buddhist heritage.

People have heard of invaders such as Mahamud Ghaznavi, Chengiz Khan, Mohammad Ghori, Alauddin Khilji, Tughlaq, Lodhi etc. There are roads and cities named after the Mogul emperors, as they settled in India, and became the citizens of Hindostan/Hindustan. There have been novels, poetry, biopic films, entertaining love-story movies, and TV serials, about the lives of prominent Hindu rulers and Mogul emperors. The temples and mosques constructed by these rulers are pilgrimage centres; and monuments such as palaces, tombs, memorials and forts are of tourist attractions.

People definitely know about the British Rule, about the first war of Independence in 1857, initiated by Mangal Pandey and led among others by *Rani* Laxmibai of Jhansi, Tatya Tope, declaring Bahadurshah Zafar, Mogul descendent at Delhi, as the Emperor of India. The freedom-fighter, V.D. Savarkar, in his book, 'The Indian War of Independence, 1857' has documented the happenings, to what the British referred as rebellion or mutiny. This 'Mutiny' resulted in transfer of power from the East India Company to British Sovereignty. People also know about the statement of Lord Macaulay advocating the British system of education in India, to break the nerve of India. Uprising in 1857 followed the Queen's Proclamation assuring Indians of non-interference of the British government in their culture, customs and rituals. This was followed by Indian national movements, for freedom from British Rule, demanding self-governance (*Swaraj*), spearheaded by Bal Gangadhar Tilak, Gopal Krishna Gokhale, Dadabhai Naoroji, Muhammad Ali Jinnah, Mahatma Gandhi, Subhas Chandra Bose, to name the few, on the platforms of Congress party, which was inclusive of all the international political ideologies. The triumvirate, Lal-Bal-Pal referring to Lala Lajpat Rai, Bal Gangadhar Tilak and Bipinchandra Pal are known as pioneers of freedom struggle. There were violent incidents against the British by freedom fighters, who became martyrs such as Rani Laxmibai of Jhansi, Tatya Tope, Bhagatsingh, Rajguru, Sukhdev, Chandrashekhar Azad, Birsa Munda, Tantya Bhil and several others, including the Naval uprising in 1946. Jallianwala Bagh massacre by General Dyre at Amritsar, on *Baisakhi* day, 13 April, 1919, has been one of the darkest spots of cruelty during British rule.

However, the non-violent model of struggle, involving the masses, by Mahatma Gandhi, received international acclaim, and continue to be pursued to express public displeasure, about the policies and practices of the ruling governments. Gandhi has been an ardent devotee of Sri Ramchandra, expressed through his prayers devoted to Ram. The impact of British rule, and Lord Macaulay model of educational system, continues to be considered as a threat to basic values of Indian civilisation, and often deprecated, as continuing the colonial mind-set. Indian Civilisation with values of *Dharma* and Truth has been symbolized, and promoted by luminaries, through historical times, representing all aspects of life, such as, Kalidas, Bhavbhuti, Panini, Vatsayan, Charak-Susrut, Aryabhatt, Ramanujam, J.C. Bose, Swami Vivekanand, Swami Dayanand Saraswati, Ram Mohan Roy, Ishwarchandra Vidyasagar, Rabindranath Tagore, R. G. Bhandarkar, Mahadev Govind Ranade, Annie Besant, Sarojini Naidu, Madan Mohan Malviya Sarvapalli Radhakrishnan, C. Rajagopalachari and several social reformers. During the feudal era of governance, the art-forms, and respect for the artists, scientists and scholars was promoted and protected by the emperors and kings.

Anthropology as history, is attempting to change the knowledge-emphasis from 'Anthropology in India' to 'Indian Anthropology', to shed off colonial mindset, and study Indian Culture and Civilisation, from the perspectives of common people of India, as lived through centuries. The indigenous knowledge and wisdom of the pre-literate, referred to as folk communities and tribal communities, have been the focused and priority areas of anthropological research. It is among these people, that Ram-

Lakshman and Sita lived during their fourteen years exile period. It is with their assistance that Ravan, the symbol of *Adharma* was exterminated. The Ramayan, the journey of Ram, to re-establish the values of Truth (*Satya*) and *Dharma*, is the subject matter of this book.

Tribal Communities in Ramayan

Ram accompanied by Sita and Lakshman travelled and lived in the forest of Dandkaranya for about 13 years. In the 14th year, Sita was in Ravan's captivity for about an year, while Ram-Lakshman were camping at Kishkindha. They lived simple lives like the local tribal communities, residing in huts, which were made by themselves, by Lakshman, and ate mainly roots, tubers and fruits collected from the forest, or sometimes shared by the tribals. At Kishkindha, Ram-Lakshman lived in the mountain caves, as guests of Sugreev, particularly during the rainy season. The army of Sugreev with veterans like Hanuman, Jambavan, Angad, Nal and several others are not reported as humans, but as monkeys, bear, birds etc. Jatayu as a bird gave up his life, while attacking Ravan, who was kidnapping Sita in his *Pushpak viman.* While no miracles are reportedly performed by Ram, as are reported about Krishna, how could the miracle happen like the monkeys, bears and birds fighting a war against mighty Ravan, on the side of Ram, for releasing Sita from Ravan's captivity? The only weapons with them were the stones, and the leaders like Sugreev, Hanuman, Jambavan, Angad had clubs. "Clubs were weighted with pear-shaped or globular stone heads in the Early Neolithic". The Old World Prehistory: Neolithic, indicates existence of globular stone heads, used as clubs by monkeys in Ramayan. The bow and the arrow, as also spear-thrower were widely used as weapons (Childe, Gordon: in Kroeber, Ed. "Anthropology Today" 1953, 203). Ravan is reported to have used primarily bow and arrow, but also used occasionally, a sword, a spear and a mace. Ram and Lakshman always used bow and arrow as weapons, which have been the conventional weapons of tribal people.

The reality of these 'animals' being humans, as certified by Rabindranath Tagore and S. Radhakrishnan support the anthropological interpretation that these so-called 'animals' were actually forest dwelling tribals, whose clan names and totems have been the monkey, bear, bird etc. Such totems are found even among the contemporary tribal communities. In anthropological ethnographic monographs, the tribal social structure is described, based on exogamous clan system, each clan or tribe having a totem which could be an animal. In Ramayan, the monkeys such as Sugreev, Vali, Hanuman, or bear like Jambuvan, or bird like Jatayu, are all tribal groups with the respective animals as their totems. Romila Thapar in her book, "*A History of India*" has reiterated this point. "It may be suggested that the reference in the Ramayana to Rama preparing for the attack against Ceylon assisted by a number and variety of animals, including Hanuman, the leader of the monkeys, is in part a memory of the totem symbols of tribes in the peninsula" (1966, reprint, 1972: 105).

Radhakrishnan in his book, "*The Hindu View of Life*" has discussed the interaction of Aryans with the local, native tribals, in a spirit of give and take, not as domination by one over another group. It is in the common knowledge of people, that Chhatrapati Shivaji in Maharashtra, and Maharana Pratap in Rajasthan, were helped by the local tribal communities. Malhar Koli from Jawhar in Palghar district in western Maharashtra helped Shivaji, and the Bhils helped Rana Pratap, against the attacks by Moghul kings. Ram's interaction with Guhak, Kevat, Sugreev, Hanuman, Bibhishan etc. is of that order. Ram had a formal diplomatic treaty with Sugreev, to restore back his kingdom and wife, usurped by Vali, while Sugreev would help Ram to locate Sita in the custody of Ravan.

"The Epics relate the acceptance of new tribes and their gods into the old family circle.... Many tribes and races had mystic animals, and when the tribes entered the Hindu society the animals which followed them were made vehicles and companions of gods. One of them is mounted on the peacock, another on the swan, a third is carried by the bull, and a fourth by the goat. The enlistment of Hanuman in the service of Rama signifies the meeting point of early nature worship and later theism" (1927, Ninth Impression, 1954: 39).

According to Rabindranath Tagore, as reported by Uma Das Gupta: "India has never forgotten that Ramchandra was the beloved comrade of *chandala*; that he appeared as divine to the primate tribes, some of whom had the totem of monkey, some that of bear. His name is remembered with reverence because he won over his antagonists as his allies and built the bridge of love between Aryan and non-Aryan." (The Poet on the Past: Rabindranath's Analysis of India's History, Uma Das Gupta) (http://jshc. org/the-poet-on-the-past-rabindranaths-analysis-of-indias-history/).

It is common anthropological knowledge that traditionally, adultery among the tribal communities is punishable with death, and continues to be so. If somebody falls in for extra-marital affair, the same has to be publicly acceptable, only after divorcing the partner, as per the prevailing norms. Divorce is a matter of mutual consent, approved by the village or tribal elders. It could be that a part of the bride price, has to be returned back by the woman, or her new spouse, to the divorced wife. Guardianship of children is also not an issue, in tribal communities, neither in case of divorce, nor in widowhood. Although social structure is patriarchal, woman is not held as property. An unsatisfied woman can walk off more easily, after the issue of bride price is settled amicably. In some cases, in case of infertility, a woman prefers to desert her husband and take another. She is not necessarily held responsible for infertility. The customary residence is patri-local but neo-local residence is preferred.

Vali, Sugreev's elder brother had kept his wife, along with the kingdom. As per Indian norms, younger brother's wife is considered as daughter-in-law, and has to be protected, while any relations with her would be considered as incest and molestation, which according to customary tribal law, is punishable with death. Elder brother's widow could be protected as wife, by the younger brother, as socially acceptable custom, expressed by the anthropological term,

Levirate. There are several cases of war widows being rehabilitated in the family, through the custom of Levirate, in the Hindi belt in India. Ram as King punished Vali, since he had molested his younger brother's wife, committing the crime of adultery, against the consent of the woman.

Sita was abducted by Ravan by deceit. Among the tribal communities, a woman is never molested by a tribal man. So, the tribal people under the leadership of Sugreev, Hanuman and Jambavan fought the war as Ram's army, to punish Ravan for kidnapping Sita, against her consent. Hanuman had testified from his personal observation, that Sita not only refused to fall in for Ravan's solicitations, even after months of captivity, under a tree like an open jail, but fearlessly rebuked him and threatened him with death, at the hands of her husband Ram. Ravan was also afraid of the moral strength of Sita, since he had been cursed by his step-brother Kuber's son, Nal-Kuber, with instant death, if he molested any woman against her consent. Ravan had molested Nal-Kuber's wife, who was his daughter-in-law, by kinship category. Nal-Kuber was the son of Kuber, Ravan's elder step-brother. The tribal communities continue to follow the moral issues, that is *Satya* (Truth) and *Dharma*, and customary punishment patterns about adultery, and forced molestation of a tribal woman by a tribal man.

While residing in an interior tribal village for anthropological investigation, I happened to ask a tribal person, as to what would happen if his wife, by chance, took a liking for another man. He said, she was free to marry him after divorcing him, after the repayment of bride price was negotiated satisfactorily. I intercepted with a hypothetical query; if the man or the woman declined to pay back the proportionate bride-price; he said, in that case, he would play black magic on him. To my further probe that the lover could also play black magic on him; he said, the man's black magic would be ineffective, since my claim would be on the side of Truth (*Satya*), as per the tribal custom.

The personalities, and attitude to life of Ram-Sita-Lakshman living in tribal areas, interacting with the tribal people, on one hand; and simultaneously with the sage-teachers from the *Gurukul-Ashrams*, must have been greatly impacted. Observing the simple life of tribal people in symbiotic relationship with nature, and discussing the philosophy of life with the sages, would develop secular approach to life. Thirteen years of peaceful life, while performing the duty to ensure peaceful atmosphere for educational pursuits of the *Gurukuls*, followed by herculean efforts to destroy the demonic leadership of Ravan, takes the major part of Ramayan. What emerges after Ram-Lakshman-Sita living their youthful years in Tribal geography is a *Maryada Purshottam* Sri Ram, who is continued to be worshipped as Divinity, by the masses of India.

2

Ramayan

Plural Versions—Uniform Essence

There are thousands of books on Ramayan, written in Indian languages and in the languages of South-East Asian countries. It is estimated that there are no less than 300 well-known versions of *Ramayan* in several Indian and foreign languages, not deviating from the main story of Ram, as detailed by *Valmiki. Ramayan* in parts is also reflected or referred in scriptures of other religions such as Jain, Buddhist and Sikh.

Ramayan: Plural Versions

In every regional language in India, Ramayan has been transcripted, based on the basic text of *Valmiki Ramayan*, with slight regional modifications and the historical period, when it was written. Ramcharitmanas, the most popular version of *Ramayan* in Hindi belt, was written by Tulsidas in the 16th Century, during the reign of Akbar. *Kamban Ramayan* in Tamil from 12th Century and *Bhavarth Ramayan* in Marathi by Sant Eknath from 16th Century are equally famous. The great scholar, politician-statesman, C. Rajgopalachari, who was the first Indian Governor-General of Independent India, succeeding Lord Mountbatten, has written Ramayan for the common man in English, which is largely based on *Kamban Ramayan*.

Valmiki in his Ramayan has dealt with full biography of Ram, until his *Samadhi* in Sarayu river. Other versions of Ramayan, in regional Indian languages, including the most popular one by Tulsidas, were written during the period when Mughal rule was established in India. *Sant* Eknath in '*Bhavarth Ramayan*' in Marathi, has put considerable blame on the behaviour of Kaikeyi, who constantly found faults with Sita, almost hinting that Sita having lived in Lanka was defiled and polluted. Eknath held Kaikeyi responsible for Sita deciding to leave the patriarchal world and join her mother, *Bhumata,* tired of her blurting taunts.

In Tamil Kamban Ramayan, Ravan, although an enemy, but as a scholar of Vedas with Brahmin descent, reportedly officiated as the priest, while Ram was installing *Shiv-ling* at Rameshwaram, during the construction process of Ram-*Setu*, meant for Ram's army to cross the ocean to go to Lanka to fight the war with Ravan's army. So, Ram duly bowed to Ravan as the holy priest, receiving the blessings for the success of his mission. It is believed that Ravan as priest, even arranged to have Sita for the rituals, meant to be performed by the couple, for the desired results. Ravan as a priest was kind to Hanuman, who had burnt the major parts of Lanka. Hanuman had gone to fetch a *Shiv-ling* from Kailash, the abode of Lord Shiva himself, but got delayed to come back. In the meanwhile, Ravan as priest asked Ram to form a *Shiv-ling* of sand to be installed at an auspicious moment. After Hanuman's arrival, his *Shiv-ling* was installed in the vicinity of sand *Shiv-ling*, made by Ram. It has been called as Hanumanteshwar or Vishwanath, and sanctified to have the honour of pilgrims, first worshipping Hanuman's *Shiv-ling*, followed by the one installed by Ram. May be, due to such regional stories, Ramayan has been denigrated by some as pure mythology, as a collection of myths, and not a reality or history. There is a Rameshwar temple near Jalgaon city in north Maharashtra, with a story that Ram had installed *Shiv-ling* at the place when he settled down at Nashik, from where Sita was kidnapped.

Goswami Tulsidas has begun Uttarkand in Ramcharitmanas, while Ram-Sita-Lakshman and leaders of Sugreev army boarded *Pushpak* on way to Ayodhya. After the coronation of Ram, the guests go back to their destinations, having been honoured with presents, personally by Ram. This is followed by description of *Ram Rajya*, ending Ramayan. So, the major controversy about abdication of Sita, until their reunion, and Sita joining Mother-earth has not been touched by Tulsidas.

As we know, Ramayan was originally composed by Sage Valmiki, written in poetic format in Sanskrit. *Ram Katha* was narrated to him by the divine Sage Narad, as a living example of a Man and his life, which symbolized 'Truth (*Satya*) and *Dharma*' as universal values, to be emulated by the humanity. Probably, Narad's story ended with the death of Ravan, who was the epitome of *Adharma,* despite being well versed with textual knowledge, and an expert technocrat, specializing in war technology, which made him invincible in the *Trilok*. Another probability could be the story ending with the formal coronation of Ram, as the King of Ayodhya, and Sita as the Queen-consort. Valmiki after completing *Ram Katha*, up to coronation, had to become an active player in Ramayan, when pregnant Sita landed in his *ashram*, abandoned by King Ram. Sri Ram was caught in the dilemma, due to conflict of his role as King, following *Rajdharma,* superimposing his *dharma* (role) as Sita's husband. His role as Sita's husband, was to protect her from all evil forces, which tried to defile her body, or her reputation, as an ideal woman, playing her role as wife and mother, to its perfection. His role as husband, and King, to protect women was achieved, with inflicting death penalty to Ravan. But he could not protect her, from the vile gossip about her 'defilement', and hence, not acceptable as the Queen-mother, by the citizens of Ayodhya. Ayodhya people had experienced King Dashrath, falling a prey to the cruel designs of a beautiful woman, Kaikeyi, inflicting outright injustice and punishment to Ram, who was totally innocent. The gossip, implicitly put Ram in the same category in relation to Sita, as his father, Dashrath, in relation to Kaikeyi. According to the prevailing norms, Sita as a wife and the queen, was easily replaceable by another princess. King Ram resisted popular desire, and ritual 'requirement' to replace Sita, with another woman, by offering to give up kingship. This monogamous resolve of Ram, also sustained the morale of Sita, and her emotional binding with Ram, despite hard life for her, in bringing up Luv-Kush in Valmiki *Ashram*. Joint family of Ram, with his three mothers, step-brothers and their wives, also present an ideal role model of joint family and kinship, in the Indian Culture, continuing to be the ideal pattern of behaviour, that is, '*Pariwar Dharma*' in Indian Civilisation.

Several lists of versions of Ramayan have been compiled. One of them has been referred as under:

"Depending on the methods of counting, as many as three hundred versions of the Indian epic poem, the Ramayana, are known to exist. The oldest version is generally recognized to be the Sanskrit version attributed to the sage Valmiki."

"The Ramayana has spread to many Asian countries outside India, including Burma, Indonesia, Cambodia, Laos, Philippines, and China. The original Valmiki version has been adapted or translated into various regional languages, which have often been marked more or less by plot twists and thematic adaptations. Some of the important adaptations of the classic tale include the 12th century Tamil language *Ramavataram*, the *Khmer Reamker*, the Old Javanese *Kakawin Ramayana*, and the Thai *Ramakien* and the Laos Phra Lak Phra Lam."

Sanskrit Versions

"Adhyatma Ramayana, Vashisth Ramayana (more commonly known as Yoga Vashisth), Laghu Yoga Vashisth, Ananda Ramayana, Agastya Ramayana, Adbhuta Ramayana; The Ramayana story is also recounted within other Sanskrit texts, including: the *Mahabharat*a (in the Ramokhyana Parva of the Vana Parva); Bhagavata Purana contains a concise account of Rama's story in its ninth skandha; brief versions also appear in the Vishnu Purana as well as in the Agni Purana."

Regional Version

"Some noteworthy examples of these additional renderings of the Ramayana tale include:

North India

The "Ramacharitamanasa" written by Tulsidas in the 16th century is the Ramayana version popular in North India.

Jammu and Kashmir

The Kashmiri "Ramavatara Charita" was written in 19th century.

Gujarat

The Tulsi-Krita Ramayana is a Gujarati adaptation of Tulisdas' Ramayana in 17th century by the poet Premanand Swami.

Maharashtra

The Marathi "Bhavartha Ramayana" written by Eknath in the 16th century. There is also reference of Ramayana being translated into old Marathi during the 12th or 13th century.

Assam

The Assamese "Katha Ramayana" or "Kotha Ramayana" in 15th century by Madhava Kandali.

Bengal

The Bengali "Krittivasi Ramayan" written by poet Krittibas in 15th century.

Orissa

The Oriya Dandi Ramayana or Jagamohan Ramayana was adapted by Balaram Das in the 16th century.

Andhra Pradesh

The "Sri Ranganatha Ramayanamu" was adapted by Buddha

Reddy and is the Telugu version of the Ramayana. The "Molla Ramayanamu" was adapted by poetess Molla.

Karnataka

The Kannada versions of the Ramayana—the "Kumudendu Ramayana" (a Jain version), written in 13th century and the "Kumara-Valmiki Torave Ramayana," written in the 16th century. There is another version titled "Ramachandra Charita Purana" written by Nagachandra during the 13th century.

Tamil Nadu

The Tamil "Kambaramayanam", a popular version, written by poet Kamban in the 12th century.

Kerala

The Malayalam language "Adhyatma Ramayanam Kilipattu" written by Thunchaththu Ezhuthachan in the 16th century.

Nepal

The Nepali language "Bhanubhakta Ramayan" written by Bhanubhakta Acharya in the 19th century. The Nepal Bhasa "Siddhi Ramayan" written by Siddhidas Mahaju in the 20th century.

Goa

Ramayanu written by Krishnadasa Shama in 15th century in Kardalipura, Goa in Konkani, manuscripts found in Portugal.

Kannada

Two prose works by Nanadalike Lakshminarayana ('Muddanna') entitled Adbhuta Ramayana (1895) and Ramaswamedham (1898).

Urdu

An Urdu language version is called the "Pothi Ramayana" and was written in 17th century.

Other Versions

Champu Ramayan, Anand Rayaman, Mantra Ramayan, Girdhar Ramayan, Shree Ramayan Mangeri, Shree Rang Nath Ramayan, Bhaskar Ramayan, Gobind Ramayan written by Guru Gobind Singh and Radhey Shyam Ramayan.

The following are among the versions of the Ramayana that have emerged outside India:

- Cambodia : Reamker
- Thailand : Ramakien
- Laos : Phra Lak Phra Lam
- Burma (Myanmar) : Yama Zatdaw
- Malaysia : Hikayat Seri Rama
- Java, Indonesia : Kakawin Ramayana
- Philippines : Rajah Magandiri

Nepal

"The Nepal Bhasa version called Siddhi Ramayan was written by Mahakavi Siddhidas Mahaju Amatya during Nepal Bhasa renaissance era and the Khas language (later called "Nepali") version of Bhanubhaktako Ramayan by Bhanubhakta Acharya marked the first epic written in the Nepali language."

Tibet

"Ramayan is found in several manuscripts from Dunhuang."

(gktoday. in/different- versions- of- ramayan/)

The famous novelist, R. K. Narayan has written a shortened modern prose version of the Indian Epic, Ramayan, as a literary product, based on Tamil version of Kamban, written in the 11th Century. In Introduction, Narayan has written,

> "The Ramayana pervades our cultural life in one form or another at all times, it may be as a scholarly discourse at a public hall, a traditional storyteller's narrative in an open space, or a play or dance-drama on stage.

Whatever the medium, the audience is always an eager one. Everyone knows the story but loves to listen to it again. One accepts this work at different levels; as a mere tale with impressive character studies; as a masterpiece of literary composition; or even as a scripture. As one's understanding develops, one discerns subtler meanings; the symbolism becomes more defined and relevant to the day-to-day life. The Ramayana in the fullest sense of the term could be called a book of "perennial philosophy". "The Ramayana has lessons in the presentation of motives, actions and reactions, applicable for all time and for all conditions of life. Not only in areas of military, political, or economic power do we see the Ravans—the evil antagonists—of today; but also at less conspicuous levels and in varying degrees, even in the humblest social unit or family, we can detect a Rama striving to establish peace and justice in conflict with a Ravan".

"The impact of the Ramayana on a poet, however, goes beyond mere personal edification; it inspires him to compose the epic again in his own language, with the stamp of his own personality on it. The Ramayana has thus been the largest source of inspiration for the poets of India throughout the centuries. India is a land of many languages, each predominant in a particular area, and in each one of them a version of the Ramayana is available, original and brilliant, and appealing to millions of readers who know the language. Thus, we have centuries-old Ramayana in Hindi, Bengali, Assamese, Oriya, Tamil, Kannada, Kashmiri, Telugu, Malayalam, to mention a few". (Penguin Books, 1972: 33-34)

Ramayan: A Comparative Study of Ramkathas

A.A. Manavalan (English translation and edited by C.T. Indra and Prema Jagannathan, Vitasta Publishing, New Delhi, 2021)

The Oriental Institute of Baroda University with a view to prepare a critical edition of Ramayana in 1951, collected about 2500 manuscripts of Ramayan, of which 86 scripts were subjected to analysis. During the period of 1962 and 1975, critical edition was published as *Bal Kaandam, Ayodhya Kaandam, Aranya Kaandam, Kishkindha Kaandam, Sundara Kaandam, Yuddha Kandam and Uttar Kaandam* (pp. 20-21).

There are several variable stories about certain happenings, such as Sita's birth and parentage, Ahilya recognizing or not recognizing Indra's identity, when he presented himself as sage Gautam, and Sita Swaymvar while Ravan was present and could not lift the bow. In Ayodhya Kaandam the variations in terms of analysis refer mainly to Manthara and Kaikeyi, Ram's state of mind and expressions accepting the commands of Keikeyi to go to forest. There are also variations with regard to arguments between Ram and Bharat at Chitrakoot about the viability of Ram continuing to obey Dashrath's wishes, blurted out by Kaikeyi even after his death.

Prof. Manavalan has done a critical analysis of '*Bal Kaandam, Ayodhya Kaandam and Aranya Kaandam* from the perspective of the discipline of Comparative Literature' published in Tamil in 2005 (Institute of South Asian Studies, Chennai) as 'Ramakaathaiyum Ramayanangalum' (Volume 1). Manavalan has cited 48 versions of Ramayan available in Sanskrit, Pali, Prakrit, Hindi, Marathi, Telugu, Tamil, Assamese, Oriya, Persian, Kashmiri, Bengali, Kannada, Malayalam languages in India. Besides he has also cited Ramayan versions in Tibetan, Japanese, Malay, Burmese, Filipino, Thai, Lao and old Javanese languages. This also indicates that the versions are given as texts in the religious context of Hinduism, Jainism, Buddhism (*Jatak* tales) or the combination of these. Besides these, there are also folk tales in regional languages or dialects, which are available in published form or as oral traditions. The original source of all these appears to be Valmiki Ramayan and the different versions are variations of Valmiki Ramayan.

Manavalan has mainly compared the editions of Ramayan by Valmiki, Tulsidas and Kamban. In *Aranya Kaandam*, there are detailed discussions about the journey through the forest, with special reference to meeting sage Agastya and Anusuya, killing of Khar-Dushana, episode of Shurpankha and abduction of Sita. There are details about Lakshman-*rekha*, not mentioned in all versions; about conversations between Shurpankha and Ram-Lakshman, Sita and Lakshman, Ravan and Mareech, Ravan and Sita, and Ram and Jatayu. There are variations about abduction of Sita, the reason and manner of it. Variations go to the extent of denigrating the lust of Ravan versus his desire for *Moksha*, getting killed by Ram, or whether real Sita or her shadow was abducted by Ravan.

There are significant controversies and variations about Sita's fire-test (*Agnipariksha*), after coming out of Lanka, after her formal release from captivity by the new King of Lanka, Bibhishan. It has been reported that Fire-God personally escorted Sita out of fire, or that only the shadow of Sita had entered fire. There are no limits to variations, but the fact remains that the main story of Ramayan as presented by Valmiki continues to be accepted as the basic document of Ramayan.

As far as Indonesia is concerned, Ramayana Kakawin is the first text to narrate the story of Rama in the Javanese language. However, the temples of Parampana in central Java reveal that the details of Ramayana had begun to be depicted in stone sculptures as early as ninth century AD. The sculptures in the inner precincts of these temples.... . bear the entire story of Ramayana from *Bala Kaandam* to *Uttara Kaandam*.... . As far as Tamil region is concerned, Ramayana sculptures are found in the temples in the Chola areas of Kumbakonam and Pulla Mangai which were built around tenth century AD (p. 360).

Manavalan has only discussed the variations in versions relating to *Balkaandam, Ayodhyakaandam* and *Aranyakaandam* (A.A. Manavalan: English translation and edited by C.T. Indra and Prema Jagannathan, Vitasta Publishing, New Delhi, 2021).

Bibek Debroy has translated the seven volumes of critical edition of Ramayana brought out by the Oriental Institute (between

1951 and 1975), now part of Maharaja Sayajirao University, Baroda, in unabridged three volumes, titled, "*The Valmiki Ramayana*" published by Penguin Random House, India in 2017.

"As with the *Mahabharata*, the Valmiki Ramayana is a text about *dharma. Dharma* means several different things—the *dharma* of the four *varnas* and the four *ashramas*, the classes and stages of life, the governance template of *raja dharma*, the duty of kings; principles of good conduct, *sadacharas*; the pursuit of objectives of human existence, *purushartha-dharma*, *arth* and *kama*" (2017, xxiv).

Swami Vivekanand and Ramayan

Swami Vivekanand who probably had discussed Vedant more in his lectures abroad, narrated the story of Ramayan very briefly at a speech delivered at the Shakespeare Club, Pasadena, California, on January 31, 1900 (some excerpts).

"There are two great epics in the Sanskrit language, which are very ancient. Of course, there are hundreds of other epic poems. The Sanskrit language and literature have been continued down to the present day, although, for more than two thousand years, it has ceased to be a spoken language. I am now going to speak to you of the two most ancient epics, called the Ramayana and the *Mahabharata*. They embody the manners and customs, the state of society, civilisation etc., of the ancient Indians. The oldest of these epics is called Ramayana, "The Life of Rama". There was some poetical literature before this — most of the Vedas, the sacred books of the Hindus, are written in a sort of metre — but this book is held by common consent in India as the very beginning of poetry.

"The name of the poet or sage was Valmiki. One day as this sage, Valmiki, was going to bathe in the holy river Ganga, he saw a pair of doves wheeling round and round, and kissing each other. The sage looked up and was pleased at the sight, but in a second an arrow whisked past him and killed the male dove. As the dove fell down on the ground, the female dove went on whirling round and round the dead body of its companion in grief. In a moment the poet became miserable, and looking round, he saw the hunter.

"Thou art a wretch", he cried, "without the smallest mercy! Thy slaying hand would not even stop for love!"

"What is this? What am I saying?" the poet thought to himself, "I have never spoken in this sort of way before." And then a voice came: "Be not afraid. This is poetry that is coming out of your mouth. Write the life of Rama in poetic language for the benefit of the world." And that is how the poem first began. The first verse sprang out of pits from the mouth of Valmiki, the first poet. And it was after that, that he wrote the beautiful Ramayana, "The Life of Rama".

"There was an ancient Indian town called Ayodhya—and it exists even in modern times. There, in ancient times, reigned a king called Dasharatha. He had three queens, but the king had not any children by them. And like good Hindus, the king and the queens, all went on pilgrimages, fasting and praying, that they might have children and, in good time, four sons were born. The eldest of them was Rama."

"Now, as it should be, these four brothers were thoroughly educated in all branches of learning. To avoid future quarrels there was in ancient India a custom for the king in his own lifetime to nominate his eldest son as his successor, the *Yuvaraja*, young king, as he is called."

"Now, there was another king, called Janaka, and this king had a beautiful daughter named Sita. Sita was found in a field; she was a daughter of the Earth, and was born without parents. The word "Sita" in ancient Sanskrit means the furrow made by a plough. In the ancient mythology of India you will find persons born of one parent only, or persons born without parents, born of sacrificial fire, born in the field, and so on—dropped from the clouds as it were. All those sorts of miraculous birth were common in the mythological lore of India."

"Sita, being the daughter of the Earth, was pure and immaculate. She was brought up by King Janaka. When she was of a marriageable age, the king wanted to find a suitable husband for her."

"There was an ancient Indian custom called *Svayamvara*, by which the princesses used to choose husbands. A number of princes from different parts of the country were invited, and the princess in splendid array, with a garland in her hand, and accompanied by a crier who enumerated the distinctive claims of each of the royal suitors, would pass in the midst of those assembled before her, and select the prince she liked for her husband by throwing the garland of flowers round his neck. They would then be married with much pomp and grandeur."

"There were numbers of princes who aspired for the hand of Sita; the test demanded on this occasion was the breaking of a huge bow, called Haradhanu. All the princes put forth all their strength to accomplish this feat, but failed. Finally, Rama took the mighty bow in his hands and with easy grace broke it in twain. Thus Sita selected Rama, the son of King Dasharatha for her husband, and they were wedded with great rejoicings. Then, Rama took his bride to his home, and his old father thought that the time was now come for him to retire and appoint Rama as Yuvaraja. Everything was accordingly made ready for the ceremony, and the whole country was jubilant over the affair, when the younger queen Kaikeyi was reminded by one of her maidservants of two promises made to her by the King long ago. At one time she had pleased the King very much, and he offered to grant her two boons: "Ask any two things in my power and I will grant them to you," said he, but she made no request then. She had forgotten all about it; but the evil-minded maidservant in her employ began to work upon her jealousy with regard to Rama being installed on the throne, and insinuated to her how nice it would be for her if her own son had succeeded the King, until the queen was almost mad with jealousy. Then the servant suggested to her to ask from the King the two promised boons: one would be that her own son Bharata should be placed on the throne, and the other, that Rama should be sent to the forest and be exiled for fourteen years."

"Now, Rama was the life and soul of the old king and when this wicked request was made to him, he as a king felt he could not go back on his word. So he did not know what to do. But Rama came to the rescue and willingly offered to give up the throne and go into exile, so that his father might not be guilty of falsehood. So Rama went into exile for fourteen years, accompanied by his loving wife Sita and his devoted brother Lakshmana, who would on no account be parted from him."

"The Aryans did not know who were the inhabitants of these wild forests. In those days the forest tribes they called "monkeys".

"So, into the forest, inhabited by demons and monkeys, Rama, Lakshmana, and Sita went. When Sita had offered to accompany Rama, he exclaimed, "How can you, a princess, face hardships and accompany me into a forest full of unknown dangers!" But Sita replied, "Wherever Rama goes, there goes Sita. How can you talk of 'princess' and 'royal birth' to me? I go before you!" So, Sita went. And the younger brother, he also went with them. They penetrated far into the forest, until they reached the river Godavari. On the banks of the river they built little cottages, and Rama and Lakshmana used to hunt deer and collect fruits. After they had lived thus for some time, one day there came a demon giantess. She was the sister of the giant king of Lanka (Ceylon). Roaming through the forest at will, she came across Rama, and seeing that he was a very handsome man, she fell in love with him at once. But Rama was the purest of men, and also he was a married man; so of course he could not return her love. In revenge, she went to her brother, the giant king, and told him all about the beautiful Sita, the wife of Rama".

"Rama was the most powerful of mortals; there were no giants or demons or anybody else strong enough to conquer him. So, the giant king had to resort to subterfuge. He got hold of another giant who was a magician and changed him into a beautiful golden deer; and the deer went prancing round about the place where Rama lived, until Sita was fascinated by its beauty and asked Rama to go and capture the deer for her. Rama went into the forest to catch the deer, leaving his brother in charge of Sita. Then Lakshmana laid a circle of fire round the cottage, and he said to Sita, "Today I see something may befall you; and, therefore, I tell you not to go outside of this magic circle. Some danger may befall you if you do." In the meanwhile, Rama had pierced the magic deer with his arrow, and immediately the deer, changed into the form of a man, died."

"Immediately, at the cottage was heard the voice of Rama, crying, "Oh, Lakshmana, come to my help!" and Sita said, "Lakshmana, go at once into the forest to help Rama!" "That is not Rama's voice," protested Lakshmana. But at the entreaties of Sita, Lakshmana had to go in search of Rama. As soon as he went away, the giant king, who had taken the form of a mendicant monk, stood at the gate and asked for alms. "Wait awhile," said Sita, "until my husband comes back and I will give you plentiful alms." "I cannot wait, good lady," said he, "I am very hungry, give me anything you have." At this, Sita, who had a few fruits in the cottage, brought them out. But the mendicant monk after many persuasions prevailed upon her to bring the alms to him, assuring her that she need have no fear as he was a holy person. So Sita came out of the magic circle, and immediately the seeming monk assumed his giant body, and grasping Sita in his arms he called his magic chariot, and putting her therein, he fled with the weeping Sita. Poor Sita! She was utterly helpless, nobody was there to come to her aid. As the giant was carrying her away, she took off a few of the ornaments from her arms and at intervals dropped them to the grounds."

"She was taken by Ravan to his kingdom, Lanka, the island of Ceylon. He made appeals to her to become his queen, and tempted her in many ways to accede to his request. But Sita who was chastity itself, would not even speak to the giant; and he to punish her, made her live under a tree, day and night, until she should consent to be his wife."

"When Rama and Lakshmana returned to the cottage and found that Sita was not there, their grief knew no bounds. The two brothers went on, seeking, seeking everywhere for Sita, but could find no trace of her. After long searching, they came across a group of "monkeys", and in the midst of them was Hanuman, the "divine monkey". Hanuman, the best of the monkeys, became the most faithful servant of Rama and helped him in rescuing Sita. His devotion to Rama was so great that he is still worshipped by the Hindus as the ideal of a true servant of the Lord."

"So, Rama, at last, fell in with these monkeys. They told him that they had seen flying through the sky a chariot, in which was seated a demon who was carrying away a most beautiful lady, and that she was weeping bitterly, and as the chariot passed over their heads she dropped one of her ornaments to attract their attention. Then they showed Rama the ornament. Lakshmana took up the ornament, and said, "I do not know whose ornament this is". Rama took it from him and recognised it at once, saying, "Yes, it is Sita's". Lakshmana could not recognise the ornament, because in India the wife of the elder brother was held in so much reverence that he had never looked upon the arms and the neck of Sita. So you see, as it was a necklace, he did not know whose it was. There is in this episode a touch of the old Indian custom. Then, the monkeys told Rama who this demon king was and where he lived, and then they all went to seek for him."

"Now, the monkey-king Vali and his younger brother Sugreev were then fighting amongst themselves for the kingdom. The younger brother was helped by Rama, and he regained the kingdom from Vali, who had driven him away; and he, in return, promised to help Rama. They searched the country all-round, but could not find Sita. At last Hanuman leaped by one bound from the coast of India to the island of Ceylon, and there went looking all over Lanka for Sita, but nowhere could he find her."

"You see, this giant king had conquered the gods, the men, in fact the whole world; and he had collected all the beautiful women and made them his concubines. So, Hanuman thought to himself, "Sita cannot be with them in the palace. She would rather die than be in such a place." So Hanuman went to seek for her elsewhere. At last, he found Sita under a tree, pale and thin, like the new moon that lies low in the horizon. Now Hanuman took the form of a little monkey and settled on the tree, and there he witnessed how giantesses sent by Ravan came and tried to frighten Sita into submission, but she would not even listen to the name of the giant king."

"Then, Hanuman came nearer to Sita and told her how he became the messenger of Rama, who had sent him to find out where Sita was; and Hanuman showed to Sita the signet ring which Rama had given as a token for establishing his identity. He also informed her that as soon as Rama would know her whereabouts, he would come with an army and conquer the giant and recover her. However, he suggested to Sita that if she wished it, he would take her on his shoulders and could with one leap clear the ocean and get back to Rama. But Sita could not bear the idea, as she was chastity itself, and could not touch the body of any man except her husband. So, Sita remained where she was. But she gave him a jewel from her hair to carry to Rama; and with that Hanuman returned."

"Learning everything about Sita from Hanuman, Rama collected an army, and with it marched towards the southernmost point of India. There Rama's monkeys built a huge bridge, called Setu-Bandha, connecting India with Ceylon. In very low water even now it is possible to cross from India to Ceylon over the sand-banks there."

"Now, when the bridge was finished, the whole army of monkeys, led by Rama and his brother entered Ceylon. For several months afterwards tremendous war and bloodshed followed. At last, this demon king, Ravan, was conquered and killed; and his capital, with all the palaces and everything, which were entirely of solid gold, was taken. "So, all these golden cities fell into the hands of Rama, who gave them over to Vibhishana, the younger brother of Ravan, and seated him on the throne in place of his brother."

"Early during the period of exile, Bharata, the younger brother had come and informed Rama, of the death of the old king and vehemently insisted on his occupying the throne. During Rama's exile Bharata would on no account ascend the throne and out of respect placed a pair of Rama's wooden shoes on it as a substitute for his brother. Then Rama returned to his capital, and by the common consent of his people he became the king of Ayodhya."

"After Rama regained his kingdom, he took the necessary vows which in olden times the king had to take for the benefit of his people. The king was the slave of his people, and had to bow to public opinion.... Rama passed a few years in happiness with Sita, when the people again began to murmur that Sita had been stolen by a demon and carried across the ocean." "In order to satisfy the demands of the people, Sita was banished, and left to live in the forest, where was the hermitage of the sage and poet Valmiki. The sage found poor Sita weeping and forlorn, and hearing her sad story, sheltered her in his Ashrama. Sita was expecting soon to become a mother, and she gave birth to twin boys. The poet never told the children who they were. He brought them up together in the Brahmacharin life. He then composed the poem known as Ramayana, set it to music, and dramatised it."

"The drama, in India, was a very holy thing. Drama and music are themselves held to be religion. Any song — whether it be a love-song or otherwise—if one's whole soul is in that song, one attains salvation, one has nothing else to do. They say it leads to the same goal as meditation."

So, Valmiki dramatised "The Life of Rama", and taught Rama's two children how to recite and sing it.

"There came a time when Rama was going to perform a huge sacrifice, or *Yajna*, such as the old kings used to celebrate. But no ceremony in India can be performed by a married man without his wife: he must have the wife with him, the *Sahadharmini*, the "co-religionist"—that is the expression for a wife. The Hindu householder has to perform hundreds of ceremonies, but not one can be duly performed according to the *Shastras*, if he has not a wife to complement it with her part in it."

"Now Rama's wife was not with him then, as she had been banished. So, the people asked him to marry again. But at this request Rama for the first time in his life stood against the people. He said, "This cannot be. My life is Sita's." So, as a substitute, a golden statue of Sita was made, in order that the ceremony could be accomplished. They arranged even a dramatic entertainment, to enhance the religious feeling in this great festival. Valmiki, the great sage-poet, came with his pupils, Lava and Kusha, the unknown sons of Rama. A stage had been erected and everything was ready for the performance. Rama and his brothers attended with all his nobles and his people — a vast audience. Under the direction of Valmiki, the life of Rama was sung by Lava and Kusha, who fascinated the whole assembly by their charming voice and appearance. Poor Rama was nearly maddened, and when in the drama, the scene of Sita's exile came about, he did not know what to do. Then the sage said to him, "Do not be grieved, for I will show you Sita." Then Sita was brought upon the stage and Rama delighted to see his wife. All of a sudden, the old murmur arose: "The test! The test!" Poor Sita was so terribly overcome by the repeated cruel slight on her reputation that it was more than she could bear. She appealed to the gods to testify to her innocence, when the Earth opened and Sita exclaimed, "Here is the test", and vanished into the bosom of the Earth. The people were taken aback at this tragic end. And Rama was overwhelmed with grief."

"This is the great, ancient epic of India. Rama and Sita are the ideals of the Indian nation. All children, especially girls, worship Sita. The height of a woman's ambition is to be like Sita, the pure, the devoted, the all-suffering! When you study these characters, you can at once find out how different is the ideal in India from that of the West. For the race, Sita stands as the ideal of suffering. The West says, "Do! Show your power by doing." India says, "Show your power by suffering." The West has solved the problem of how much a man can have: India has solved the problem of how little a man can have. The two extremes, you see. Sita is typical of India — the idealised India. The question is not whether she ever lived, whether the story is history or not, we know that the ideal is there. There is no other *Pauranika* story that has so permeated the whole nation, so entered into its very life, and has so tingled in every drop of blood of the race, as this ideal of Sita. Sita is the name in India for everything that is good, pure and holy — everything that in woman we call womanly. If a priest has to bless a woman he says,

"Be Sita!" If he blesses a child, he says "Be Sita!" They are all children of Sita, and are struggling to be Sita, the patient, the all-suffering, the ever-faithful, the ever-pure wife. Through all this suffering she experiences, there is not one harsh word against Rama. She takes it as her own duty, and performs her own part in it. Think of the terrible injustice of her being exiled to the forest! But Sita knows no bitterness. That is, again, the Indian ideal." (Ref., *The Complete Works of Swami Vivekananda*, Vol. IV, 63-76, 1989).

This story of Ramayan coming from Swami Vivekanand clearly indicates the reflections that such great person of modern India has internalized, with an impulse to educate the foreign audience in a prestigious club, about the spirit of India. This is a testimony how Vivekananda was projecting Indian values to the world.

Essence of Ramayan

Valmiki's poetic talent flowered with the observation of hunting of male Kraunch bird, resulting in the heart-breaking death of female bird partner also, while they were merrily romancing with each other. Valmiki's impromptu anguish, blaming the hunter, was expressed in poetic format, which surprised himself. Having discovered the poetic talent, and with blessings from the supernatural powers, Valmiki dramatised the tender love of Ram and Sita, which had flowered in the forest journey and dwelling. However, both of them sacrificed their love to please the hounding male values in a patriarchal society of Ayodhya. Thus Valmiki has presented the malefic gossiping in Ayodhya about King Ram, doting on 'polluted' Sita, similar to that of the hunting of birds who were engaged in blissful romance. However, it was left to the next generation, to Luv and Kush in the role of bards, to inform the people about the facts, and change the mind of people. This was complemented and strengthened by the resolve of Ram as a person, not to replace Sita, whom he loved, by remarrying. In a patriarchal society, with feudal political system, the people, that is the vocal males, could not conceive as to why a person with political power, particularly the king, would not marry more than one woman. However, the women who could not be publicly vocal about such issues would obviously have great respect for a man in power-position, who would insist on practicing monogamy in spirit and letter. Particularly, the women could easily identify themselves with Sita, as one of them, representing the womanhood in the patriarchal society. The masses of India thus address Ram as Sitaram or Siyaram, not separating the two. Actually the masses worship Ram, Sita, Lakshman and Hanuman as one entity in the thousands of Ram temples in India.

It is debated by scholars as to how much of what is called as original Ramayan, was written by Valmiki and what additions and subtractions were made subsequently. However, the people of India who celebrate Ramnavmi and enjoy Ramlila, accept the basic story given by Valmiki. People visit thousands of temples which have idols of Ram, Sita, Lakshman and Hanuman and express Sita's Ram (*Siya Ram*) as an ideal human being, in his different roles as son, disciple of *rishis*, seeking their counsel in times of wavering of mind; as brother, as king, a compassionate person at heart, but performing his duties as the king, to protect the people and punish the wrong doers. *Ramrajya* as referred by Gandhiji is not equivalent to traditional, or current statutory *Panchayati Raj*, but credits Ram, who gave due importance and respect to the wishes and desires of the people. He sacrificed his love for Sita and his duty to take care of her pregnancy, as an husband, and surrendered to the unjustified gossip of the people by deserting Sita. His moral stature as a person went high in public mind, by not replacing Sita with another woman in his life.

Although electoral democracy in India has replaced the feudal chiefs, who governed large number of 'Princely States', the chiefs of government are expected and respected, if they follow *Rajdharma* as enunciated in the Constitution of India, which becomes visible, when the Ministers take oath of office. Persons occupying positions of governance are expected not to follow any discrimination on the basis of caste, religion, region, race, or other such ethnic identities in discharging their duties, as per the secular spirit of the Constitution. The President of India, Governors of States, and Speakers of legislative bodies, who might have been elected due to their political affiliations, are expected to shed off their political identities, once they hold such offices. That is *Rajdharma*, the ideal of which was laid down by Sri Ram, when he sacrificed his loving relationship with Sita, due to her status as the Queen, with the role-identity of mother, to the citizens of the nation. Even the witnesses in the courts of justice vow in the name of god, or putting the hand on *Gita*, or may be *Bible* and *Quran*, or those who profess to be agnostic, in the name of '*Antratma*', to speak nothing but Truth. In common communication, people express an oath (*shapath*) in the name of a person, whom one loves, like father, mother or a child, to ensure that they are telling Truth.

Mahatma Gandhi played the role, as a patron, supervising the freedom struggle, to become independent from the British Rule. In order to confront the two nation theory, based on religion, initiated by some Muslim leaders and promoted by the British, in line with their 'Divide and Rule' strategy, Gandhiji propagated equating Ram and Rahim, clarifying that he was talking about the concept of Ram, not the Ram as the son of Dashrath. Despite this, he could not prevent the partition of the country into India and Pakistan, which meant temporary victory to the Ravan forces who had the greed of power, sacrificing the lives of thousands of people. While communal violence erupted on the eve of Independence, in the process of large scale migrations of Hindus and Muslims, Gandhiji undertook fast for communal harmony to stop the violence.

However, the paradox about the division of India by creating Pakistan as an Islamic State, back-fired when muslim people of Bangla Desh rebelled againt the Ravanic tendencies of West Pakistan leaders, to crush the cultural-linguistic identity of the people, violating the basic principles of *Rajdharma*. Creation of Bangla Desh as an independent nation brings to the fore the understanding of the concepts of nation, culture and civilisation. It also leads to introspection about the plurality and diversity of cultures, which may be the soul of civilisation, which may or may not be co-terminus with the nation. Nations are created, civilisations evolve historically based on certain humanistic values. Incidentally, the National Anthems of the two countries, India and Bangla Desh, originate from *Gurudev* Rabindranath Tagore's lyrics and musical composition.

There are technologically superior powers, like Ravan, in the world, who benefit by fostering war and sickness. They are technologically advanced in the commercial production of war machines. The are also technologically advanced in laboratory sciences, related to biological, chemical and pharmaceutical sciences. They manufacture allopathic pharmaceutical products, which seem to provide temporary relief to symptoms of sickness. But the people get hooked to continue consumption of medicines, to get relief from the side-effects of earlier treatment. Mahatma Gandhi advocated nature cure, without the use of processed drugs. One of the indicators of growth in the new suburbs in a metropolitan city, is the multiplication of pharma shops. Does superior technology providing ephemeral material comforts, ensure Truth (*Satya*) and *Dharma?*

King Ram did not colonise or annex Lanka or Kishkindha to the kingdom of Ayodhya, while bestowing the status of brother to Bibhishan and Sugreev. He declined the gift of *Pushpak Viman* from Bibhishan. Special gifts given to King Bibhishan and King Sugreev on the occasion of Ram's coronation as King, were the bejewelled thrones, symbolizing the recognition of their sovereignty. The moral essence of Ramayan is thus *Satya* and *Dharma*, which continues as the soul of Indian Civilisation.

3

Ram Katha

Journey of Dharma in Search of Truth

Mahatma Gandhi has characterised Ramayan as a love story written by Valmiki, triggered by observing the love of Krounch bird-couple with a tragic end, with an arrow from the hunter, killing the male-bird and the female-bird instantly, dying in grief. C. Rajagopalachari has narrated his dialogue with Gandhi.

"On one occasion Gandhiji and I were talking about a girl very dear to both of us." I said:"How did she get all these ideas and phrases of love without having read any of present-day love stories?" Gandhiji said in answer: "But has she not read the Ramayana? Is the Ramayana not a love story too? This struck me as profound." (1951, 29th Edition, 1996: 309).

Valmiki Ramayan

Swami Vivekanand, the greatest visionary in contemporary India, has paid a handsome tribute to Sage Valmiki, for presenting Ramchandra, the soul of Indian civilisation to keep us breathing and taking us to new heights. "Rama, the ancient idol of the heroic ages, the embodiment of truth, of morality, the ideal son, the ideal husband, the ideal father, and above all, the ideal king, this Rama has been presented before us by the great sage Valmiki. No language can be purer, none chaster, none more beautiful and at the same time simpler than the language in which the great poet has depicted the life of Rama" ("Thus Spake Rama", Sri Ramakrishna Math, Chennai, 2004).

Ramayan refers to the biographical path of the King of Ayodhya, Shri Ramchandra, son of Dashrath and Kaushalya, written by Valmiki in poetic format. Valmiki has presented Ramayan in seven chapters commensurate with seven phases of Ram's journey of life, in a time sequence, such as *Balkand, Ayodhyakand, Aranyakand, Kishkindhakand, Sunderkand, Yuddhakand* and *Uttarkand.*

Valmiki: *Adya Kavi* (First Poet)

Sage Valmiki was in an exhilerating mood at sunrise, by the side of river, Tamsa, a subsidiary of sacred river, Ganga (Ganges), near his *ashram,* in the woods. He and his disciple, Bharadwaj were enjoying chirping of birds making sweet sounds. A *Krounch* (Crane) bird-couple was seen romancing, soliciting each other, kissing each other with their beaks. Suddenly, an arrow struck the male bird and it came down wounded, blood oozing, falling on the ground, breathing for life, with the incessant fluttering of wings. The female bird, shocked and grieved, made crying sounds, and whirled around the wounded male bird. In a few moments, both the male and female birds breathed last. The pleasant romantic scenario of blissful happiness of bird-couple, turning into death, within minutes, shattered the compassionate emotions of Valmiki. He saw the culprit hunter at some distance, with a bow and arrow in his hands. Valmiki in great grief, blurted the curse at the hunter: that no more would he enter this forest for a long time, and no more would he remain a happy person, for the sin committed by him.

"मा निषाद प्रतिष्ठाम्त्वमगम शाश्वती समाः।
यत्क्रौन्च मिथुनादेकमवधिः काममोहितं।।"

"O! Nishad, you will not get respect in the society, for you have killed crane birds who were absorbed in enjoying conjugal love."

Valmiki composed himself, wondered and introspected; what he had uttered as an emotional outburst at the hunter, happened to be a metrical verse, a rhythmatic *Shloka*, which could be rendered as a musical composition. He shared this enlightening revealation with his disciple Bharadwaj, who quickly memorized the *Shloka*. This verse by Valmiki is considered to be the first poem in the world, which earned him the title as *Adyakavi*.

Later, in the day, while Divine Sage, Narad, happened to visit him, Valmiki, visibly unhappy and sad over the behaviour of bird-hunter, inquired with Narad, whether there could be any ideal human-being on the face of the earth. Narad said, 'Yes', there is one. He praised and narrated the life of the ruling king of Ayodhya, *Maryada Purshottam*, Sri Ramchandra. Narad then entreated Valmiki, to write the story about the life of Ramchandra, in the poetic format. He advocated wide dissemination of the legendary story, about difficult biographical path of Ramchandra, traversed by him with equanimity. Narad was confident that Ramayan scripted by Valmiki, would provide guidance to the humanity; to tread the path of Truth and *Dharma,* howsoever difficult it may be. That scripture is immortal Ramayana, the *Ram Katha*.

Life History of Ramchandra

Dashrath was the Sovereign king of Ayodhya in *Tretayug*. Ayodhya means and refers to a city which cannot be subjugated through war. Dashrath literally means ten chariots, or a chariot with ten wheels, or may be one, driven by ten horses. Dashrath was a great warrior, whose help was sought by celetial kings like Indra, in their fight against the demons. He had three wives as queens. Kaushalya was the principal queen, followed by Sumitra and Kaikeyi. The King had no son who could be his successor. However, he had hopes, paradoxically due to a curse given by old parents of Shravan.

Story of Shravan

Dashrath was an expert hunter, who could aim the target with his arrow by the sound (*shabdbhedi*), that the target would make, although the target may not be visible. Once at night, he went for hunting by the side of a river, thinking an animal would visit the river for drinking water. He heard the sound of walking on dry leaves and sound of drinking the water. He shafted an arrow in the direction of the sound. Instantly he heard human voice of agony. He rushed to the spot to see a young boy, who identified himself as Shravan, hit by the arrow. Shravan said, his old parents who were blind, were waiting for him to give them drinking water. While he was carrying the parents in the open baskets on his shoulder (*kavad*), during travel, they felt thirsty. He requested Dashrath to quentch their thirst. Shravan collapsed to death. Dashrath took water to the parents, but could not respond immediately to their inquiry about the cause of delay, which they sought, thinking he was Shravan. Dashrath had to reveal his identity to them, and told them that he was inadvertently responsible for the death of their son. Both the parents collapsed to death in shock. But before they breathed last, father of Shravan cursed the King, that he would also die like this, longing for his sons. Dashrath cremated the three and performed appropriate cremation rites and rituals.

Although Dashrath was very distressed due to death of three innocent humans at his hands, his hope of begetting sons was rekindled, due to the curse by Shravan's father. On return to Ayodhya, he narrated the incident to sage Vashisth, who was official *Guru* and mentor to the King and the kingdom. The King would always seek his advice on moral and religious issues, and abide by such advice. All religious functions and rituals, would be guided and monitored by *Guru* Vashisth. Vashisth advised the king to perform '*Putrakameshti yagnya*' for begetting sons.

Balkand: Summary

This period details the '*Putrakameshti yagnya*' performed by Dashrath, father of Ram and his brothers, to beget children by divine blessings, since he had no children from the three queens, Kaushalya, Sumitra and Kaikeyi. After basic education, sage Vishwamitra took Ram and Lakshman with him to protect the *yagnyas* performed by sages, which were attacked by demons. They were taken to the kingdom of Janak where Ram got married to Sita and other brothers to Sita's cousins.

BALKAND

Birth of Ram, Lakshman, Bharat, Shatrughna

Sage Vashisth invited a great scholar, Shring-*Rishi*, who knew all the four *Vedas* by heart, to perform the *putrakameshti yajnya*. Sage Shring came with his team of Brahmins to perform the '*Yaag*'. (term used by Rajgopalachari). At the completion of the *yajnya*, elixir, pious '*kheer*' or '*payasam*' as '*prasad*' (sacred gift) was handed over to sage Vashisth to be consumed by the three queens. Vashisth gave half of the '*prasad*' to the senior queen, Kaushalya, and the rest was to be divided equally between Sumitra and Kaikeyi. Kaikeyi expressed displeasure to receive the '*prasad* ' last, expressing that, she was the most beloved queen of the King. She had saved the life of King Dashrath in a battle with the demons and was entitled to receive it first. Vashisth was pleading to take the '*prasad*' quickly, to avoid any mishap. A bird '*Ghar*' (Hawk) swooped and snatched the leaf-cup of '*prasad*' from Kaikayi's palms and flew away. Kaikeyi was crest fallen. Kaushalya and Sumitra counselled Kaikeyi and shared their '*prasad*' with Kaikeyi. While the '*prasad* ' was being divided for distribution, small portion was left which was again given to Sumitra. After about an year, four sons were born to three queens. Sumitra gave birth to two sons, since she received the '*prasad*' twice. Guru Vashisth performed the naming ceremony. Kaushalya's son, eldest among the four was named Ram, Kaikeyi's son was named Bharat. Sumitra's sons were named Lakshman and Shatrughna. There was great joy in Ayodhya and King Dashrath distributed sweets and gifts to all the citizens.

Birth of Hanuman

A female monkey who was known as Anjani was in penance, praying God Shankar, for a long time, to beget a son. The '*Ghar*'

(Hawk) which snatched the '*prasad*' from Kaikeyi's hands was flying over the place where Anjani was seated. The Wind God, *Vayu*, swept the '*prasad*' from the bird's beek, and it fell in the lap of Anjani. Coming unexpectedly from the skies, as God's gift, she consumed it with great reverence. After about nine months, Hanuman was born on full moon day (*Purnima*), i. e. the 15th day of lunar calendar, while Ram was born on the 9th day (*Navmi*) of Hindu new year. Every year the birth anniversary of Ram is celebrated across India as '*Ramnavmi*', which is also declared as public holiday. Birthday of Hanuman as '*Hanuman Jayanti*' is also celebrated by the devotees of Hanuman, as he is also addressed as '*Sankat-Vimochan*' (Remover of hurdles), since he helped Ram in locating and liberating Sita from the captivity of Ravan.

After the birth of Hanuman, while Anjani went to collect fruits for herself and the baby, Hanuman saw the sunrise, and the Sun looking like a red fruit. The baby leapt to get the Sun. Rahu and Ketu who used to create solar eclipse were greatly worried about a new competitor. They complained to rain god Indra and the care-taker of heaven, whereupon Indra hurled his most powerful weapon, '*Vajra*' to vanquish the baby. The weapon hit the lower jaw, (*hanuvati*) injuring it, but the hard weapon broke. As Hanuman fell on the ground, his foster father, wind god (*Vayu*), who had managed to deliver the procreative elixir to Anjani, suffocated the lives of all living beings, by refusing to whirl, and remain deadly static. The humanity felt suffocated without the flowing wind. All celetial beings apologised to wind-god for harming the baby Hanuman, and blessed the baby with the boon of immmortality. Thus, Hanuman has been literally a co-brother of Ram and his brothers, born out of the same divine elixir consumed by their mothers. Hanuman has rendered maximum help to Ram and Sita, in their difficult times, during war with demon-king Ravan. There is no single temple of Ram-Sita and Lakshman, without the idol of Hanuman, in a sitting posture, paying obeisance to Ram-Sita-Lakshman. There are thousands of Hanuman temples across India. Hanuman as a god of valour, has been an inspiration to all those, who want to fight the enemy. Hanuman is also worshipped, as *Sankat-Vimochan*, since he is known to face and vanquish obstacles, with great wisdom and quietness. Hanuman as a deity presides over all traditional gymnasia and places of physical exercise, for body-building and martial arts. He is also referred as *Bajrangbali* and *Maruti*. Tulsidas, who has written '*Ramcharitmanas*' has also written *Hanuman-Chalisa* in praise of Hanuman, which is recited by millions of Indians, as a sacred hymn.

First *Ashram* of Life-cycle: *Brahmacharyashram*

The sacred thread ceremony (*upnayan*) was performed for Ram and his brothers at their age of eight, as per cultural convention and Hindu *Dharmashastra*. They learnt the basic rituals to be performed after *upnayan,* and took lessons from *Guru* Vashisth about *Vedant*. The four brothers were sent on pilgrimage to sacred rivers and Shiva temples, accompanied by minister Sumant. They met the people at these places, interacted with them, and gave *Dakshina* to local priests, and gifts to others. They attained the age of twelve, while they received training from Vashisth, about basic knowledge of Vedas, as also training in the use of arms for self-protection, and protection of the sages and people, from the demons.

Prince Warriors

One day, the Great Sage, *Brahmarishi* Vishwamitra arrived at Ayodhya. King Dashrath welcomed him and offered him the seat of honour, and provided hospitality appropriate to his spiritual stature. Vishwamitra said, he had not arrived to ask for any material gains. He narrated his anguish, that, when he and his peers performed *yagnyas*, the demons in the forest desecrated the sacred fires, by throwing dead bodies in it and polluting the fire, or even killed the priests. He requested the King to allow him to take Ram with him for protection and safe performance of *yagnyas*. Dashrath was shocked and flabbergasted. He said, he would be happy to go himself with his army for the safe performance of spiritual rituals. He entreated that Ram was still a child and had no knowledge of actual fights. Viswamitra was crestfallen and thought of leaving Ayodhya. However, he said, "Oh King, how do you call Ram, who is trained in *Vedang* and *Yoga*, as a child?" Vashisth advised Lakshman to go with Ram to give him company and to be of assistance to him.

Knowing the spiritual and moral strength of Vishwamitra, Vashisth assured king Dashrath that Ram and Lakshman would be safe with Viswamitra. There could be a general querry as to why should Vishwamitra with his moral strength, require the martial services of the King, to protect them and their spiritual rituals from being attacked and destroyed by the demons. It is believed, that if the realized souls, such as that of the great sages, used their moral powers for routine issues, they would be depleted with their moral powers. There are any number of examples, whereby the sages had to use their strength to correct the deviant behaviour of heavenly demi-gods, when they transgressed the moral code of conduct, by violating the principle of Truth. It was considered the duty of the King, to protect his subjects and particularly the Brahmin sages, who performed *yagnyas* for the welfare of humanity.

Vishwamitra and Vashisth

Vishwamitra used to be a great king. He happened to visit Vashisht *ashram*, with his army. Vashisth offered him sumptuous hospitality which astounded Vishwamitra, organized at a forest hermitage. Vashisth explained that his cow '*Sabala*' was the fountain-head of this abundance. Thereupon, the king Vishwamitra sought his cow as his right, as a king. Neither Vashisth nor the cow wanted to join Vishwamitra. When physical force was attempted to carry '*Sabala*', the holy cow created an army, at the instance of Vashisth, which defeated Vishwamitra's army. Realising the spiritual and moral strength of the *Rishi,* Vishwamitra passed on his kingdom to his son, and proceeded to Himalayas for penance and austerities. Pleased with him, Lord Shiva gave Vishwamitra all the weapons which the celestial demi-gods possessed. Armed with these, he again went to Vashisth's *ashram* and challenged him. But the weapons proved ineffective before the spiritual strength of Vashisth. Vishwamitra again proceeded for severe austerities. Indra, the patriarch of the kingdom of heaven, felt threatened by Vishwamitra's further penance and austerities, which would make him morally and spiritually strong enough to threaten his position. Indra directed the celestial *apsara* (nymph), Menaka, to seduce him, so as to vanquish his moral strength. It is well-known that a daughter, Shakuntala was born out of their union, who was reared by Sage Kanva, since the baby was abandoned by Menaka. The great poet Kalidas has written a play '*Shakuntalam*' about the love story of Shakuntala and King Dushyant, which is very famous in the world of literature and art. It is believed that India is called '*Bharat*', after the name of great King Bharat, son of Shakuntala and Dushyant. Out of remorse, Viswamitra further went into penance and austerities, until Vashisth complimented him as a realized soul, as *Brahma-Rishi*, his equal. Vishwamitra as a Kshatriya king could become a Brahmin, through his austerities. This example of change of *Varna* from Kshatriya to Brahmin, is often cited to argue that *Varna* system has not been a closed system of social hierarchy. Since then, Vashisth and Viswamitra became friends, respecting each other.

Orientation of Ram-Lakshman

Ram asked Sage Vishwamitra that since they were being taken where they would have to fight the demons, it was obvious that as soldiers, they were at risk of loosing their lives. So they would like to be educated about such concepts as *Jivatma* and *Parmatma* Kindly illuminate our minds with such philosophical knowledge", Vishwamitra directed them to get this knowledge from Vashisth, who was their *Rajguru*.

Vashisth discussed with Ram-Lakshman such concepts as Truth and Illusion. What is ultimate truth and God? What is *Maya*? What is the purpose of life? What is *Satva, Raja, Tama*? What is morality? What is soul and body? Ram-Lakshman meditated about these issues, to be mentally prepared to face the consequences of their future course of action, under the guidance of Vishwamitra, with equanimity. We see so many things with our eyes or listen through ears. Is there eternal truth, what we perceive through our sense organs, or could truth be different than what we perceive? The advice (philosophical treatise) given by Vashisth is textualised as '*Yoga-Vashisth*'.

Truth and Moral Strength

The principle of moral strength is universal in humanity. That is how, we find Jesus, Prophet Mohammad, Mahavir, Buddha, Guru Nanak, Saibaba and several other human beings elevated to the level of Divinity, adored and worshipped by the masses. They had the moral power to perform miracles, which they used very rarely. We have the recent example of Mother Teresa being elevated as Saint with the certification of her miracles, which saved lives. In India, we have had saint poets such as Dnyaneshwar, Tukaram, Ramdas, Eknath, Gora Kumbhar, Chokha Mela, Janabai in Maharashtra, from all the caste groups; Mirabai, Kabir, Thyagraj and several such spiritual leaders, in all geographical regions, who continue to be respected, remembered and followed by the masses.

Although Ram and Krishna are considered the incarnations of God Vishnu, there is great difference in their biographies. There are any number of miracles in the life of Krishna, while none in the life of Ram. Ram had to undergo all the miseries as a human being, and did not possess any supernatural powers to get Sita released from the captivity of Ravan. He could not kill Ravan by miracles, but had to fight like a warrior and strategies the war front like any other war. Ravan on the other hand, who happened to be a son of a Brahmin, was technologically superior, in the war-game.

The governance protocol would require the king to protect the people at large from the invaders, more particularly the Sages as teachers and advisers to the king. They are the fountain-head of knowledge, and respected as conscience keepers to maintain the moral balance. The sages on the other hand, would not interfere with the routine affairs of governance, unless their counsel was sought by the king. This tradition in Indian civilisation continued, whereby several saints and saint-poets were treated with great respect by the respective rulers, including by the Muslim rulers in India, who had come from outside, but subsequently settled down to rule India. The most recent example has been that of Vinoba Bhave, spiritual disciple of Mahatma Gandhi, who was treated by the Prime Minister, Indira Gandhi with great reverence.

Vishwamitra with Ram and Lakshman, went ahead towards his *Ashram*. On the way, by the side of river Ganga, Sage gave them further training about *Dhanurvidya*, about the expert use of bow and arrow. Sage also provided them with various superior weapons which he had received from Lord Shiva. As they entered the forest region, a demoness Tatika attacked them. Being a female, Ram was reticent to kill her. But Vishwamitra said she did not make any difference when she killed both men and women. She deserved to be killed. Ram killed her with a single arrow. Next day, in the *Ashram*, *Yagnya* rituals started. Seeing the fire and smoke from the ritual *yagnya* fire, the two demons. Subahu and Mareech arrived to destroy the *yagnya*. Ram-Lakshman fought with them and killed Subahu. Mareech was thrown miles away, at a great distance by a single arrow from Ram. It is believed, Mareech took to spirituality, since then, till Ravan forced him to take the form of golden deer, to kidnap Sita. The *Yagnya* was completed without any further hindrance.

On Way to *Grihasthashram*

Sage Vishwamitra received an invitation from the king of Mithila, Janak, to grace the function of *Swayamvar,* whereby his daughter Sita would choose a person worthy of her to be her husband. As per the prevailing common practice, besides the notification to several kingdoms for the kings and princes to attend the ceremony, as eligible husbands, to win the hand of princess, several spiritual gurus were also invited to grace the occasion and bless the princess for her worthy choice. Janak was a prominent king in the country. He had in his possession, a sacred bow which originally belonged to Lord Shiva. Sita in her childhood used to play with it as if it was a horse, in the compound of the palace. Janak announced a condition that a person who would put a '*pratyancha*' (bow-string) to it, would be considered by Sita as a suitable life partner for her. Vishwamitra accepted the invitation of Janak to visit Mithila on the occasion and decided to take Ram-Lakshman with him. Actually, Ram-Lakshman wanted to go back to Ayodhya and meet Dashrath. However, Vishwamitra counselled them that probably, they would meet Dashrath at Mithila.

On the way, they came across an *Ashram* which appeared to be desolate and abandoned. There were lots of rocks around. They inquired with the Sage about the desolate *Ashram*. Vishwamitra told them the story of Ahilya while going through the *Ashram*.

Story of Ahilya

Ahilya, as the most beautiful woman in the world was created by Lord Brahma. At marriageable age, Brhama announced intention to marry her. As per the condition, the person who would circumambulate the earth first would be considered eligible to marry her. Several demi-gods, including Indra in their respective vehicles, raced to win the hand of Ahilya. Sage Gautam, an elderly Rishi circumambulated a cow, 'Surabhi', three times, who was in the process of giving birth to a calf, in labor, the head of the calf being visible. Brahma decreed that the act of Gautam was equivalent to circumambulation of earth and married her to Gautam. Indra had set his eyes on Ahilya and was keen to unite with her. On the day of total solar eclipse, Gautam and Ahilya had gone to the river for the ritual bath. Ahilya returned back to their hut, while Gautam was continuing with his prayers at the riverside. Indra arrived, feigning as Gautam, and sought the sexual favours from his 'wife', rather urgently. Ahilya expressed her displeasure at such a demand, particularly on the day of solar eclipse, but surrendered to 'husband's desire'. While Indra was at the doorstep to leave, Gautam arrived and saw Indra. He cursed Indra that he would become impotent, having commited a sin of defiling other person's wife, by caprice. He also cursed Ahilya to become lifeless as a rock, unseen and unnoticed by anybody. Ahilya pleaded with him that she was fooled by Indra, coming in the disguise of Gautam. The sage expressed displeasure with this argument, countering that if she had high moral stature, she could have recognized Indra as a fake person. However, taking her by her word, Gautam expiated the curse, directing her to go in for penance and austerities, till the Prince of Ayodhya, Ram would come with sage Vishwamitra, and liberate her. Indra went in hiding with disgress. He being in-charge of managing rain, drought like situation arose everywhere. Other demi-gods requested Gautam to expiate the curse on Indra. Indra profusely apologized to Gautam seeking pardon. Gautam went to Himalayas for penance and austerities, feeling sorry for punishing innocent Ahilya. It is believed that those who want to go up the ladder of divinity and spirituality, should refrain from anger and giving curse, and control their senses. Otherwise, their spiritual power would get depreciated. Gautam felt sorry on that count for hurling a curse on Ahilya.

At one place, in the desolate *Ashram*, Ram-Lakshman and Vishwamitra heard a human voice, chanting some *mantras*. As they went near the rock, a beautiful woman, who looked sacred and spiritually blessed, appeared and gave a respectful smile. She touched the feet of sage Vishwamitra and showed due respect to Ram-Lakshman, the princes of Ayodhya, the *Ashram* being located under the sovereign jurisdiction of Ayodhya kingdom. She offered hospitality by way of giving fruits. Ram and Lakshman also showed respect to her. Gautam Rishi arrived after some time, and greeted the guests at the *Ashram*. He expressed satisfaction at the penance of Ahilya, and rejuvenated the *Ashram*. Ahilya is rated as one of the *Panchkanya* in Indian cultural traditions, others being Tara (Harishchandra's wife), Sita (Ram's wife), Mandodari (Ravan's wife) and Draupadi (wife of five Pandavas), for devotion and loyalty to their husbands.

Sita: Birth and Upbringing

It was reported that Janak had no child. A peasant while ploughing the field of the king, found a decorated box. On being reported to the king, he immediately rushed to the field. On opening the box, Janak found a beautiful baby girl, with a smiling face. Janak and his queen, Sumedha were very happy to get this celestial gift from mother earth, *Bhumi-Mata*. They reared the baby with great affection. While once sage Parasuram visited Janak, he had kept his bow outside in the compound. After some time, he was surprised to find, child Sita playing and running in the compound, using the bow as a horse. Parasuram left the old bow with Janak, as a gift. The bow which was very heavy, was kept in the store room of the palace.

When Sita reached marriageable age, Janak sent messages to all prominent kingdoms about her '*Swayamvar*'. The eligibility criteria for marriage was that the king or the prince, who would string the bow, would be considered by Sita, eligible for selection as her life-partner.

Marriage

Ram-Lakshman led by sage Vishwamitra proceeded towards Mithila, which was not very far from the Gautam *Ashram*. King Janak welcomed Vishwamitra with respect, and inquired about the two young princes. Ram as Prince from Ayodhya, made polite inquiries about the well-being of King Janak and about Sita, for whose *Swayamvar*, they had arrived as visitors.

When Vishwamitra and Ram-Lakshman entered the hall, it was full with several kings from all parts of India. Sita was led in the hall sitting on a decorated elephant. The bow carried on an eight wheeled cart was placed at the centre of the hall. At the announcement of the beginning of the *Swayamvar* proceedings, several kings came one by one and tried to lift the bow, but failed to move it. At the last, as one story is reported, the demon-king Ravan, who was not specifically invited, came bragging, that since he had defeated all the demi-gods, including Indra, this contest was a child's play for him. He lifted the bow, but he fell down on his back, with the bow on his chest. It was difficult for him to move. With great difficulty, Janak's soldiers lifted the bow, and restored it back on the cart. It was reported that Ravan left the hall in a huff, greatly embarrassed. However, Ravan's presence on the occasion and the episode has not been universally accepted by people at large. It is considered as a myth. There was hush-hush in the hall about the impending failure of *Swayamvar* ceremony.

Thereupon, Vishwamitra signalled Ram to undertake the task. There was visible concern on the face of Janak and queen Sumedha, as to how this young man could lift the bow. Sita and her friends were appreciative of the handsome Rama, whom they had glanced as he came with Vishwamitra, but were concerned about his attempt. Queen Sumedha thought that Sita would have to remain unmarried. Ram went to the cart and meditated with closed eyes for few moments. After saluting the bow, which originally belonged to Shiva, and was presented by the celestial sage Parasuram, he lifted it with great ease with one hand. As he bent the bow for putting the string, there was a great sound, since the bow broke into two pieces. Complete silence ensued in the hall for a moment with great surprise. Sita accompanied by her friends walked graciously with a blissful smile towards Ram, and garlanded him as solicitous approval as life-partner. There was thunderous applause in the hall. There are several folk songs in Bihar about how Sita fell in love with Ram, as she saw this handsome prince. These romantic songs about how *Janaknandini*, that is, Sita, felt stunned when she saw handsome Ram first time, continue to be sung during marriage ceremonies in Bihar, and now at the musical concerts by professional singers. A folk song refers to a call to young woman to get ready with their best adornment of dress and jewellary (*Shringar*), since Ram broke the bow and established 'relationship' with Sita, meaning, to get ready for the marriage ceremony and festivities.

Messages were sent to King Dashrath, about the happenings, and inviting the Royal family, i.e. the Queens, brothers of Ram, Bharat and Shatrughna, for a ceremonial wedding of Ram and Sita. Sage Vashisth was invited, as also the ministers of Dashrath. On arrival, by mutual consultations, it was decided to offer Janak's other daughters, born after Sita was adopted as daughter from *Bhumata,* and his brother's daughters, in marriage to three brothers of Ram. Accordingly, Urmila was married to Lakshman. Janak's brother's daughters, Mandavi was married to Bharat and Shrutkirti to Shatrughna. The four brother-princes marrying four sister-princesses was unique, and made Ayodhya royal family, a remarkable joint family. On arrival back to Ayodhya, there were great celebrations. The citizens were hosted with delicious food and with gifts.

Kaikeyi's brother, Sangramjeet, also known as Yudhajeet, who had come for marriage celebrations, at Mithila and at Ayodhya, took back with him Bharat, Shatrughna and their wives, for a month-long holiday, to their kingdom at Kaikas, on Afganistan border.

Ayodhyakand: Summary

Dashrath had an idea of coronating Ram as the *Yuvraj* who would succeed him as the King. Kaikeyi insinuated by her hunchback maid Manthara forces Dashrath to accept to coronate her son, Bharat, as the *Yuvraj* and banish Ram to forest for 14 years. Ram, Lakshman and Sita leave for forest and visit the *ashrams* of sages and seek their advice about location for settling down in the forest. Dashrath breathes his last in shock. Bharat refusing to accept to get coronated as King, goes in search of Ram with the entire family, to persuade him to return to Ayodhya and accept the Kingship. Ram declines the offer in view of commitment to father Dashrath to be away in the forest for 14 years. A compromise solution is reached whereby Ram as a king would be installed in Ayodhya symbolised by his *Paduka* and the duties of kingship being performed under the leadership of Bharat. Accordingly, Bharat settles down at the outskirt of Ayodhya, at Nandigram as a hermit, and conducts administration.

Ayodhyakand

Ram-Lakshman continued with their training and practice in the use of arms, under the supervision of Vashisth. Dashrath desired to witness the battle-prowess of Ram-Lakshman. At a special stadium, the show was arranged by Vashisth, to be witnessed by the King, ministers and some prominent citizens. After paying obeisance to the various arms exhibited there, both brothers showed their use, riding the chariot and on the ground. The skill of using one arrow to hit several enemy heads or one arrow multiplying into several arrows were exhibited. The arms given by sage Vishwamitra were also practised. The skill of creating fire or rain was stupefying. Dashrath and Vashisth were very happy with the presentations by Ram-Lakshman. Sita and Urmila were with the queen-mothers-in-law, Kaushalya and Sumitra, serving them and learning the duties as daughters-in-law, receiving great love and affection.

King Dashrath was ruminating about annointing Ram as Crown-Prince (*Yuvraj*) to take over kingship from him, at an appropriate time. He consulted *Rajguru* Vashisth and his ministers, who concurred with the King that Ram was capable of taking over the responsibilities of kingship. An auspicious day (*muhurta)* was chosen in the month of *Chaitra*, first month of national lunar calendar, in the spring season, when *Pushyanaksatra* coincided on Thursday (*Guru-Pushya*), which is supposed to be very auspicious. On this day, currently, it is considered auspicious for the people to purchase gold from the market, which is visible by the customers making a bee-line at the jewellors' shops. The sacred day of proposed coronation was not far off.

The administrative machinery was geared to make the preparations to decorate the city and to invite the guests and arrange for their hospitality. The ritual arrangements were being supervised by sage Vashisth and administration was to be supervised by the minister, Sumant. King called for Ram and informed him of his desire to coronate him formally as the Crown-Prince (*Yuvraj*). Ram said, he would abide by the orders and desire of the father and the King. Vashisth advised Ram-Sita to observe fast on the previous day of coronation and sleep on the sacred grass (*Darbha*).

King Dashrath personally went to the palace rooms of Kaushalya, where Sumitra and Lakshman were also present. Both the queens were very happy to know the desire of the King to coronate Ram as the Prince. Lakshman expressed his happiness by saying that he would be happy to assist brother Ram in discharging his duties as per his directions.

Kaikeyi's Boons

While this process was on, queen Kaiakeyi's personal maid, Manthara, who was a hunch-back and had been with her since her marriage, having come with her from the maternal kingdom, became irritated about the gossip that Ram was to be coronated. She had seen Kaikeyi since her childhood, probably as her distant kin. She asked Kaikeyi, whether she had heard about Ram's coronation as the Crown-Prince. Kaikeyi expressed pleasure, at the news from Manthara. Manthara blurted out that Kaikeyi was a fool, not understanding her interests and that of her son, Bharat. "Was it not a conspiracy that the coronation was planned while Bharat was away?" Kaikeyi did not accept her argument, but knowing Manthara's loyalty to her, she said, "If you are right, what is the problem? And what is to be done?"Manthara said, "Have you forgotten that the King had offered you two boons, when you saved his life during a battle, in which he participated to assist Indra? You have forgotten that there was a big fight between the King Sambara and Indra, and Indra sought the heip of Dashrath. You wanted to see the heaven ruled by Indra and you sought the permission of *Guru* Vashisth, to accompany the King. During the actual battle, when Dashrath was attacking Sambara, you became the charioteer. Dashrath was critically injured and you very cleverly took the chariot to a safe place. You nursed him and he revived. He expressed that you had given him another life. So he offered you two boons to be complied with immediate effect. You said, you were happy about the king being out of danger and his availability to her as the youngest and most beautiful queen, for his exclusive affections. You thanked him for the boons and said, you would ask for them at an appropriate time. So, my dear Kaikeyi, now is the time." "And what do you think, I should seek from him?" asked confused Kaikeyi. Manthara said, "By one boon, ask him to coronate Bharat as the

Crown-Prince. And by another, ask him to send Ram to forest, in exile, for 14 years. Use your feminine charms and demand your right obstinately. You are his youngest and most beautiful queen. He is fond of you. The two senior Queens are jealous of you on that count. People in Ayodhya gossip about King's special love for you. They say that your romantic affection keeps him young. So this is the time. You will live your life as King's mother. If Ram is coronated, you will be a slave of Kaushalya, and Bharat will face a risk of life from Ram." Kaikeyi took time to absorb the advice of Manthara which was in her son's interest. Knowing well that the King had gone to meet the other Queens, he was expected to reach her shortly. Manthara again reminded that the time was too short, since the King was expected any moment.

Kaikeyi swiftly removed her royal jewellary and royal dress, and lied down in a desolate room on the floor, not on the bed, in the mourning mood and posture. When King arrived to meet Kaikeyi, unlike on other occasions, whence he would be greeted with a smile and romantic posture, she was not to be seen in her royal palace. When he asked Manthara about the whereabouts of Kaikeyi, he was directed to the desolate room with a remark, that it was inconceivable as to what was wrong with the queen, that she was in a mourning mood. "She was eagerly awaiting your arrival and was very upset with all of us, for no reason."

King went to the room and seeing Kaikeyi lying on the ground was shocked. He affectionately fondled her face and inquired as to what was wrong. He said that he had come to tell her that her son, Ramchandra, was to be coronated as Crown-Prince rather expeditiously, next day morning, since the auspicious *muhurta* of planetary constellation was available. The priests advised not to miss out such an auspicious and rare constellation. He wondered, on such an auspicious occasion, what was wrong with his sweetheart? He entreated her to tell him the cause of her grief, which he could instantly remove, and make her happy and lovable as always. She said that she could not trust the King anymore. The King could not understand anything. He only said, whatever she wanted as a Royal queen would be done without any delay, rather instantly. There was nothing that could create hurdles in the coronation ceremony. She said, "You have forgotten the two boons you gave me." He said "Yes, indeed I had forgotten about it. But you ask for it, and it will be given instantly, that is my promise as the King, following the traditions of our Raghu dynasty." She said, "Please swear in the name of our dear Ram, that you will keep your promise." He again reiterated that she was not to suspect and question the traditions of Raghu dynasty. "Then listen, Oh, great King of Raghu dynasty: By one boon, I want Bharat to be coronated as the Prince in place of Ram". The King said, by doing that, we would be breaking the traditions of kingship, universally followed all over the world. She said, "You have to decide whether you want to break the promise given to me just now, and become a laughing stock, that your word of honour was not to be trusted." King said, "Okay, I will send message to Bharat to come back for his coronation, finding some other auspicious day. I am sure, Ram will have no ill-feeling for Bharat to be anointed as crown-prince. At the assembly, he had shown reluctance to accept to become crown-prince. Are you satisfied now queen Kaikeyi? And what is your second demand?" Kaikeyi said, "By another boon, I want Ram to be sent to forest for fourteen years, to live hermit's life." It was as if lightening struck the King and he lost his balance, while sitting by her side. She further said, "You may not accept my demands, but then, you would be violating the noble traditions of your ancestors." King swooned and in semi-conscious state, blurted that she could ask for anything else, except sending Ram to forest. "I will not survive without Ram with me." Kaikeyi said that there was no going back on her demand. "Either Ram goes to the forest in the morning, or my dead body leaves this palace." It was for him to accept or reject it, and face the consequences of public ridicule. The King fell on the ground in an unconscious state.

As the dawn was approaching, Sage Vashisth felt concerned, that there was no further message from the King. He asked the minister Sumant, to personally go and inquire with the King about further procedures and get Ram-Sita ready for the rituals. While Sumant finally traced King to the palace of Kaikeyi, he was informed by Kaikeyi that the King having kept awake whole night, was sleeping and asked Sumant, to send Ram expeditiously to meet the King. As Ram arrived at Kaikaeyi's palace, he was surprised to see King Dashrath lying on the ground, unable to speak. Lakshman seeing Ram rushing towards Kaikeyi's palace, also followed him. Ram asked, "Mother, what is wrong with the father. Why is he crying and lying on the ground?" Kaikeyi said, "The King was ill and not in a position to tell his mind. I will tell you what he intended to tell you." She then narrated that the King had given her two boons, when she saved his life in a battle. She asked for those two boons now, the one being that Bharat be annointed as the *Yuvraj* to become the next king, and that you should go to the forest for fourteen years. The King following the traditions of your royal dynasty accepted to honour his word and for that purpose, he called you here. Ram said, "Oh! Why should he become ill on this count. Bharat is my brother. He is very affectionate and competent. I would have willingly proposed his name for the kingship. As for going to the forest, I am being given the whole forest, full of nature, and where the *Rishis* dwell. This would be a good opportunity for me to learn at their feet. I have experienced the bliss of forest life and these *ashrams,* when I and Lakshman went with sage Vishwamitra. I have absolutely no problem in fulfilling the promise he made to you." Dashrath moaned and said, "This was between me and Kaikeyi. You are not bound by my foolish acceptance of the cruel demands of wicked Kaikeyi. I do not know, why she has become mad. As we know, Bharat has great regard and affection for you. I know, he himself would not approve of what his mother desires for him." Lakshman did not say anything. However, one could see from his expressions and body language, and knowing his short temperament, that, he would be bubbling to attack Kaikeyi. Ram said that this was not a matter of debate. He felt honoured to obey and comply with his father's and mother's wishes. He then proceeded to Kaushalya's palace to seek her blessings. Queens Kaushalya and Sumitra were expecting Ram to arrive to seek their blessings, before getting ready for the coronation rituals. However, Ram arrived, followed by Lakshman, to report what had happened in Kaikeyi's dwelling. The queen mothers were shocked to hear such catastrophic happenings, in a flash, like an earthquake or lightening, without any premonition. Mother Kaushalya composed herself and said, "As your father has commited you to his boons to Kaikeyi, I as your mother ask you not to follow his desires. You are also bound to follow what your mother orders you." However, Ram said, "Father was also the King and his wishes need to be followed in letter and spirit." Kaushalya said, "In the backyard of this palace, there is a dense forest. You could stay there in a hut. Otherwise I will come with you to the forest for 14 years."Ram appreciated this show of concern and affection. But the essence of Ram to go to forest, as promised by the King in fulfilling the boon given to Kaikeyi, was not something, which could be met by such white-wash actions. This kind of circumvention would make a mockery of the promises made by the King, and would be liable to public ridicule. Lakshman said that, he would accompany Ram to the forest, and be on guard against the attacks of demons, who considered themselves as the masters of forest territory and forest resources. They had experienced demons attacking the Rishi *ashrams* and demolish their *Yagnya*. Lakshman's mother Sumitra supported the idea of Lakshman, accompanying Ram. Actually, one of the ideas of Manthara advising Kaikeyi to seek banishment of Ram to forest for 14 years was that Ram could not survive the attacks of demons for 14 years, and thereby would never be a risk or threat to Bharat's rule as the king of Ayodhya. When Sita came to know of these happenings, she came rushing to Kaushalya's palace. She said, she had not married Ram to be away from him. As his wife, she was like his shadow, all the time. She pressed that she would accompany Ram to the forest. Ram tried to dissuade her, saying that the life in the forest was very difficult, and frought with dangers, from wild beasts and demons. However, Sita would not give up. She touched the feet of Vashisth and prayed him to allow her to be with Ram, as his shadow, all her life. Ultimately, Sage Vashisth consented that Ram, Lakshman and Sita would go together to the forest for 14 years.

King Dashrath had no choice. He said, his position was like an elephant, who would fall in a muddy pond; or a tiger trapped by a hunter; or like a fish stuck in the throat. He suggested that they could take a protective army with them and accept all the state facilities to be comfortable in the forest. Kaikeyi said that they were not going for a pleasure trip, but to live the life of hermits. The hermit's clothes were provided to Ram-Lakshman and Sita by Kaikeyi. Sita was helped by Kaikeyi and Ram to drape her forest clothes. Sage Vashisth who was otherwise silent, reprimanded Kaikeyi in front of everybody, when he found Sita being draped in very coarse clothes, which could hurt her. At the insistence of Dashrath, they were to be carried in a chariot, up to Ayodhya border, by the minister Sumant personally. While Ram, Lakshman and Sita touched the feet of Dashrath, Kaushalya, Sumitra and Kaikeyi, and left the palace to ride the chariot, King Dashrath followed them to the main gate of the palace, and then went up on the balcony to see their chariot.

Thousands of citizens of Ayodhya followed the chariot. Many citizens expressed the resolve to accompany Ram, Sita, Lakshman to the forest. As they were to cross the boundary of Ayodhya, Ram addressed them and thanked them for their affection. He said, "Please go back and look after your families and the welfare of the Kingdom. King Dashrath needs your support in difficult times. We will be back soon to be with you." Majority of the people returned back. However, some of them followed them till they camped for the night halt, at the bank of Sarayu river, to cross it over next day morning. The citizens also had a night halt, to accompany them next day morning, to the forest.

The people of Ayodhya could not understand this turnabout in few hours, from impending coronation ceremony and festivity, to the exile of Yuavraj to the forest. Some of the servants and maids who were attached to the palaces of the Queens had witnessed the rushing of Ram, Lakshman as also Sumant and sage Vashisth from one palace to another in a huff and puff. It was obvious that the centre of activity was centred in Kaikeyi's palace where King Dashrath was closeted with Queen Kaikeyi for the whole night. This led to considerable gossip in the town, about unreasonable demands by Kaikeyi, conceded by King Dashrath, leading to sudden exile of the crown-prince. Ayodhya citizens were shocked to see Ram, Lakshman and Sita doning the hermits' apparel in the royal chariot.

People were blaming the carnal affection of King Dashrath for Kaikeyi. There was gossip among the citizens blaming King Dashrath, to agree to the wishes of a woman, Kaikeyi. People knew that being the youngest and beautiful, Dashrath was fond of her. She used to accompany him even on his official tours, including some battlefields, to see the places around. Actually, when Dashrath was injured in a battle, whereby she nursed him in the chariot, taking it aside, she had accompanied him to see the heaven, since he was scheduled to meet Indra. It was inconceivable for citizens to understand, as to how could a King fall a prey to the wishes of a woman, about recommending her son's coronation, who was not even present in Ayodhya; setting aside the age-old traditions of the eldest son succeeding the father-King. So, the stereotypical image of women under patriarchy was expressed, that women were never to be trusted. When all preparations had been made for the ritual ceremony of coronation, guests and sages, priests having arrived, how could things change overnight, not only denying the right of Ram to be the Crown-Prince, as decided by the King himself, but banish him from the kingdom to forest for a long period of 14 years? They were all praise for Ram for showing disinterest in his anointment as Crown-Prince, and for being an obedient son, to a fault. They were wondering as to what would King Janak feel about Ram-Sita going to the forest? Where had the manliness of Dashrath vanished that he should dance to the tune of a woman? Many people felt, King Dashrath would be punished by destiny, for falling prey to the capricious wishes of a woman. Dashrath had clearly violated the principle of *Rajdharma,* and falling prey to the machinations of a woman.

Ram-Lakshman-Sita for *Vanvas*

At the bank of river Sarayu, before dawn, Ram-Lakshman-Sita and Sumant got away in the chariot in a different direction, before the citizens woke up. They reached an area which was ruled by Guhak, the chieftain of Nishad community, who are forest dwellers, under the surveillance of Ayodhya kingdom. While Ram relaxed under a banyan tree on grass, Guhak came to inquire about the guests. The chariot appeared royal while Ram-Sita-Lakshman were doning the robes of hermits with the distinct hermit hairstyle. Guhak inquired with Sumant as to who were these handsome young men and the beautiful young woman. Guhak was surprised to know their real identity, as from the royal family of Ayodhya. They had heard that Ram was to be coronated as the *Yuvraj,* destined to become the next King. They had also heard the story of Ram, liberating Ahilya. Guhak offered them to reside in his chieftaincy, offering full protection. He invited them hospitality, but Ram declined saying they would take only fruits. Ram requested Guhak to arrange for them, to cross the river Ganga in a boat. Guhak's mother said to her son, "How can you ask them to go in a small boat?" Guhak ensured his mother, that he would personally go with them in the boat to cross the Ganga. Ram embraced Guhak with great affection. Ram advised Sumant to go back to Ayodhya and report about their safety. He advised Sumant to report to the King and Queen-mothers, not to feel concerned about them. "We will be back after 14 years as promised and directed". Kevat, the boatman who navigated the small boat to cross the Ganga river, was very happy to meet Ram, Lakshman and Sita. He and his wife offered great respect to Ram by washing his feet with Ganga water, and subsequently of Sita and Lakshman, before taking them on the boat . . . Significant folk literature and folk songs are available on the dialogue of Ram and Kevat, the boatman.

After crossing Ganga river, the three then proceeded to *ashram* of Sage Bharadwaj, near Prayag. The sage was very happy to provide them hospitality, having heard the happenings in Ayodhya. Ram inquired about a good place to stay in the forest for a considerable period. Bharadwaj directed them to go and settle down at Chitrakoot hills, and gave them topographical directions to reach the place. Several seers had their *ashrams* in that area. Accordingly, the three followed the path and crossed Kalindi river, on a raft of wood, made by Lakshman, and covering it with grass, for Sita to sit comfortably. They enjoyed the beautiful nature, full of birds and trees, laden with flowers and fruits. They saw the Chitrakoot hills, and selecting a small plateau, decided to settle down. Lakshman like an expert architect, constructed a hut from wood and grass, as is made by the tribals. There were enough roots and tubers in the area to collect as food. Rituals like *yagnya* by way of '*Vastushant*' (house-warming) was performed by Ram, before entering the hut. Food consisted of roots, tubers, eatable leaves, fruits and some small game roasted on open fire. They visited the *ashrams* of Sages in the region, and gained knowledge about the area, during conversations. Sita thoroughly enjoyed the nature. Ram and Sita used to walk around, enjoying nature and identifying the various kinds of trees and birds. From a plateau, they could also witness the movements of tribal men and women, engaged in collection of roots, tubers and fruits, as food.

Death of King Dashrath

Sumant was very reluctant to leave Ram-Sita-Lakshman with Guhak, and report back to Ayodhya. He had no courage to face King Dashrath and queen-mothers, Kaushalya and Sumitra, without bringing back Ram-Sita and Lakshman with him. Ram ultimately had to tell Sumant that going back to Ayodhya was his formal directive, which had to be complied. Sumant went back alone to Ayodhya in the chariot, covering his face, while entering Ayodhya. When he reached the palace, he found King Dashrath was still moaning, and uttering nothing but Ram, Oh! Ram. He was still hoping that Ram-Sita and Lakshman would be back with Sumant. Kaikeyi and Manthara were concerned, whether Ram could be back with Sumant. When Sumant reported to the King about Ram crossing the Ganga to go further beyond Prayag, Dashrath's hopes were totally shattered. He also remembered the curse by Shravan's father about his death, while longing for his sons. However he made anxious inquiries about where they stayed, where they slept, and what food they ate, and from where. He was concerned about Sita, as to how she could walk distances and felt apologetic and guilty. He was wondering as to how to face King Janak, who had brought up Sita with affection, and married in his family. Kaushalya and Sumitra were in the room when Dashrath talked to Sumant. After Sumant left the room, Dashrath breathed his last. It took quite some time for Kaushalya and Sumitra to realize that he was no more.

News of Dashrath's death spread like wild fire. Sumant informed the *Rajguru*, Vashisth, who came forthwith. It was a piquant situation, that not a single son was present to perform the last rites. Vashisth directed Sumant to arrange to reach out to Bharat and bring them back expeditiously. He was careful in his instructions. He said, "The messengers after reaching Kaikas, the kingdom of Kaikeyi's brother, should tell Bharat, that they were called urgently for some official work by the ministers. The messengers should not show any grief on their face. Not only that, they should carry the gifts for the king's family, as per usual protocols."

In the meantime, Vashisth arranged for the body of Dashrath to be preserved in a trough full of oil, till the return of Bharat. He said that the funeral rites had to be performed by the King in office. Kingdom could not be without a ruler, without the king.

Return of Bharat

As Bharat-Shatrughna were approaching Ayodhya, they found eerie silence all the way. Bharat was received by Sumant. Bharat proceeded to his mother Kaikeyi's dwelling. Shatrughna went to the chambers of his mother Sumitra. Bharat could sense that everything did not seem to be normal. His mother was not in her usual exuberant self. She was not wearing her royal attire or jewellary. His mother, Kaikeyi welcomed him in a low voice and inquired about his journey, and about her maternal family. Bharat asked about his father Dashrath and about Ram and Sita. Kaikeyi said, "I have to appraise you about the happenings at Ayodhya in your absence, the good and the bad of it." Bharat said, "I do not understand anything. I do not know why we were called expeditiously from Kaikas. The messengers with the chariot would not say anything. The minister Sumant received us but did not tell us anything, except asking us to take rest after a long journey. Please tell, what is what?" Kaikeyi said, "Please listen carefully, since you have to shoulder and perform onerous responsibilities as a Prince in the Raghu-kul. The King wanted to anoint Ram as the Crown-Prince to head the kingdom and made preparations for his coronation. At the last moment, he changed his mind and wanted you to be the Crown-Prince instead of Ram. Many citizens and officers of the Kingdom, including sage Vashisth were not in agreement with the King. The King took ill, and he breathed his last. So, you were invited expeditiously to take over the reigns of Kingdom, and rule as a kshatriya as per the glorious traditions of your ancestors. You have to perform obsequies of your father, whose body has been preserved in oil, awaiting your arrival. Be brave and perform your duties." Bharat was flabbergasted, but keeping cool, inquired as to where have been Ram and Lakshman, when the King expired, and where were they now? Kaikeyi said that Ram-Lakshman and Sita had left for Dandkaranya forest, before the death of Dashrath. Bharat was totally confused and asked as to why these changes at the last moment, and why they left for forest? In the meantime, Sage Vashisth and Sumant arrived. Before Vashisth could say something, Kaikeyi said, the changes were brought about by her in the interest of Bharat, to become king, instead of Ram. Bharat was shocked, and blurted out in anger, as to what prompted her to break the age old traditions of the eldest son, as crown-prince, to be the next King, and how could his father, King Dashrath agree to break such glorious traditions? Thereupon, Kaikeyi told him the story of getting boons from the king, for nursing him in a battle, that helped him to revive fast from the injuries. It was a kind of rebirth for him. So the king was pleased with her, and asked her to seek two boons from him. Kaikeyi said, she sought the crown for Bharat and sending Ram to the forest for 14 years. The king reluctantly agreed, since he had given the sacred promise to sanction the boons, and acted on it, as per the traditions of the ruling dynasty of Ayodhya. The destiny had it, that having completed his life-time responsibilities and ensuring transfer of Kingship to Bharat, he left his mortal body, as it happened with every mortal being. Now, we are sure that his soul will rest in peace, after the soul is freed from the body. She again asked Bharat to be brave like a Kshatriya and perform the duties of an obedient son, to perform the funeral rites, and prepare to guide the kingdom as the king. "As your mother, I could get for you to be the King of Ayodhya, which you eminently deserved."

Bharat was livid with anger. He said, "Are you a mother, wife of the King or a snake who poisoned and murdered him to death? How did you think, that I would accept and commit such a preposterous sin? If you were not my mother, I would have killed you forthwith. Instead of Ram, you should have been banished. I can imagine how much the King must have gone through agony, which led to his sudden death, when none of his sons were here. So, he did not die a natural death. You murdered him. Shame on me, that I was born of your womb. I do not want to see your face in life." Saying this, he walked off her place, and went to meet Ram-Lakshman's mothers, Kaushalya and Sumitra, followed by Vashisth and Sumant. Manthara was keeping a distance and was not visible, hiding herself behind a pillar. After Bharat left, she counselled Kaikeyi, assuring that after Bharat's coronation, everything would become normal. "You will be the Queen-mother. May God bless you."

The news about Bharat's return to Ayodhya reached Kaushalya and Sumitra. They were thinking of meeting Bharat, while Bharat arrived in their dwelling, crest fallen. Kaushalya knew that Vashisth and the ministers had sent the chariot to bring Bharat-Shatrughna forthwith, for taking up the kingship and for performing obsequies. As Bharat touched the feet of his two mothers, Kaushalya and Sumitra, the queen-mother Kaushalya said, "My blessings to you to accept the kingship, ensured for you by your mother, Kaikeyi for you. We have one request to you, as the King. Please allow us to join your father in death, on the funeral pyre. Or, let us join our sons in the forest." Hearing such words, Bharat started sobbing and clung to the feet of Kaushalya. He said, "Do you think mother, that I would ever agree to be the King of Ayodhya, in place of our dear Ram? I knew nothing about all these happenings till I reached here just now. It is a miracle, how I am not dead, with this shocking news." Sage Vashisth intervened to say that Bharat knew nothing about these tragedies and machinations, until he arrived here. We had instructed the messenger who had gone to fetch him from Kaikas kingdom, to keep it a secret and control the body language, lest it would arouse any suspicion. He further said, that women with sons were not expected to self-immolate themselves, on the funeral pyre of their husbands. Anyway, Ram-Lakshman will return to Ayodhya after 14 years. We can also go to forest to meet them. But now that seven days are already over, since the mortal remains of the King have been preserved, we should prepare forthwith for the funeral. It is our bounden duty to help release the soul from the mortal remains, by conducting the funeral rites, as per traditions. Saying this, everybody left the palace to make further arrangements for funeral, worthy of the great King.

The cremation of the King was carried out with due solemnity on the bank of Sarayu river, in the presence of citizens of Ayodhya. The funeral procession through the streets of Ayodhya provided opportunity to the citizens to have the last glimpse of the mortal remains of the King and pay their respects. The ashes were collected for immersion in Sarayu river and at the confluence of holy rivers at Prayag. After 14 days of death, a portion of the ashes were immersed in Sarayu river and some preserved to be immersed at Prayag, possibly by Ram-Lakshman.

The formal meeting of the ministers and advisers was convened to take further action about the smooth administration of the kingdom, under the leadership of Bharat, as the new king to be coronated, following the traditional religious rituals. Minister Sumant requested sage Vashisth to initiate proceedings about Prince Bharat to be coronated as the King, as agreed by King Dashrath to the proposal of queen Kaikeyi. Sage Vashisth addressed Bharat. "You are now aware about the unfortunate situation in which the Kingdom of Ayodhya is placed. Kingdom cannot remain unheaded without the King. As desired by King Dashrath, and agreed by Ram, please take over the reigns of Kingdom as the King and follow the dynastic traditions of this kingdom. Let the Kingdom be restored to normalcy and let it rise to new heights under your benign leadership." The general assembly of ministers, advisers and representatives of citizens lapsed into hush-hush silence with the address by Vashisth, but showing concurrence to Guru Vashisth's proposal, by their body communication with shaking heads in assent.

Bharat became emotional, and addressed the Assembly, with tears in his eyes. He thanked particularly sage Vashisth, who was a father figure as *Guru* and minister Sumant, to take steps to organize the affairs of the kingdom with the unimaginable tragedy of King's sudden demise, in grief of Ram-Lakshman and Sita going to the forest. He thanked the citizens for maintaining peace and fortitude, in such an unprecedented and unforeseen calamity, which came as lightening. He also expressed gratitude for proposing him to take over the affairs of the State as King, as per the traditions and customs of governance. He said. "With due respects to all of you, I hereby decline to accept the office as King, which rightfully belongs to the eldest son, and my dear brother Ram, as announced by King Dashrath. It is very unfortunate that through machinations and playing with the emotions and dignity of the King, the tragedies have occurred. I am getting everything, and being offered by you, in good faith, being born to Kaikeyi. What do I do as King Dashrath's son and as brother of Ram? Do I accept what Kaikeyi planned, for what reason, I do not know, without consulting me? So, I am unable to accept your proposal, which you are making in the interest of kingdom. Your *bona fides* are not questionable. They are noble and practical. What Kaikeyi wanted from the King, digging the past and reminding the King of the boons, at the behest of wicked Manthara, was given by him, as promised, but paying the price of his life. So, that matter is over. I am not complying with the wishes of Queen Kaikeyi, for which she could curse me. Ram is already in the forest. When he left Ayodhya, Ayodhya was being ruled by King Dashrath and as per his promise under duress, he was to train me in kingship by anointing me as Crown Prince. However, the situation has now totally changed, for which we have to find a new solution. Ram has already followed the wishes of the King and Queen, without any grudge or complaint. Why should my compliance to what queen Kaikeyi wanted me to do, without my knowledge and consent, be the cause of suffering to Ram-Lakshman and Sita? Why should I be the cause of their suffering and my father's death? I refuse to be a party to this great sin which does not befit a Prince of the Raghu dynasty. Please correct me, Oh! Honourable Sages, Seniors, and wise and knowledgeable noble persons, if I am wrong."

"I have an alternative proposal for your kind consideration. It is in our hands, and it is our ethical and moral responsibility, to undo the situations which caused these tragedies. I propose to go to the forest, to meet dear Ram and persuade him to return to Ayodhya, and take over the Kingship as per the traditions, and as desired by Late King Dashrath, for which all the preparations were completed. I would request you to accompany me in this mission. I am confident that God will accept our wish, and persuade Ram to lead us. Otherwise, I will have no choice but to live with Ram in the forest, and Shatrughna to perform the functions of kingship."

The ministers, advisers and sage Vashisth were greatly impressed with the spirit and commitment of Bharat's arguments. They readily agreed with Bharat, and complimented him for his wisdom, and affection and respect for his elder brother, Ram. He then asked Sumant to make arrangements for the travel to the forest. "Since

Sumant had left Ram-Lakshman and Sita up to the banks of river Ganga, under the stewardship of our friend, Guhak, he could lead us to seek Ram's further destination." Bharat also requested *Guru* Vashisth, to accompany them to persuade Ram, and if possible to have his coronation, at his present residence in the forest. He requested Sumant to carry the King's crown to the forest for coronation of Ram, as the King of Ayodhya. He also requested to keep King Janak informed about these decisions.

Bharat meets Ram (*Bharat-Bhet*)

Bharat-Shatrughna, with a large contingent of army, to protect the entourage from unforeseen attacks on the way, accompanied by Queen-mothers, Kaushalya-Sumitra, sage Vashisth and minister Sumant started the journey in search of Ram. Guhak's informers appraised the chieftain about an army contingent approaching their territory and formed themselves in defending position. However, Guhak recognized the flag of Ayodhya and saw Sumant in a chariot. So, he welcomed them at the border and offered hospitality. After introduction with Bharat-Shatrughna and Queen-mothers, and paying respects to sage Vashisth, they discussed the route of Ram towards the forest via Prayag, crossing Ganga river. They proceeded to the *ashram* of Sage Bhardwaj with which Vashisth was familiar. Bharadwaj also offered hospitality to everybody including the troops. He was particularly happy to meet his spiritual senior Vashisth. He was also appreciative of the efforts of Bharat to get back Ram to Ayodhya as a rightful Ruler. He told them about the abode of Ram at Chitrakoot. Guhak helped all of them to cross Ganga river.

As they were approaching Chitrakoot, Lakshman could see, from their location on the pleatue, a large army approaching in their direction. He also identified the flag of Ayodhya on the chariots and some *palanquin*. Not knowing about the death of King Dashrath, Lakshman was perplexed as to the motive of Ayodhya army heading towards them. However, Ram counselled him and identified Bharat approaching him with great speed. Bharat and

Shatrughna also saw some smoke at a spot on the mid-portion of the hill. As per directions of Bharadwaj *rishi,* they surmised, that could be the habitation of Ram-Lakshman-Sita. Smoke would indicate the *'Homa'* (sacred fire/fire worship) that would be performed by Ram as daily ritual.

Bharat asked his troops and some citizens of Ayodhya, who had accompanied them to camp at an open space at ground level. Bharat-Shatrughna, Sage Vashisth and Sumant went walking, and the two queen-mothers following them in a palanquin. Coming face-to-face with Ram-Lakshman in their hermit dress and hairstyle, Bharat embraced Ram while sobbing. This embrace has been immortalized in Indian expression as '*Bharat-Bhet*', the meeting of two souls in great affection.

Ram also saw Kaushalya and Sumitra getting out of the palanquin, at a distance, wearing white sarees, and was perplexed. Sita was inside the hut, but came out with bustle, hearing movements and multiple voices. As Queen-mothers walked slowly towards Ram, both Ram-Lakshman followed by Sita touched the feet of Vashisth and the mothers, and became emotional with tears, rolling down the eyes. Sage Vashisth announced to Ram about the death of King Dashrath. Sumant briefed about the sequence after his return to Ayodhya, while Ram-Sita-Lakshman crossed river Ganga. For sometime, nobody could speak anything, as Ram-Lakshman-Sita were stunned. Suddenly, everybody present at the site started sobbing with the sad news. Then, they were seated on the grass mats, in the verandah of the hut. The mats prepared by Lakshman were the beds of the three.

Vashisth narrated briefly about the details of King's sudden death, saying he never recovered after Ram left for the forest. He also told about the meeting of General Assembly to request prince Bharat to agree for formal coronation and take up the responsibilities as King. Bharat declined to be the King of Ayodhya in Ram's lifetime. He did not want to share the sin committed by Kaikeyi. So, they had come there, as per Bharat's proposal to request Ram to return to Ayodhya and accept the responsibilities, as were designed by the King for Ram's coronation as Crown-Prince. Bharat said, "Dear brother, you have already followed your father's wishes in letter and spirit. Our father has left for his abode. Now you come to your abode, that is, Ayodhya." There was total silence. In the meantime, Sita brought the fruits from the hut and kept them on leaf-plates. She informed about the natural products of Chitrakoot, which were in abundance, and requested everybody to taste them. Everybody became fresh with a wash from the river water, and settled down to enjoy the fruits. There was brief conversation about the Chitrakoot area. The area had several *ashrams* of *rishi-munis*. Ram-Lakshman used to visit them for philosophical discussions. There were some local communities in the forest around, known as Kol, Kirat, Bhil, who collected roots, tubers, fruits and edible leaves of trees, and shared with them.

After the hospitality and polite discussion, Vashisth informed Ram that the funeral ashes were partly immersed in Sarayu river, and some were brought in an urn, to be immersed at the confluence of sacred rivers at Prayag. Since the chariots and horses were available, it would not be time consuming to make a trip to Prayag. In the meantime, the troops with assistance from Ayodhya citizens, erected few temporary huts for the guests. Next day morning, the four brothers with sage Vashisth and Sumant went to Prayag to perform the rites of immersion of ashes. They again called on Bharadwaj *rishi* briefly.

King Janak had kept himself informed about the affairs at Ayodhya. All the four princes were sons-in-law of King Janak's family. There was no point in going to Ayodhya, while Dashrath's mortal remains were preserved in oil, in the absence of Bharat-Shatrughna. There was a big row between Bharat and his mother Kaikeyi after his return, whereby he disowned his mother. While Janak got information about the princes and their mothers having gone to Chitrakoot, Janak and Queen Sumedha headed for Chitrakoot to meet all and share their grief. They did not go to Ayodhya.

Dharma and Rajdharma: Ram-Bharat Dialogue

Pressure was getting built up on Ram to return to Ayodhya and take up the position, which was originally designated by the King. The public opinion expressed, that there was no moral violation any more on the part of Ram, of disobedience to the wishes of King Dashrath, which was made under duress. Ram had already complied with the wishes of King Dashrath by going to the forest. It was a matter of opinion as to what was *Dharma*. There was a difference of opinion between Ram and Bharat on this point. Kaushalya, Vashisth and Janak saw the logic on both the sides, and decided not to intervene using their position and authority. They preferred to be silent on the issue, and quietly listened to the arguments of Ram and Bharat. Neither Ram, nor Bharat were willing to get coronated for kingship. Dashrath had desired Ram to be the next King, but agreed for Bharat's coronation, with the joyful consent of Ram. This had happened in the absence of Bharat, who had gone to Kaikas kingdom. If Bharat had agreed to be the king of Ayodhya, that would have meant that he assented to the demand of Kaikeyi, which she extracted from King Dashrath, by caprice, leading to his death. Bharat also put up a proposal, that he would remain in the forest for 14 years in lieu of Ram, while Ram would be the King of Ayodhya as was originally designed. That would also teach a lesson to Kaikeyi of the consequences of her adamant action, blackmailing the King, without any consultation with Bharat, for whom she played a dirty game. Bharat was willing to volunteer the punishment which his mother had inflicted on Ram, for no fault of his. Ram smiled and said to Bharat, "Hey, this is not a business transaction in a market, that such an exchange is transacted. I am obeying the wishes of my father and King, which I am morally bound to fulfil. Nothing changes because the King is no more. I am alive. Lakshman and Sita could go back since they were under no obligation to come with me. They came out of their deep affection for me. I am enjoying forest life with them. I am quite happy here. I will take up my responsibilities after the period of 14 years and 14 days were over. I promise to be in Ayodhya on the 15th day."

A compromise and workable solution was struck after discussions, at the initiative of sage Vashisth. Ram agreed to be formally coronated as King after 14 years of hermitage. In the meanwhile, Bharat would govern the Ayodhya kingdom on behalf of Ram, as his Agent. However, he would not do so from the authority throne of the King of Ayodhya, which belonged to Ram. Ram would be present at Ayodhya, symbolised by his '*Paduka*' (wooden footwear) honourably installed on the throne. There was a great satisfaction about this arrangement, till Ram returned to Ayodhya after 14 years. So, Ram was '*de jure*' King of Ayodhya, 'King-in-waiting', while Bharat was '*de-facto*' administrator-king, both of them owning the moral responsibility and authority of the King.

This arrangement set a record in human history, of*Vairagya*, *Virakti*, about dispassionately playing up the formal role of authority, but agreeing to discharge the duties for public good. The Self has been totally missing in this arrangement.

As the King, everybody was equal as public (*praja*), including the dear ones such as parents, children or wife. One has to sacrifice one's likings, your biases, your affections, for public good. The status as King was different from other statuses, that one may have as son, father, husband, friend etc. One may play those roles in private life. But as King in his official position, he was to treat everybody equally.

That is the *Dharma* of the king, *Raj-Dharma*, to keep the good of the people at the highest pedestal without favour or fear; to perform your duties without getting emotionally involved into it, for your subjective or personal gains. . Key message or term is 'Sacrifice Before Self'. The universal and eternal moral value, respected as the greatest virtue is: 'Truth (*Satya*) and *Dharma* become synonyms as concept, and in action'.

Before Bharat left for Ayodhya, they had several discussions about the duties of the King. Vashisth summarized by saying that the King represented or symbolized as God, in his kingdom. So, he had to treat everybody with equanimity without favour to anybody. Everybody is '*Praja*' including the dear ones in the family. Finally, Ram counselled Bharat not to treat his mother Kaikeyi with harshness. "She had nothing but goodness and intense affection for you. Her intentions about you were pure, which were conceded by the King. But she was mislaid by the destiny, again to ensure your safety and position, throughout life, without any hindrance from your brothers. Being the third Queen, probably she had not absorbed the values of solidarity of family, of brothers, of unflinching loyalty to parents. She was advised to be self-centred, out of affection for you, and that hurt our father, from which he could not recover. She is in the process of repentance. Understand, what is destined could not be avoided. We have to face it with the "Divine principle: that the Truth shall prevail, and there would be light after darkness". Bharat thanked Ram for his advice, whose approval was clearly seen in the eyes of sage Vashisth. After touching the feet of all elders, Bharat-Shatrughna departed for Ayodhya with sublime mental peace, and feeling of divine bliss. Bharat reminded Ram that if he did not reach on the 15th day after 14 years and 14 days, 'Bharat would have to depart for heavenly abode'. Bharat carried the *Paduka* of Ram as symbol of King's authority, on his head.

Bharat at Nandigram

After returning to Ayodhya, Bharat decided to settle down at Nandigram on the outskirts of Ayodhya. He got a hut constructed and lived like a hermit, donning the saffron clothes and the hairdo, as Ram-Lakshman were living in the forest. He kept Ram's '*paduka*' as deities, kept on a high pedestal. The administrators from Ayodhya would visit him to report to him and seek directions. Shatrughna was at the palace in Ayodhya, and would look after the Queen-mothers, and supervise routine administration, managed by Sumant. Sage Vashisth settled down in his own *ashram*, at the outskirts of Ayodhya, in a natural ambience without urban structures. When needed, he would be consulted on behalf of Bharat. For the past few months, particularly, during the last few days of King Dashrath and after his demise, he had to make several trips to Ayodhya, to be available, or take initiatives in the absence of the King.

Aranyakand: Summary

Ram, Sita and Lakshman continue their journey in the forest, Dandkaranya, visiting various sages in their ashrams, before settling down at Panchvati, which is currently a part of Nashik city in Western Maharashtra. Demon king Ravan's sister, Shurpankha soliciting the love of Ram and Lakshman and threatening to destroy Sita, was punished by defacing her nose (*Nasika*). Her other brothers, Khar and Dushan attacked Ram and got killed Shurpankha reports to Ravan in Lanka and advocates kidnapping beautiful Sita to be one of his queens. Ravan conspires to kidnap Sita with the help of demon Mareech who takes the form of a golden deer, grazing near their residential hut, so as to be seen by Sita. Sita attracted by the golden colour of the deer pleads with Ram to get it for her. While Ram is chasing the golden deer, in the woods, Ravan taking the form of a mendicant kidnaps Sita and carries her to Lanka, in his flying chariott (aircraft), '*Pushpak*'. The bird king, Jatayu tries to intercept Ravan and engages him in a fight but gets grievously injured, and dies after telling Ram about kidnapping of Sita, by demon king Ravan. Ram and Lakshman in search of Sita reach Pampa lake, in the vicinity of what is currently known as Hampi in Karnatak. They meet tribal old lady Shabari. She shows the way to reach out to Sugreev, the monkey-king, living at Kishkindha hills, with his trusted colleagues, such as Hanuman and Jambavan. She consoles them that Sugreev would help to locate Sita in Ravan's captivity.

Aranyakand

Ram and Lakshman decided to go further in the forest of Dandakaranya, realizing that Chitrakoot was in the easy reach of Ayodhya. So, the citizens could make trips to Chitrakoot more frequently. Large gathering of people from Ayodhya, and the battalion of security troops, that accompanied Bharat, disturbed the eco-system in the area, by way of consumption of natural food, and also disturbing the serene atmosphere of the *ashrams* of *Rishi-Munis*.

A very elderly Jabali *Rishi* told them that Chitrakoot was very close to '*Janasthan*' area inhabited and ruled by the demons, Khar, Dushan and Trishira, who were the younger siblings of Demon-king Ravan. Having heard about Ram-Lakshman killing the demons, when they had accompanied sage Vishwamitra, they were waiting to attack them and kill them. So, the *Rishis* at Chitrakoot felt threatened and wanted to shift from there. Sage Jabali advised Ram-Lakshman to go to *Dandakaranya,* in the the deeper forests, instead of settling down at Chitrakoot.

Sati Anusuya and Sita

One of the first major stops was the *ashram* of Sage Atri whose wife *Sati* Anusuya was tested by the Trinity gods, Brahma, Vishnu, Mahesh, about the spiritual power of her penance and austerities. She had transformed the trinity into babies, while they tried to test Anusuya by making some unethical and immoral requests. The legend refers to the request made by trinity to serve them food, without any clothes on her body. As babies, this condition became totally ineffective. The wives of Trinity, Laxmi, Parvati and Saraswati, approached Anusuya and begged to release their husbands, punished by her, due to the pranks played by them against Anusuya. A new deity, Dattatreya, with three faces, representing Trinity, was formed, commonly known as Datta-Guru, who is worshipped by the people in distinct Datta temples. A sacred tree, *Audumber*, indicating the water-body in the vicinity, is associated with Datta temple. Mahasati Anusuya became very fond of Sita who was about 18 years then. She presented her with some divine clothes, which would not get dirty, and would not require cleaning. She also gave her some ornaments, saying that a married young beautiful woman, without ornaments was not appropriate. Ram appreciated her in her clothes and ornaments. Anusuya also blessed her to be totally fearless from any calamity, and to face adversities with courage and grit. Sati Anusuya told Sita, that no extra penance or austerities were required by a married woman, than total devotion to her husband. She complimented Sita for opting to go with Ramchandra, during his exile. Sage Atri recommended them, to settle down at Panchvati (place with five banyan trees), on the bank of river Godavari. He also cautioned that this area of travel, which was known as '*Janasthan*' was the abode of *Rakshasas*, who troubled the inhabitants of *ashramas.*

We are aware that the term '*Jana*' refers to tribal people. In current official terminology, in India, tribal communities are referred as '*Janjati*'. So, Dandakaranya has been the abode of tribal communities, and continues to be so. The current tribal area, referred statutorily as 'Scheduled Area' covers the geographical area of Bastar in Chhattisgarh, and spreading through Nashik to Nandurbar district, in Satpuda hills, and going further in Gujarat. It is also believed that Ashwathama, son of Dronacharya, from *Mahabharat*, moves in Satpuda region, searching for medicinal oil, to apply to the wound on his brow, inflicted by Draupadi's curse. The sages chose some places in the forest to establish their *ashrams* (hermitage), as small residential educational institutions, in serene atmosphere, close to nature. Ravan's brothers ruled the area, probably for using the natural resources, for their greed. One could indulge into wild guess, as to whether the gold for golden Lanka went from this area, from the gold mines.

Interaction with *Rishis*

A little while after some travel, a demon who introduced himself as Viradh attacked Sita. Ram-Lakshman killed him, after breaking his hands. He declared while dying that he was a *gandharva* (celestial musician), cursed to become demon by Kuber, elder half-brother of Ravan, since he had evil designs about Rambha, Kuber's daughter-in-law, which also led to dereliction of his duties. He thanked them for destroying his demon-form and liberating him from the curse. With death, he could get back to his form of Gandharv and get entry in their exclusive abode. Viradh recommended them to visit the *ashram* of Sharbhang Rishi. It appears, Sharbhang Rishi was afflicted with *Galit-kushta*, i. e. leprosy. Ram paid respects to him, and inquired about his well-being. The sage requested him to provide hot water bath, which could cure his affliction. Thereupon, Ram used a powerful arrow to dig a hole in the field, from which emerged hot water. Sharbang Rishi got cured of leprosy. The lake of this hot water springs is currently located on the border of Maharashtra and Gujarat and is called '*U, nou lake*'. People visit the place to bathe to cure skin ailments. The story written at the lake says that Sita sought permission of Ram to bathe in the lake, which in Gujarati language would be '*U, Nou*?' (shall I take bath?). Sharbhang Rishi then directd them to visit the *ashram* of sage Suteekshna. Ram-Lakshman-Sita visited the *ashram* of old sage, Suteekshna, who was very happy to offer them hospitality and shared his spiritual merit with them, to increase their prowess in the event of attack by the demons.

Agastya Rishi and Ram

Sage Suteekshna advised them to visit the powerful Agastya *Rishi*. On way, they spent a day with the brother of Agastya, who was also a *Rishi*. Agastya almost owned a forest which was full with fruit trees, sacred trees like Banyan and fragrant trees like *chandan* (sandalwood), flowers and birds, as also ducks etc. Demons were afraid of Agastya who also used arms against them. There have been many legends about his powers, about monitoring forces of nature like hills and sea. Ram-Sita-Lakshman stayed with Agastya for about a month. During this time, Agastya discussed the philosophy of life with the three. He was telling them that 'God meant Truth'. Unless we control our senses, particularly the mind, we cannot attain Truth. We are too much involved and give in to our affections, in our likes and dislikes, constantly making efforts, using any means to seek pleasure. We forget that everybody has to die. Birth has to end in death, like sunrise, sunset, night and day. All the demons who go in for stringent penance to seek the blessings of Shiva and Brahma, ultimately ask for immortality. The blessing they get has always a chink which is used by God of Death to kill them. After getting the blessings of so-called immortality, they invariably seek pleasures by troubling the spiritual leaders, and by amassing wealth and molesting women. As we know, ultimately, they have to pay the price for their sins, for violating the '*Dharma*, that is, *Satya* (Truth)'. Agastya advised them to settle down for the rest of the period of their forest life, at Panchvati (five Banyan trees), on the bank of sacred river Godawari. Agastya presented Ram with the inexhaustible strings of bows, so the strings would never break, and inexhaustible arrow basket (quiver), which would never become empty, and would always remain full of arrows.

On way to Panchvati, they met with the 'vulture-bird-king', Jatayu, who was a friend of King Dashrath. Jatayu assured that he would protect them at Panchwati, particularly Sita, when they went to the forest for collection of food. Lakshman constructed a hut, not far from the river, with a compound wall of bamboo and a small gate, the like we find in the tribal areas even today. The Bhil women interacting with beautiful Sita, would bring the fruits for them from the forest almost everyday.

Shurpankha Episode at Panchvati

In the nearby forest lived Ravan's sister, Shurpankha and her son, Shambari or Samb, who was undertaking penance to procure a super '*astra*' (weapon) from Lord Shiva. It so happened that the benedicted '*astra*' dropped from the skies and fell near Lakshman, who happened to have gone to the forest. As per one legend, the '*astra*' chose to go to pious Lakshman, who was in the vicinity, where the demon Samb was doing penance. Lakshman was surprised to see an unusual weapon, picked up the '*astra*' and thought of testing its sharpeness. So, he threw it at some place which had lots of shrubs and small trees. He was shocked to see a flood of blood flowing out from the place. Lakshman realized, that some human being had been killed accidently, may be some sage, pursuing the ritual penance. He reported the matter to Ram, with his suspicion that probably, a sin had been commited at his hands, inadvertently. As directed, Lakshman visited the site to confirm, and found that a demon had been killed, not a human being, which did not incur any sin.

Shurpankha on her routine visit to the place saw that her son had been killed. Unfortunately, her husband had also got killed accidently, by her brother Ravan. Looking around, she saw a handsome and strong man, Lakshman. She realized that he must have killed her son. With the intention of taking revenge, she transformed her demoness form into that of a beautiful woman. She approached Lakshman and sought his identity. Knowing that he was a prince of Ayodhya, she expressed desire to marry him. Lakshman directed her to his elder brother, Ram, who was supposed to take all the decisions about the family. She approached Ram and saw beautiful Sita performing household chores. She said, she was directed by his brother, Lakshman to him. She expressed the desire to marry him, whereupon Ram said he was already married to Sita, the princess of Janakpur. He sensed that since she did not appear to be a Bhil woman, who inhabited the forest area around, she could be from the demon race. His doubt was confirmrd when he carefully looked at her eyes. He again directed her to Lakshman, saying that Lakshman was without his wife in the forest. She threatened, that in case of treachery, she would kill and devour Sita; the threat confirming her demoness stature. At her insistence, to give message to Lakshman, Ram wrote a message for Lakshman, on her open back, that being a woman, she could not be killed, but she could be punished and made more ugly by cutting her nose. As she approached Lakshman, with the romantic posture, he deftly flattened her nose with one stroke of sword. Instantly, her form changed to that of demoness. She was wild with anger and said, she was sister of Demon-king Ravan, and her brothers Khar, Dushan and army-chief, Trishira ruled the Janasthan forest. She immediately reported to her brothers about the two handsome humans, Ram and Lakshman and a beautiful woman, Sita as wife of Ram, who had encroached upon their territory, and had temerity to attack her. The three brothers with their army attacked Ram-

Lakshman. However, the three brothers of Shurpankha and their army was totally exterminated by Ram-Lakshman. The Godavari region became totally safe for the *Rishis* to follow their penance.

The current pilgrimage city of Nasik, in Marathi, pronounced as Nashik, at the bank of Godavari river, refers to nose, meaning '*nasika*'. It is believed that the name of the town, Nashik comes from the legend, since Shurpankha's nose was severed here. The name Panchavati continues for the area with temples of Ram and some banyan trees. Ram-Lakshman-Sita had their hut under these banyan trees, enjoying the shade provided by the trees.

Thus began the direct enmity of Ram-Lakshman with Ravan family, which culminated in Sita's abduction and deadly war with Ravan. Shurpankha then headed straight for Lanka to meet Ravan and beseech him to take revenge about the killing of his brothers and making her ugly. She further said, she had not seen a more beautiful damsel than Sita, who deserved to be his queen. She advised him to kidnap her and marry her. If he was really powerful to challenge the heavenly king, Indra, whom his son Meghnad defeated, and got the title of Indrajeet, Ravan should bring Sita to Lanka as one of his queens. Ravan who had a weakness to seduce beautiful women for his pleasure, agreed to the suggestion of Shurpankha. He remembered the embarrassment whereby, he could not lift the bow of Shiva at Sita's *Swayamvar*, but fell down with the heavy bow on his chest. Ravan continued to nurse the inflated ego, and boasted that no woman would ever spurn his romantic company, being the King of the richest State of Lanka. Everybody in *Trilok* knew about his martial power, of which even the heavenly kings were mortified. He assured his sister that at an appropriate timeand in an appropriate manner, he would kidnap Sita and bring her to Lanka.

Story of Ravan

In Ramayan, several times, it has been mentioned that Ravan was a scholar, had studied Vedas, and was a son of a Brahmin. In Valmiki Ramayan, in Uttarkand, details of Ravan's origin have been documented. Lord Brahmadeo or Prajapati had a foster son, named as Pulastya, who followed in his father's spiritual footsteps, with long penance and austerities, in *ashrams*. He went to *Ashram* of a senior sage Trinbindu, located on Meru hills. The place was very scenic and romantic, in all climatic seasons. This place attracted the *apsaras* (nymphs), and adolescent daughters of *Rishis* and Kings, to visit the place for entertaining themselves with music, dance etc. Pulastyafelt disturbed in pursuing his spiritual penance. He warned them to vacate the place, lest one catching his eye would get impregnated. Everybody vanished except Trinbindu's daughter, who had not heard this warning. While she went in search of her friends, she heard the sage reciting*Veda*. Feeling attracted by the melodious recital, she went closer to the place where the sage was seated. Her body size and complexion got changed resembling that of a pregnant woman. Her father noticing this change, went to meet Pulastya and requested him to take his daughter as a life-partner, who would take care of him and provide services during his penance. Pulastya was happy with her services. Since she had heard *Veda* recitation when she became pregnant, the son born was also of spiritual inclination, and was named Paulasti, with other name as Vishrava. Sage Bharadwaj married his daughter to him, begetting a son, named Vaishravan, who later became known as Kuber, the *Lokpal* in-charge of the treasury of the gods. Brahma gave him '*Pushpak*' aircraft, for his mobility and asked him to reside at Lanka, in the south, on Trikoot hills. He was designated as '*Rakshas*', the one who would provide *raksha,* that is, protect the people.

Earlier, *Rakshas* like Sumali and his elder brother, Malyavan were the inhabitants of Lanka. They got into conflict with Lord Vishnu and were defeated. So, they migrated to *Patal-Lok* for some time, vacating Lanka. This Lanka was handed over to Kuber, by Brahma. Malyavan had a beautiful and well behaved daughter, named Kaikasi. When she became eligible for marriage, father told her that offers were not coming for her, with the fear in the minds of eligible young persons or their families, that he may not approve them. He advised her to present herself to sage Paulasti, also known as Visrava, so as to beget children like Kuber. She went to meet him in the evening while he was offering *Agnihotra.* He inquired about her parentage and the purpose of her visit. She said, her father advised her to meet him, since the other suitors were not approaching them for fear of her father. She wanted to be mother of his children who would be like him. He regretted that she came at inappropriate hours, while he was engaged in performing sacred and spiritual rituals. So, she would beget *Rakshas* (demons) as children. When she begged for children like him, he said the youngest would be like him, with spiritual bent of mind. So, Ravan, Kumbhakarna, Shuparnkha and Bibhishan were born to her. Ravan, Kumbhakarna and Bibhishan went for penance and austerities, and earned the attention of Brahma. Ravan sought to become immortal, in his fight with *Danav, Dev, Yaksha* and other celestial species. He did not seek protection from human species, whom he thought below his dignity to seek, as a blessing. Kumbhakarna asked for long sleep, for major part of his life, and Bibhishan requested for pious life, company of good people and offering services to the people. Brahma accepted and bestowed these boons, as per their wishes.

Ravan claimed privileges from Kubera, being his half-brother, and challenged him to a battle. Brahma advised Kuber to shift to Kailash mountain and give Lanka and *Pushpakviman*, to Ravan, asking him to rehabilitate the *Rakshas*, who had fled to *Patal- Lok*, due to fright of Vishnu. He asked Kuber to have another aircraft. Later, Ravan on another occasion of his visit to Kailash, saw a young beautiful woman with whom he wanted to enjoy the pleasures. She introduced herself as Rambha, the wife of Kuber's son, Nal-Kuber, reminding Ravan that she was his daughter-in-law. Despite that, Ravan who was heavily intoxicated, molested her. So, Nal-Kuber cursed him that if he ever tried to molest a woman against her desire, his head would burst into pieces and he would instantly die. That could be the reason for Ravan soliciting the love of Sita, but not touching her for molestation, except when he lifted her to kidnap and brought her to Lanka in *Pushpak*. Even during the aerial journey, he did not physically molest her. He kept on talking about his greatness, about the pleasures he could offer her, denigrating her husband Ram, who was a forest-wandering beggar, exiled by his own father. This event of the curse inflicted by his half-brother Kuber's son was not publicized and remained a closely guarded secret. Ravan bragged, he never had to molest any other woman, since women never refused favours to him, due to his martial and monetary status. They enjoyed the pleasures of his position. His married wife, Mandodari accepted him as he was, but kept on warning him and advising him to send back Sita to Ram, with dignity. Mandodari knew Sita's spiritual demeanour and the powers of Ram, who had protected the *Rishis* performing their *Yagnyas* from the *Rakshas*. Ram had killed Ravan's brothers in *Janasthan*, located in Dandakaranya forest. Ravan ruled Dandakaranya which had abundant natural resources of food and minerals, but had not tried to capture Ayodhya, which literally means invincible. So, here was a Princess-Queen of Ayodhya in his custody, who was refusing to be his queen. His ego was hurt, since never before any woman had declined his favours to join his harem. Ravan's ego about his martial prowess and wealth, resulted in his downfall.

His textual knowledge of *Vedas* was never put to analyse the difference between *Dharma* and *Adharma*. He kept on specializing on *Tantra* techniques and wrote books about it. He had mastered the technique of changing his form, at will, and trained his son, Meghnad, and other army personnel to do that. He had changed his form to that of a mendicant when he kidnapped Sita. Mareech was also ordered by Ravan to change his form, to that of a golden deer to entice Sita. Shurpankha had changed her form, to present herself as a beautiful and sensuous woman to attract Ram and Lakshman, asking them to marry her. So, these were the characteristic features of *Rakshas* of Lanka. Even Bibhishan, belonging to demon race, travelled in air, while he went to join Ram, to seek his protection. Ravan and Meghnad disappeared in the space several times during war with Ram-Sugreev's army. So, Ravan with his knowledge, was superior in technology, specifically war technology.

Sita Kidnapped

Having made up his mind to abduct beautiful Sita, for his sensual pleasure, and also as revenge, whereby Ram and Lakshman had exterminated his hegemony over Dandkaranya, by killing Khar and Dushan, he went to meet one of his trusted and senior warrior, Mareech. Mareech had become a recluse after he was flung far away by one arrow of Ram, when young Ram had accompanied Vishwamitra to protect the *Yaga*. Mareech was an expert imposter who could take any form as desired. Ravan sought his help in kidnapping Sita, from Panchvati. He advised Mareech, to take the form of a deer with golden skin, to attract Sita, who would desire to have it. When Ram would go after deer, Ravan would kidnap her and take her to Lanka. Mareech who had an experience of Ram's prowess counselled him not to antagonize Ram. He also said, it was not proper to seek somebody else's wife, while he had such devoted queen as Mandodari. Ravan mocked at him, about being careful with a mortal human, while he had captured the heavenly deities, defeating them in battles. While Mareech persisted in not undertaking the task, Ravan threatened him with instant death, unleashing his sword. Mareech understood that his death was certain. He preferred to risk death at the hands of Ram, rather than by Ravan. Ravan took him to Panchavati forest in his *Pushpak* aircraft. Mareech turned himself into a very attractive deer with golden skin, and started dalliance near the dwelling hut of Ram-Lakshman-Sita. While Ram-Lakshman were busy with their morning chores of religious rituals, Sita noticed the golden deer which came quite close to the gate of their compound. She had never seen such a beautiful deer in her life and had a craving to possess it. She showed the deer to Ram and requested to capture it for her. She said, they could keep it, as a pet in their house, and take it to Ayodhya, which would be an exclusive novelty in the palace. Ram also liked the deer and felt pleased, that Sita for once, had sought something from him. Otherwise, she had a drab life with no friends, and doing everything by herself, without any help. He asked Lakshman to get him his bow and arrow to capture the deer.

Sita also said that if the deer could not be captured live, it could be hunted and the skin could be taken to Ayodhya. She also thought, that a blouse could be made of the golden skin, which would be an exclusive attraction among the women in Ayodhya. Lakshman had doubt about the deer being a natural animal. But Ram was keen to satisfy the desire of Sita, which for the first time, she had expressed since their marriage. So, Ram followed the deer in the forest with an intention to capture it alive. As planned, Mareech as deer, with its dalliance, ran through the trees and shrubs, and led Ram to a considerable distance from the hut. When Ram realized that it was not possible to get the deer alive, he thought of killing it for the skin, as desired alternative suggested by Sita. Known for his precision, Ram's arrow targeted the deer. Struck with the deadly arrow, wounded deer reverted to the original form of Mareech. Mareech started shouting loudly for help from Lakshman, feigning the voice of Ram, saying that he was in danger. "Oh! Lakshman, Lakshman, Help, Help. I am in danger. Come fast." Sita and Lakshman both heard the voice of Ram. Sita became panicky and asked Lakshman. "Are you not hearing the call from Ram for help? How you are so cool?" Lakshman said, "Oh! *Bhabhi*, Ram can never get into danger. This must be some treachery. We are in an area inhabited by demons. Ram asked me to be with you for your protection. So, I am doing my duty as directed. Please do not feel panicky about the safety of Ram. He is the greatest warrior on the face of the earth." When the shouting for help continued, Sita lost temper. She used the harsh words for the first time in her life. "What kind of brother and younger brother you are, that despite call for help, you are not moving at all. Do you have evil designs on me? Have you accompanied Ram to forest with the evil design that let Ram be killed, so that you could marry me? If you do not comply to what I am asking you to do, I will get drowned in Godavari or set myself to fire." Lakshman could take this no more, since he had always treated Sita equivalent to his mother. He said, "Okay, I will go. But please listen. For your safety, I am drawing a line around our hut which would protect you. Please do not cross that line under any circumstances. You will remain safe till we come back." And with his arrow, the deep line was drawn, before he went in the direction of alleged call for help from 'Ram'. This line continues to be addressed as '*Lakshmanrekha*', that is; the concept of line or limit, not to be crossed, which otherwise would invite danger. In common usage, a threat of tolerance limit is hurled with an expression, "You are crossing the line, the *Lakshmanrekha*; or don't cross the line; Enough is enough." Women may be restrained from crossing the threshold of the house.

Ravan was in hiding in the vicinity of the hut. As Lakshman left for the interior forest in the direction of 'Ram's voice' for help, Ravan changed his form into that of a mendicant and started chanting loudly, the prayers in praise of Lord Shiva, near the gate of the hut. Sita heard the chanting and came out in the verandah of the hut. She inquired with mendicant *(sadhu)* as to who he was and from where he came. He said, he moved in the Bhil area, and told them about Shiva, whom their deities worshipped. He asked about Sita's family, since he found the hut of recent construction. She told him about them coming from Ayodhya, and walking through Dandkaranya, meeting the *Rishis* and visiting their *ashrams*. They had settled down here for a while, before returning back to Ayodhya. He asked about the whereabouts of her husband. She said, her husband and his younger brother had gone to capture a deer for her, who had golden skin. They should be arriving shortly. While this dialogue was going on, Ravan opened the bamboo gate and entered the compound, coming quite close to the protective line made by Lakshman. He said, "Oh! Gracious lady, I was quite hungry. When I saw this hut, I thought I would get some fruits. That is how, I am here. Please give me some fruits to eat." He sat on a grass mat under a tree, and again asked for the fruits. Sita went inside the hut and on a leaf-plate brought some fruits, and kept close to inside of Lakshman's protective line. She requested the mendicant to take the fruits. However, Ravan realized that he could not put his hand crossing the line, lest it might burn. So, he stood near the line and said to Sita, "Dear lady, you know that a guest is not asked to lift any gift by himself, particularly to a spiritual person like me. I am not a beggar. Please put it in my bowl, so that you will earn spiritual merit and my blessings." Sita knowing such courtesies shown to spiritual visitors at her father's place, as also at Ayodhya, picked up the plate and taking her hand across the 'protective line' started putting the fruits in his wooden bowl (*Kamandalu*). Instantly, Ravan caught the hand and pushed her outside the line, almost falling on his chest. She was flabbergasted and frightened by this behaviour. She shouted, "Hey! What are you doing? Do you want to die at my husband's hands by touching me and dragging me?" Ravan laughed loudly.

Ravan instantly transformed himself to his imperial form. He said, "Oh! Heavenly Beauty, I am Ravan, the most powerful King in the world. I had defeated all the kings in the *Trilok.* I have fallen in love with you. Why do you want to live like this? I will make you my principal queen. You had wanted a mere deer, who had golden skin. The deer is my man, in the form of deer, who would kill your husband and his brother. I am offering you not just the golden skin, but the whole city, Lanka, which is made of gold." Sita said, "Hey Ravan, You are inviting death at the hands of my husband Ram. You know as to who killed your demon brothers and his army, and what happened to your sister." Ravan bragged, "I am not afraid of even heavenly powers, what of a mere human, that your husband is." Ravan lifted her on his shoulder and got into his *Pushpak* aircraft, and took off in the air instantly. Sita was shouting for help. Jatayu, the royal eagle, who was resting on a tree heard her voice for help. He immediately took to the skies and accosted Ravan in the *Pushpak*. He asked Ravan to release Sita forthwith, if he did not want to die at his hands. Ravan only laughed at him. Jatayu started biting him with his sharp beak all over his body, blood oozing out at several places. Jatayu also hit his crown which fell on the ground. However, Ravan mustered all his strength, and attacked Jatayu with his sword, and cut a wing of the bird-king. Jatayu fell on the ground. Sita was constantly shouting for help and chanting Ram's name. Seeing Jatayu's fall, Sita was crestfallen. While Ravan was nursing his wounds, caused by Jatayu, Sita took out her ornaments given by Anusuya, and threw couple of them on the ground, thinking Ram would identify and track the direction of Ravan's journey. While they were crossing a hill of considerable height, she saw five or six figures who looked like humans or monkeys, sitting at one place. She tore a piece of cloth from her dress, kept the rest of the ornaments in it, tying it neatly and threw them on the ground in the direction of the human-like figures. She was quite confident that Ram-Lakshman would try to locate these ornaments and reach her.

Ravan was successful in taking Sita to Lanka, crossing the ocean, immediately after the hill. Sita had almost become unconscious. He had a feeling of tremendous success of procuring beautiful Sita, as recommended by his sister, Shurpankha. He took her to his exclusive palace and showed her his glory and riches, to impress her. He even took her to his bed-room and showed her the bed where he would make love to her. However, Sita kept her eyes closed and only kept on cursing him, and chanting Ram's name. Ravan then sent her to *Ashok-van (Vatika)*, a beautiful forest garden, full of trees of fruits, flowers and fragrant trees like sandalwood, situated at the outskirts of Lanka. The garden forest was not open to the citizens of Lanka. It was exclusively meant for the visits of his queens. He posted female demoness guards, with instructions that they should constantly goad her and threaten her, with an intention to agree to the desires of King Ravan. Fortunately, one of the female guard, Trijata, took pity on her and was sympathetic to Sita. With the knowledge of what happened to Khar-Dushan and Shurpankha, Trijata counselled her that Ram would surely find her and get her released from the clutches of Ravan.

Sita Search

As Lakshman reached Ram, where he had killed Mareech, Ram expressed surprise as to how Lakshman left Sita alone and came to meet him. However, both of them realized, seeing the golden deer was in fact a demon, that there was a treachery directed towards them. Lakshman was very apologetic about leaving Sita alone, but with the unkind words from Sita, about his character and intentions, he had no other choice. However, he assured Ram that he had drawn a protective line which would protect her from evil forces. When they reached near their residence, Ram started calling Sita from a distance. There was no response. As they entered the hut, there was no trace of Sita. Ram became panicky and started running helter-skeltor, around the hut, calling Sita. But there was no other sound except that of the chirping birds and the rustling sound of the leaves of the trees. They also looked for her by the riverside. Not finding anywhere, Ram-Lakshman started moving southwards. After some time, they saw some precious pearls of a male necklace, scattered on the ground. As they wondered, they heard moaning sound of a wounded creature. And sure enough, they saw wounded Jatayu without his one wing, who was moaning. When they approached him, and Ram placed his head on his lap, Jatayu opened his eyes and seeing Ram, apologized that he could not protect Sita, from the clutches of Demon-King Ravan. He told Ram that Ravan kidnapped Sita, and took her in his *Pushpakviman* towards Lanka, his capital. Sita was shouting for help, taking your name. I attacked him and wounded him, but he managed to sever my wing. The pearls you saw were from the necklace of Ravan, which must have broken during my attacks on him. Jatayu told them the direction of Ravan's flight and breathed his last, on the lap of Ram. Ram-Lakshman collected firwood and cremated Jatayu's body, who was like their father, being father's friend. As they moved forward, they were attacked by a demon, who gave his name as Kabandh. Ram cut his hands, whereupon he said, he had become a demon by curse, given by some *Rishi*, due to his ill behaviour with the *Rishis*, during their penance and *yaag*.

Kabandh gave direction of the hermitage (*ashram*) of the Late Matang *Rishi* where his disciple, an old woman, Shabari, was staying. She belonged to the forest tribal community, commonly believed now, to be from the Bhil tribe. They proceeded towards the *Ashram*. They gave their introduction to the old lady. She said, her *Guru* knew about the kingdom of Ayodhya and about

King Dashrath. My *Guru* had told me that I was destined to meet you some time. So, I was waiting for you. She offered the berries. However, to ensure to offer only the sweet berries, and not the sour ones, she took a small bite of each berry and offered only the sweet ones. Lakshman was reticent about eating the berries which were already tasted by the old tibal woman. But Ram appreciated the depth of pure affection of a mother, and praised her for that. All mothers give the best of food to their small children, which they taste before offering to them. Ram told her about the kidnapping of Sita by Ravan, and their search for her. She assured them, that further south, by the side of Pampa lake, on the hill of Kishkindha, lived the king of monkeys who could help them to trace Sita at Lanka. After profusely thanking her, they moved southwards and came across Pampa lake, where they took bath.

So, Valmiki in *Aranyakand* has described the journey of Ram-Lakshman-Sita after leaving Chitrakoot, through the forest, until they settled down at Panchvati. They visited the *ashrams* of *Rishis* who were teachers, some of them staying with their students. These were the residential schools. They got an opportunity to discuss the philosophy of life and about eternal values. They could see that the *Gurus* led a very simple life, and were more knowledgeable than the heavenly demi-gods who were living the life of comfort. The *gurus* treated Ram-Lakshman and Sita with great respect, knowing that Ram, who was legally the King of Ayodhya was leading a life of a hermit and ascetic, for no fault of his, but due to capricious behaviour of one of the queens, who was also responsible for her husband-king's death. But Ram was taking it in a stride, as a matter of destiny, and did not show any imbalance in mind. He only became tense as Sita was abducted by Ravan, who was a formidable enemy.

Kishkindhakand: Summary

They meet Hanuman, the powerful monkey warrior of Sugreev who introduces them to King Sugreev in exile, due to quarrel with his elder brother Vali, who kept Sugreev's wife with him. Ram entered a diplomatic treaty with Sugreev to restore his kingdom and wife to him, while Sugreev would help to locate Sita, in Lanka. Ram punishes Vali by killing him, restores Sugreev to his kingdom, and anoints Vali's son, Angad as the *Yuvraj,* as wished by Vali. Hanuman takes a big leap-jump over the sea on way to Lanka in search of Sita.

Kishkindhakand

Near Pampa lake, a steep hill full of greenery was visible with no sign of habitation. Ram-Lakshman were wondering whether this was Rishyamook hill referred by Shabari. On a plateau of a hill, Sugreev and his ministers such as Hanuman were sitting. Sugreev spotted two human beings who were armed, with bow and arrow, loitering at the foot of the hill. He was wondering whether his elder brother, King Vali had sent these human warriors to kill him. He went in consultation with Hanuman, and asked him to enquire. Hanuman changed his form into that of a human being, as a Brahmin priest. He walked towards Ram-Lakshman, with a smiling face. Ram-Lakshman were very happy to meet somebody with whom they could inquire about King Sugreev. The priest said, "You appear to be strangers here. You are fully armed warriors. What are you searching here?" Lakshman was apprehensive as to whether the priest was a demon in the garb of a human being. Ram asked the priest as to whether this was the Rishyamook hill. The priest asked the reason as to what was their interest in the hill. He also asked for their identity. Lakshman was little reticent. But, Ram told about them being the sons of King Dashrath of Ayodhya. They also told about kidnapping of Sita by Ravan. Ram said, Shabari advised them to seek the help of King Sugreev in locating Sita. The priest, i. e. Hanuman was familiar with the names of Ayodhya and Dashrath, since his mother had told him about the '*Prasad*' she received, which caused the birth of Hanuman. So, the priest changed his form into that of Hanuman and touched the feet of Ram-Lakshman. He informed them about Sugreev, living on this hill with his small army, after his kingdom and wife were usurped by his elder brother Vali. Since, there was no proper road to climb the hill, Hanuman offered to carry them on his shoulders. He increased his form to show the wide shoulders, for comfortable seat on the shoulders. They were presented to Sugreev who could not offer any formal seats for the guests to sit. They were seated on the logs of wood, cut from the trees for them. Sugreev paid respects to them knowing their origin from the great kingdom of Ayodhya. Sugreev desired their help in getting back his kingdom and his wife, from the mighty Vali. Ram told him about abduction of Sita by Ravan, and desired Sugreev's help in locating Sita. Hanuman intercepted to say, that they had witnessed a lady shouting for help, while she was being carried away by a demon. She threw a parcel (*potli)* of jewelry tied in a piece of cloth, directing towards them. We retrieved it. Hanuman promptly brought the *potli* (parcel) for their inspection. Lakshman could identify the ornaments, which Sita was putting on her ankles, since he always used to stand in front of her, with his downward look as a mark of respect. Ram identified all other ornaments, some of which were gifted by *Sati* Anusuya. Ram-Lakshman were happy to have identified the route taken by Ravan and the help received from Hanuman and Sugreev.

Sugreev talked about the strength of Vali and was apprehensive about Ram-Lakshman capable of fighting with Vali. Lakshman could understand Sugreev's apprehensions, from his body language. He told Sugreev about the demons they killed during their journey. Ram was impatient about getting Sugreev's help in locating Sita, since they were knowledgeable about Ravan and the geography of the region. So, Ram took out his bow, and twinged the string which made a very loud and challenging sound. In an instant, he targeted the trees standing in a row. One arrow pierced seven trees and came back to his quiver. Sugreev and Hanuman had never witnessed such expertise. So they were convinced about the battle strength of Ram-Lakshman, capable of fighting with Vali.

Vali and Sugreev

Ram asked Sugreev about the dispute among the two brothers, between Vali and Sugreev. Sugreev told the story of the dispute. "In this area, Dundubhi was a notorious son of a demon, Mahisasur. He would trouble the people and *Rishis*. He was challenging and seeking an equal, who would fight with him. He was advised to challenge Vali to a fight. Vali was too powerful. He lifted him and killed him, by repeatedly smashing him on the rocks. His body was thrown on this Rishyamook hill, which also hit several *ashrams* of the *Rishi*. So, Matang Rishi, whose disciple, Shabari you met, and who directed you to me, warned Vali not to visit this hill. He was cursed that the visit here would bring death to him. That is how we have taken a safe refuge here. Ram again asked him, as to what was the dispute with his elder brother Vali, which made him flee from Kishkindha? Sugreev narrated the happenings like this. "Dundubhi's son, Mayasur attacked Kishkindha, to take revenge about his father's death. We were chasing him. Mayasur entered a deep cave followed by Vali. He asked me to wait outside. I waited for a long time. I noticed blood draining out of the cave. It was obvious that one of them had been killed. However, nobody came out. I thought Vali must have been killed. I closed the entry of the cave with a rock, thinking that if Mayasur came out, he would continue with his terrorist activities. I returned to Kishkindha. The kingdom without a king was attracting the attention of *Yaksha* and *Gandharva* to capture Kishkindha. The people asked me to take over kingship and govern. I ruled like this for more than a year. One day, Vali appeared with the head of Mayasur in his hand. It seems, it took time and effort for him to locate the opening of the cave, which I had closed with a rock. He somehow broke the rock with his nails and came out. Seeing me as King, he was very annoyed and wanted to kill me. Somehow, my trusted colleagues, Nal, Neel, Jambavant and Hanuman saved me. We came on this hill, since Vali could not attack us on this hill, due to curse of Matang *Rishi*. Vali also kept my wife. For no fault of mine, he is bent upon killing me."

Ram only remarked that nobody could avoid the destiny. Ram and Sugreev entered into a formal diplomatic treaty, circumambulating the open fire thrice, with the terms, that Ram would kill Vali, and install Sugreev as the King of Kishkindha, with his wife as queen. Sugreev would delegate his entire army to search Sita's whereabouts. Although it was known that Ravan had kidnapped her, nobody knew about Lanka, or where had he kept her in hiding in Lanka, or somewhere else. Ram embraced Sugreev and designated him as his brother, like Lakshman.

Vali's wife Tara informed Vali that their son, Angad, heard *Rishis* discussing the arrival of two great warriors, Ram-Lakshman, staying with Sugreev. Vali roared, that he would have to kill Sugreev. He sent a message to Sugreev, to come out of the cursed hill for a duel. Sugreev agreed and they had a duel at an agreed spot. Ram was present with an intention to kill Vali. However, Vali and Sugreev looked identical like twins. So Ram could not dart his arrow to kill Vali. Since the duel remained inconclusive, they decided to continue it next day. It was decided, that Sugreev would put on a flower garland, around his neck for his identification. Vali-Sugreev were fighting with a mace. Ram-Lakshman and Hanuman were witnessing the fight from a distance, not noticed by Vali. Vali was cursing Sugreev, that he brought two humans to kill him, so that Sugreev could become King again. He said, "What these humans could do, when even Ravan could not defeat me. Ultimately, Ravan had to enter in friendship treaty with me." When Vali and Sugreev separated for a while, for taking renewed attack positions, Ram darted an arrow which hit Vali, and he collapsed on the ground, heavily injured. When Vali looked around, he saw Ram and Lakshman, with Hanuman, approaching him. He asked Ram, "What kind of a Prince you are from the great kingdom of Ayodhya that you wanted to kill me by treachery? How am I your enemy? By hitting me like this, you have acted as a coward, in the same way that demons commit the sin of '*adharma*'. Ram said, "Sugreev is our friend, as close as a brother. You are now talking of '*Dharma*'. What *Dharma* you followed by throwing away Sugreev, who was governing Kishkindha on your behalf, as your agent, in your absence? What *Dharma* is that, to keep younger brother's wife, when you should have treated her as your daughter? I had promised Sugreev to help him, having accepted him as a friend, and having entered into a friendship treaty with him. Don't you deserve death penalty for the sin commited by you? Is not adultery punishable with death, in your community?" Vali said, "You made friendship with a coward, to get back your wife, from the clutches of mighty Ravan. Do you think, you could be successful in your aim with Sugreev's help? If you had approached me, I could have brought back your Sita in a minute. Don't you know how many times did I defeat Ravan and humiliated him, when Angad was a baby, until his father intervened for his release? Ravan was forced to have Peace Treaty with me." Ram said, "You treated your younger brother with cruelty, for no fault of his. He had accompanied you to kill Mayasur. He had to return back in the interest of the people of Kishkindha. Why did you not consult your ministers, Nal, Neel, Jambavan and Hanuman? None of them are with you. Why so?" Vali kept quiet. He said with folded hands, requesting to make Sugreev the king and look after Angad as a son, and to treat him like a prince. Repeating this with folded hands, Vali breathed his last breath. Sugreev was crowned King of Kishkindha and Angad was coronated as Prince.

Search Parties

This was the time, when rainy season started in full swing, and the normal movements were disturbed. Ram and Lakshman continued to live in a cave, not affected by heavy showers. But search operations to locate Sita by Sugreev's army could not be started. Sugreev as a King, who lived a hard life on Rishyamook hill, started living the royal life, with entertainment like dance, music, drinks, food etc. As the monsoon retreated, there were no signs of any effort to search for Sita. Ram was visibly annoyed with Sugreev, and expressed to Lakshman, that such people who did not keep their word, deserved punishment. He told Lakshman to go to Kishkindha and remind Sugreev about his promise. Knowing Lakshman, Ram told him not to be harsh to Sugreev, since he was now our friend. Lakshman who was a short tempered person, and could not hide his facial expressions of annoyance, headed for Kishkindha, with his bow and arrow, to question Sugreev about his inactivity. Hanuman could foresee danger, and sent a message to Sugreev, reminding about the treaty with Ram. As Lakshman reached the palace of Sugreev, Vali's widow Tara, and Sugreev's wife Rumi, welcomed him and assured him, that Sugreev was organizing the search teams to locate Sita. Sugreev welcomed Lakshman and accompanied with ministers, went to meet Ram to plan the search strategies.

Accordingly, four teams were formed for four directions and dispatched to return back with their exploration findings, in a months' time. It was almost certain, that Ravan was headed to south carrying kidnapped Sita, in his *Pushpak*. So, a strong team, under the leadership of Angad, with seniors like Nal, Neel, Jambavan, Rishabh and Hanuman, and hundred monkey-soldiers headed towards south. Hanuman asked Ram, as to how would Sita trust them as your messengers. Ram said, "You could tell her that Ram personally helped her in Kaikeyi's palace to wear the hermit clothes, which she could not manage by herself." Hanuman further asked whether they could carry any identity object from him, which would confirm, that we were sent by you. Ram gave his special ring (*mudrika*) which was also used to stamp official documents. On the way, they met with demons who attacked them. However, they were killed. The search party came across a cave, at the entry of which a beautiful woman was sitting for penance. She made inquiries about so many of them going together, and about their mission. That was the cave of Hema, a celestial nymph, who was cursed to be there for some time. The attendant of Hema, told the search party, that she would rescue them, to the sea coast, by a shorter route, through the cave. Inside the cave, there were beautiful gardens, with lots of fruits, which the monkey-team enjoyed. Ultimately, they were on the sea coast. There was a hill nearby on which a big eagle was sitting, who appeared disabled. His name was Sampati. While the monkey team leaders were discussing about Sita-Ram-Lakshman, Sampati heard the name of Jatayu, who was his younger brother. Sampati enquired about Jatayu and was very sad to know, that he got killed at the hands of Ravan, while Jatayu was trying to rescue Sita. Sampati who had a long vision said, "I can see Lanka of Ravan, across the sea, and Sita under a tree at Asokvan." There was a sense of satisfaction in the search party, about the confirmation that Sita was located in Lanka. The problem came up, as to how to cross the sea, and who would do that, to reach out to Sita, hoodwinking the security systems of Lanka?

Sundarkand: Summary

Hanuman locates Sita, kept in captivity in Ashokvan in Lanka, guarded by demonneses. He consoles Sita-*Mata* and offers her to take to Ram, sitting on his shoulder or back. She, however, declines to go out surreptitiously, desiring Ram to release her after punishing Ravan. Hanuman surrenders, respecting the *Brahmastra* used by Indrajeet, and gets captured, to be presented in Ravan's Darbar. Hanuman extricates himself and burns Lanka. Hanuman reports back the message of Sita to Ram, to get her release from Ravan's captivity, by duly punishing Ravan.

Sundarkand

Hanuman was sitting quietly, as if in meditation. Jambavan knew that Hanuman had the power to cross the sea, since as a new born baby, he had leapt to sun, thinking it was a fruit. Jambavan had to remind Hanuman about his in-born power. Hanuman had never taken a leap so long after his adventure as a neonate, although he had changed his form and size, to carry Ram-Lakshman on his shoulders to the Rishyamook hill, to meet Sugreev. Hanuman then offered prayers to Shiva and Wind-god *Vayu*, who was also his foster father. He realized that he got back the power, to fly long distances. He extended his size, so that he could navigate with large and long hands. He took a leap and crossed the sea, and reached the gates of Lanka, which were heavily guarded by the demon-guards. He again changed his form to a small size to enter Lanka, unnoticed, from the top of entry gate. He felt elated about reaching Lanka. While he was seated on the top of entry gate, he could see the opulent city of gold. He could see the wide roads, the food people were eating, and their dwelling places, which were very attractive. He focused his mind on searching for Sita. But then, the mind was filled with concern and questions. Was Sita alive? Is she not already living with Ravan? How to find out? He thought of entering big houses appearing like palaces.

The first one he entered; he found a warrior like young person, speaking to his wife. He thought, she could be Sita. The woman was asking the man, as to why his father should have indulged in immoral behaviour by abducting Sita, who was Ram's wife? (Meghnad/Indrajeet and Sulochana). Then he entered another palatial building. There, he could here only loud snoring from a huge demon, lying in bed. He did not see any woman. Hanuman then entered a huge palace. He went from room to room. In several rooms, he found several women sleeping without attention to their dress. Hanuman, the bachelor monkey-god closed his eyes, and rushed out of the rooms. He found in a spacious bed-room, a majestic and well-built person talking to a gracious and beautiful woman. He thought, she could be Sita. However the lady said, "My lord, why have you brought Ram's wife Sita? Why do you want enmity with the powerful Ram?" Thereupon, Ravan called a maid, and asked her to go to Ashokvan, and find out what was Sita doing, and whether the female guards were in their respective positions. Hanuman instantly understood the location of Sita in Ashokvan, and he stealthily followed the maid to Ashokvan. He also remembered Sampati, brother of Jatayu, saying that he could see Sita in Ashokvan. The maid went to Ashokvan and called the female guards in a corner, to inquire about Sita's behaviour. The guards told her, that Sita was only chanting the name of Ram. We keep on telling her, to accept the proposal of mighty King Ravan, to be his queen. But she does not respond at all, as if she did not hear, what we told her. She only communicated with Trijata, who visualized the dreams about the fall of Lanka, due to capture of Sita. The maid went and reported to the King, Ravan, that the female guards were doing their duties well. They were constantly trying to persuade Sita to accept the proposal of Ravan, to live with him in the palace.

Hanuman at Ashokvan

Hanuman reducing his size, was listening to this conversation, sitting on a branch of a tree, hiding himself behind the leaves of the tree. After the maid was gone, the female guards had their alcoholic drinks, and were tipsy. Hanuman went closer to Sita's tree, where she was sitting, resting her back by the trunk of the tree. Hanuman instantly recognized her as Sitamai, Sri Ram's wife. He had not seen such a blissful, shining face of purity and spiritual power. He instantly thought of bowing down and touch her feet, showing his respect. However, he stationed himself on the branch of the same tree, under the shadow of which, Sita was sitting. He started singing prayers in praise of Sri Ram in a very melodious and low voice. Sita was quite surprised to hear Ram's name in Ashokvan, around her.

In the mean time, Ravan decided to visit Ashokvan, with one of his queens. As he arrived, the female guards kept a distance, to ensure privacy to the King. Ravan addressed Sita, "Oh! Beautiful woman. Why are you here, instead of in my palace, as the chief queen? All queens and maids will be at your service. All the pleasures of life would be at your command, including me. Why are you after that hermit Ram who was thrown out by his father, at the wishes of his younger queen? With him, you did not have even a proper bed to sleep. I care so much for you. Why don't you agree to my proposal of love? I do not propose to force myself on you, since I love you so much. Have pity on me, instead of hoping that your forest wandering husband, will take you from me. Even the celestial powers are afraid of me. Many of them are languishing in my prison, begging to be released." Sita plucking a blade of grass near her, and holding it in her hand, replied to Ravan, "Hey! King Ravan. You are supposed to be a wise person, having studied the ancient scriptures, and as a son of a Brahmin sage, and brother of Kuber. How do you imagin that I woud agree to your solicitation? I am married to somebody. You know of my father's family, and the dynasty of Ayodhya kings. Follow the rules of *Dharma*, if you do not want Lanka and you, to be destroyed. Why don't you look after your queens? What would be your reaction, if somebody else would kidnap one of your queens? Would you not protect them? Don't you know what happened in *Janasthan*? How your brothers and their armies were vanquished by Ram-Lakshman? Why did you have to kidnap me by treachery, if you were not afraid of Ram's prowess? When I asked you to come to the hut, and pick up the fruits offered to you, you had no courage to cross the line, which was drawn around the hut by Lakshman for my protection. By deceit, in the form and dress of a mendicant, you persuaded me to cross the protective line, to kidnap me. I followed all the courtesies, which are offered to the mendicants, in good faith. That is your character, which deserves punishment by death, which you will get from my husband, Sri Ram. However, he is a kind-hearted and compassionate person. If you send me back and seek pardon from him, he will pardon you, and spare your life. You seem to have forgotten that, you had come for my '*Swayamwar*', uninvited. You could not even lift the bow, which was a condition for selecting a suitor by the bride. Ram broke the bow in the process of putting a string to it. Oh! Ravan, have you consulted your queens, before making offers to me? Don't you have any elders or *Guru* in your family, whom you could consult about the sins being committed, heading for severe punishment?" Ravan was wild with anger by Sita's retort. The queen Dhaanyamaali, who had accompanied Ravan to Ashokvan said, "Oh! My lord, why are you after this stupid human woman, while we are there for your enjoyment. Let us go away and enjoy ourselves. Let us ignore what she is blurting out, as an insane person. She does not even know as to with whom she is talking."

Hanuman sitting on the tree was carefully listening to this dialogue, and he felt proud of Sitamai, for her fearlessness and courage. Sita also remembered that she was blessed by *Sati* Anusuya, to be confident and courageous. After Ravan left, and Hanuman could see that the female guards were not in immediate vicinity of Sita, Hanuman gently dropped Ram's '*mudrika*' on the ground, near Sita. She was alarmed. She picked up the '*mudrika*' and looked around. Hanuman descended from the tree, as a small monkey, and respectfully bowed down to her. She asked him, "Who are you and how are you here? Are you again another demon spy of Ravan? How and where are Ram-Lakshman?" Hanuman told her, "*Prabhu* Ram and Lakshman were searching for you. When they met us, we showed your ornaments, which you had thrown in our direction, and picked up by us. Our King, Sugreev, has taken an oath, to use his army to locate you and seek your release." Sita was very happy to know this, and also see the personal '*mudrika*' of Ram. However, she was apprehensive. She again asked as to how could she trust him. Then Hanuman said, "Ma, when you had to accompany Ram-Lakshman to the forest, Sri Ram personally helped you in Kaikeyi's palace to adorn the rough hermit clothes, which you could not manage by yourself." With this, Sita was sure that this little monkey, Hanuman, was indeed a messenger of Ram. Hanuman told briefly about Ram meeting Sugreev, killing of Ravan's friend Vali, and about his taking a leap to cross the ocean. He assured Sitamai, that soon Ram-Lakshman with Sugreev's army would invade Lanka, to seek her release. Hanuman made an offer, "Mai, I had carried Ram-Lakshman on my shoulders, to jump to the hill to meet Sugreev. Likewise, I can carry you just now, across the ocean, and join you with Sri Ram." Sita said, "What you say is nice on your part. You do have the prowess to do that, knowing about your parentage. But, that would not be appropriate. It would be similar to how Ravan brought me here. He brought me stealthily, committing a crime which deserve death penalty. Ravan should send me back with honour, or Ram should punish him, and get my release, as would be done to establish Rule of Law, i. e. *Dharma*, to uphold the eternal Truth.

Hanuman sought her permission to satisfy his hunger by eating the fruits in Ashokvan. Sita said, "Please do that by all means, but take the fruits which have fallen from the trees." Hanuman sought her permission to leave with an assurance, that he would again meet her, before finally leaving Lanka. In the meanwhile, he requested for an object from her to be shown to Sri Ram, as a proof of their meeting. She gave him an ornamental hair-bun cover (*chudamani*) from her hairdo, as her personal identity, which Ram could identify as her own, since he had first helped her to adorn it after marriage, at Ayodhya. She also narrated an incident happened at Chitrakoot. Indra's son appreciating her beauty, turning himself into a crow, tried to kiss her body with his beak, which made a bloody wound and hurt her. Ram who was then following morning religious rituals, hearing Sita's agony, darted a blade of sacred grass, '*darbha*' after the crow. The crow unable to avoid it, and everybody including Indra, expressing inability to help him; the crow surrendered to Ram and begged apology. Ram spared his life, but made him blind, with one eye, and cursed him to eat the faeces for food. The celestial fellow further begged apology. Ram atoned the curse, and blessed him, that unless he touched the rice balls (*pinda*) which are offered to the dead, on 13-14th day, after funeral (obsequies), usually at the river side, the dead would not be eligible to get '*moksh*'. Sita told Hanuman to narrate this story, which would ensure, that he indeed met Sita. This ritual of crow touching the rice balls, is still followed among the Hindus. Crow continues to be identified as wily, and his sight on the roof top as inauspicious. There are several proverbs at local level, connected with crow. At the cremation site, relatives of dead do wait for a crow to touch the balls of rice, kept there, with the belief, that it would ensure the departed soul to attain '*moksh*'.

Hanuman sought leave of Sita-*Mata* with an assurance, that before he left Lanka's boundary, he would revisit again. He had in mind to threaten Ravan about the consequences, if Sita was not released, with honour. So, he assumed the big form, to be visible to the citizens of Lanka. Since Sita-*Mata* had forbidden him, to pluck the fruits from the trees, and take only those fallen on the ground, he shook some fruit trees, and uprooted others, near the gate of Ashokvan. The female *Rakshsini* guards attacked him, but he threw them away, using his strong tail as a weapon. The guards reported the matter about a big monkey, destroying Ashokvan, to Ravan, for whom it was a coveted garden, meant exclusively for his queens. He sent his son Aksha, with some soldiers, to kill or arrest the monkey. But Hanuman killed all of them. Thereupon, the great warrior son, Indrajit came. But Hanuman could not be tamed by Indrajit's arrows, although they hurt him. Ultimately, Indrajit used *Brahmastra,* the ultimate and unfailing weapon, given by Lord Brahma to Indrajit, by way of a reward for his penance. Although Hanuman had spiritual strength, not to be hurt by *Brahmastra,* since he also had the boon of immortality, he showed respect to *Brahmastra*, by getting bound by the weapon, immobilizing him. He wanted to see Ravan, and convey the warning to him. Hanuman was produced in the grand court of Ravan, who was sitting on a magnificent throne of diamonds.

Burning of Lanka

The Prime Minister of Ravan, Prahast, asked Hanuman as to whose agent he was, and why did he come there? Hanuman replied that he was a messenger of Sri Ram whose wife was kidnapped by Ravan by deceit, and is in captivity. This is against *Dharma*. He further said that Ram was now with King Sugreev. Addressing Ravan, he said, "Your friend Vali has been killed for committing *Adharma* of keeping Sugreev's wife, who was like his daughter, being younger brother's wife. So, Sugreev has asked me to convey to you that you will meet the same fate as that of Vali." Ravan was red with anger, and ordered to kill Hanuman forthwith. Bibhishan intervened to say that it was against the ethical protocol, to kill the messenger of another king. Then Ravan roared that the tail of the monkey was precious to him. So burn it. The tail was wrapped by rags of cloth. But Hanuman kept on increasing the length of his tail, till there was shortage of rags in Lanka. However, the tail was lighted with fire. Hanuman left the court and jumping from one building to another, he set the whole Lanka on fire, taking care that the fire would not reach Ashokvan. Ultimately, he put off the fire of the tail, by dipping it in seawater. Afterwards, he again went to meet Sita-*Mai*. The female *Rakshsini* guards had already seen Lanka on fire. So, they maintained a distance from Hanuman and Sita, talking to each other. *Ma*-Sita was greatly impressed by the powers of Hanuman and blessed him. She expressed to convey to Ram, that Ravan had given her some time limit to join him as his consort. That time limit would expire in two months. If not released by then, she would be left with no other option, but to exterminate herself. Hanuman counselled her, that now since her location was known, and he had met her, Sugreev's army under the leadership of Ram would soon invade Lanka. He prayed her not to loose her patience, at the last moment. Sita wished him safe journey back, and blessed him, addressing him as Son.

Hanuman has been portrayed not only as brave but also as a wise person. "Hanuman is described as a master of tact and diplomacy and *vakpatutvam* (skill of speech). For example, when he was bound and taken to Ravan after he destroyed *Asoka Van*, Hanuman praised Ravan for being an illustrious and mighty king. Although Hanuman was furious with Ravan for having kidnapped Sita, at that point, in the court of Ravan, he thought discretion was the better part of valour. Since he wanted to collect information about Ravan, his intention and his strength, Hanuman acted with great tact. (Ramkrishna, Dr. Lalita: *Ancient Indian Greats*, Sri Ramkrishna Math, Chennai, 2014, 151-152).

Hanuman's Report of Lanka Visit

Hanuman leapt across the ocean to join his team under the leadership of Prince Angad. All the members of the team, Nal, Neel, Jambavan, Rishabh went to meet King Sugreev and apprised him about Hanuman's successful expedition, in locating *Mata* Sita, and communicating with her. Sugreev was very happy having redeemed the promise of locating Sita. They all rushed to meet Sri Ram and Lakshman, near Pampa Lake, to report to them, about the good news, and discuss further plan of action. Ram hugged Hanuman with great affection, having met Sita. Hanuman narrated all the details of his exploits in Lanka, including his meeting with Ravan in his grand Court. About *Ma*-Sita, he said, she looked radiant but thin. She had nothing around her, in her expression, accept the name of Ram. She conveyed her sincere apologies to Lakshman, for misunderstanding his protective actions, and having expressed unkind words. She also regretted her desire for a golden deer, which led to her kidnapping, despite the prowess of Ram-Lakshman. He presented to Ram the '*chudamani*' given by her, and narrated the incident of crow troubling her at Chitrakoot, as evidence of having met her. Ram became mute, overcome with emotion, and closed his eyes. He collected himself and said, "What Hanuman has done, nobody else, in the world can do that." And, he embraced Hanuman in a very close and affectionate embrace. He further said, "The time is very short to get release of Sita, by waging a bloody war, with the powerful demon-king Ravan, and his huge organized army, with all the war resources at their command. Let us organize ourselves fast, as armed forces. One of the invincible task would be to cross the ocean."

Ram further asked Hanuman about the defences of Lanka. Hanuman first narrated about the wealth of Lanka, and the confidence and affection, that the citizens had about King Ravan. He said, there were fort-like structures at each gate, guarded round the clock. There was moat surrounding the town, with drawbridges. The sea coast was guarded on all the sides. King Sugreev and Hanuman assured Ram, that whatever obstacles, our army will get over it, under your command. They started marching towards sea. When they reached Mahendra mountain, Ram reached the peak, sitting on Hanuman's shoulder and surveyed the ocean.

On the other side, in Lanka, Ravan's informers appraised King Ravan, about movements of Ram, Sugreev and Hanuman, in the direction of the ocean. Ravan was little apprehensive, and felt ashamed about Hanuman's exploits in Lanka, single-handed. He called the ministers for consultations. He addressed them asking for their frank opinion, about the impending attack by the enemy, who had reached the coast of ocean. Each one of the ministers, starting with Prahasta, the General Commander-in-Chief of the army, hailed the King and said, "Everybody knows that our army was the strongest in the world. Sir you first defeated Kuber, captured Lanka and got his *Puspak* aircraft. You defeated *Devas* and *Yakshas*, Indrajit defeated Indra. One monkey might have indulged into some pranks, since we were caught unawares. Each of us here could defeat their entire army single handed. We are also experts in black magic, whereby we can fool them, by assuming different forms, including those of the humans.

Bibhishan's Dissent

However, there was a dissenting voice from one person, Bibhishan, brother of Ravan. He said, "Oh, brother King. It is nice to hear such sweet bravado from our colleagues. But, let us look at the ground realities. Have they come to attack us, to capture Lanka? We have committed a sin, by kidnapping Sita, by deceit, not defeating Ram in a battle. They killed our generals and army in *Janasthan*, since our people were engaged in continuous destruction of the *Yagas* of *Rishis*. In retaliation, we captured his wife, using some black magic of creating a golden deer. Are we aware of the extent of their forces? One Hanuman created so much destruction in Lanka. So, let us not underestimate their strength. I am saying these bitter words for your good. We should first correct our faults and act as per *Dharma*. You are a scholar of *Vedas*. You can think and act accordingly."Ravan adjourned the meeting and decided to meet again. Next day, at the Council meeting, Bibhishan repeated again, what he had said earlier, pleading to return Sita, and live in peace. Ravan refused to accept the suggestion of returning Sita, since he liked her, and as a great warrior, would like to have her. He said, he had not forced himself on her. At her request, I have given her time, to consider joining me, as my consort. She has been foolish to think, that Ram would come, and release her from our custody. We have to only decide, how we could kill Ram, and his army of monkeys, who are camping on the other side of the ocean, since they could never cross the ocean in such large numbers. Kumbhakarna, another brother of Ravan had joined the assembly, rising from his long sleep. He said, "You are now seeking our counsel. But you made a mistake of bringing Sita without a battle with Ram and defeating him. However, we support you as a King and in the interest of Lanka and its people. We are on your side in war and peace." However,

Bibhishan continued to disagree. He counselled the King to send back Sita with honour and grace, to save the race of demons. Ravan was very annoyed with Bibhishan's persistent advice to surrender to Ram. He said, if you were not my brother, I would have killed you here. Ravan asked him to get out, and asked not to show his cowardly face to him any more.

Bibhishan went to his mother and told her everything. She was distressed at the behaviour of Ravan, but knew, he would not listen to anybody, due to his power and ego. She advised him to find his own ways, to avoid war and bloodshed. Bibhishan decided to meet Ram with his four colleagues and surrender himself to the *Dharma*. As he was on way to Rama with four others, Sugreev and others identified the five persons on the sky-walk. They thought of devils coming from Lanka, with bad intentions. Sugreev, Jambuavan. Angad were discussing about the action, to be taken against these intruders. Bibhishan announced from the sky-walk their identity, and the intention of surrendering to the *Dharma* of Ram. He expressed desire to be presented to Ram. Sugreev reported the matter to Ram and cautioned against meeting them. Sugreev said that they must have been sent by Ravan. Being demons, they could play tricks, like becoming invisible at will and strike. Since Hanuman had been to Lanka and had peeped in the dwellings of all kin of Ravan, Ram sought his opinion. Hanuman said, in Bibhishan's house, there was spiritual atmosphere. He was known in Lanka as an upright person, different from his other brothers. If he had evil designs, why should he approach openly and not stealthily? Ram after listening to everybody, who had suspicion about the motives of Bibhishan said, if somebody came to you to surrender, would it be proper to refuse him outright? If Ravan came to surrender, what shall we do? Let us meet Bibhishan, and assess whether his offer of friendliness, would be beneficial to us, in meeting our objectives. We can offer him the Kingdom of Lanka, after we exterminate Ravan. Sugreev appreciated clear and diplomatic thinking of Ram, and offered to welcome Bhibishan and his four friends.

Bibhishan greeted Ram and others, with great respect and humility. He recounted all that happened in the meetings of Ravan's council. Ravan almost deported him, threatening to kill him. He also reported about Kumbhkarna castigating Ravan for his fault, but owed allegiance to the King. He reported that Queen Mandodari, Ravan's mother and her father, that is, Bibhishan's grandfather were unhappy about Ravan kidnapping Sita by deceit. But Ravan's ego of being the greatest warrior in *Trilok*, and his desires to be fulfilled, not questioned by anybody, was his greatest enemy. How could Ravan be afraid of two humans, Ram and Lakshman, supported by monkey army? He was not amenable to reason or being reminded that a monkey, Vali had defeated him, forcing Ravan to seek his friendship. He could not reason out, as to how another monkey, Hanuman destroyed Lanka, single-handed, or how easily his brothers in *Janasthan* could be killed by Ram and Lakshman. Following Bibhishan's exit, Ravan sent a spy to meet Sugreev, and offer him a friedship treaty, saying that his brother Vali, was his great friend. So, the king of Kishkindha had to be his friend. There was no logical reason for Sugreev to stake his army to help Ram. However, Sugreev rejected the offer forthwith, in no uncertain words.

Ram accepted the adherence of Bibhishan, and crowned him the future King of Lanka, performing *abhisheka* with sea water.

Ram-*Setu*

Bibhishan, Ram-Lakshman and Sugreev, deliberated about crossing the ocean by the army. As decided, Ram prayed to sea god, to make way for the forces of *Dharma*, to cross the ocean and demolish the forces of *Adharma*, which tried to amass all the wealth of the forest people and exploit women for sexual pleasures. As he was getting exasperated, he received a message like a flash, that amongst them was Nal, who was a foster son of celestial architect and builder, Vishwakarma, and had the technical skill to build a causeway, to cross the ocean. Nal was very happy to undertake the task. With large labour force of Sugreev's army personnel, who quickly collected boulders and trees, the task was completed in three days.

Nal was an expert to identify the shallow portion of the ocean, and chose low tide period to work fast. While all were busy collecting boulders, clay and trees, to make the causeway, there was a squirrel, who was also collecting clay, by rolling in it and offloading it near the sight of the causeway. Everybody observed these movements of a small squirrel, and laughed at the efforts. Ram also watched the swift movements of squirrel, and appreciated the efforts. He patted on the back of squirrel in appreciation, with his fingers. It is believed that the verticle marks of fingers seen on the squirrel's back, were made by Ram, continuing and visible to us. When small contributions are made or contemplated about participation for a worthy cause, it is expressed as 'squirrel's contribution'.

All the troops crossed the ocean causeway and camped, at the foothills of a small hill, at some distance from the gates of Lanka. Ram was carried by Hanuman on his shoulder, while Lakshman was carried by Angad, across the sea.

Yuddhakand: Summary

Ravan's brother, Bibhishan and their mother's father counsel Ravan to release and restore Sita to Ram. He however banishes Bibhishan who takes refuge with Ram. Ram sends Angad as his emissary to meet Ravan with an aim to avoid war and bloodshed, by releasing Sita. However, with certainty of war as the only solution for the release of Sita from Ravan's captivity, a bridge, *'Ram-Setu'* had to be constructed for Ram's 'Sugreev army' to cross the sea. In the ensuing war, all sons of Ravan and brother Kumbhakarna get killed. Ram punishes Ravan by killing him in a prolonged battle. Bibhishan was coronated as the sovereign King of Lanka.

Sita was formally released from captivity at Ashokvan, by King Bibhishan. She joins Ram after taking a ritual bath, performing a brief ritual of purity to undo the ritual pollution of living in the custody of the enemy, combining with thanks giving to Divinity.

Ram, Lakshman, Sita accompanied by Hanuman and other important leaders return to Ayodhya in '*Pushpak*'. Ram is officially coronated as the King, with Sita as the Queen, and Bharat as the Yuvraj.

Yuddhakand

Ravan was carefully planning the defence of Lanka, posting Prahasta, the Chief Commander at the eastern gate, Indrajit at the western gate, another commander at the southern gate, and he decided to guard the northern gate himself. Ram, Sugreev, Bibhishan, assisted by Hanuman and Lakshman comprised the war council. Ram accepted the suggestion of Sugreev that Ram should be the Commander-in-Chief of the forces. Ram posted Neel at the eastern gate to face Prahasta, Angad at the southern gate, Hanuman was to counter Indrajit, while Ram-Lakshman were to face Ravan. Sugreev, Jambavan and Bibhishan were to be with the main army. All the commanders from Ravan's side and Ram's side were looking on the other side, for their own assessment. While Ravan was reviewing from the top of the main gate, Ram and Lakshman were looking at Lanka from the top of the hill. Ram was very appreciative of the beautiful city, and felt sorry that the city could be destroyed during the war. But there was no other option. While Ravan was reviewing from his gate, in an inkling of an eye, Sugreev, without anybody noticing, sprang at Ravan, and the crown of Ravan came down tumbling. Ravan was alert, and the two got into wrestling bout. Ravan played *tantra* magic and disappeared. Sugreev came back. Ram appreciated his valour, but counselled him from desisting such adventures, which were unbecoming of a King. Sugreev apologized, but confessed that he lost his balance of mind, seeing villain Ravan who insulted *Ma*-Sita.

Espionage

In the meantime, Ravan sent his spies, who disguised themselves as monkeys, to assess the strength of Sugreev's army. However, Bibhishan could locate them as demons and captured them. They were produced before Ram for punishment. Ram said, take them to the entire camp, and let them make their assessment, to report back our strength, which would break the nerve of Ravan. Accordingly, the spies were taken around and they saw the committed warriors and soldiers. They were impressed with the disciplined behaviour of all army personnel, and were all praise for the treatment meted to them. Back in Lanka, they reported to Ravan and Prahast about the strength of Sugreev army and their resolve to vanquish Ravan's *adharma*, once for all.

Ravan got confused. Then he called their sorcerer and asked him to make an exact replica of Ram's head. Ravan made a war-time last trip to Ashokvan, to tell Sita that the Sugreev army was defeated, and Ram was killed. As a proof, the socerer placed before her the head of Rama. Sita got into swoon, muttering that she had no other option but to go with Ram. As Ravan left, due to urgent meeting of the war council, the replica of Ram's head disappeared, due to expiry of the magic time. Trijata woke up Sita, to consciousness, and told her to listen to the sound of drums of Sugreev army. She told her, that what was presented was only *tantric* magic, knowing the sorcerer, who brought the replica of Ram's head. Sita recovered to her self-confidence, and knew that the days of Ravan rule were numbered, and within sight.

Diplomacy

The relevance of Ramayan is conspicuous in the civilisational context even today. The epics, *Mahabharat* and *Ramayan* have a common message of victory of good over evil. The ultimate and most lethal instrument of state used by the King to administer justice is the use of his military. Use of military causes destruction, loss of lives, economic and social degradation of the vanquished and public humiliation, hence use of military to wage a war, is the last option, to be used only when all other means of settling a dispute have been exhausted; these would include diplomacy, persuasion, coercion, and such other steps. While using military as an instrument to settle a dispute, victory is ensured when the soldiers are convinced that they are fighting a "just war" (principle of *jus ad bellum*). It was only after the First World War that the United Nations declared waging war as illegal, except accepting the right to self-defence. Lord Ram had displayed this foresight in that era when waging a war was commonplace to assert one's power.

The importance of having a "moral high ground" to justify waging a war was what prompted Sri Ramchandra to seek help from the oppressed Sugreev. Sri Ram first helped Sugriva to defeat his stronger brother Vali; in that battle too, when Vali questioned Ram's intervention and called it illegal/immoral, Ram had admonished Vali as having no right to speak of morals, and further justified his actions as against the fight being of good (Sugriva) over evil (Vali). Vali, who had not only usurped Sugriva's kingdom but more importantly his wife, which was an immoral act, had no moral standing, and thus had to be vanquished. Thus, Ram showed apt statesmanship in choosing his allies well, Sugriva having suffered the ignominy of having his wife kidnapped would surely help Ram to get back Sita, who too had been abducted immorally by Ravan. Vali was the stronger of the two brothers and had the capability to defeat Ravan, but Ram chose to align with Sugriva, who though weaker of the two brothers, was morally correct and an oppressed party.

Ram could have sought support of the mighty armies of Ayodhya or Janaka (his father-in-law), but he chose the tribals of Dandakaranya as his allies. Ram's selection of the correct allies in battle is relevant even today. Chanakya in his treatise "*The Arthashastra*" too has given views on how a King should carefully decide his choice of the correct allies.

Intelligence Gathering

Ramchandra had gone hunting the golden deer when Sita was abducted. Ram had no means to locate Sita, the first information was given by Jatayu who unsuccessfully tried to rescue Sita. Thereon, Ramchandra started gathering intelligence about the likely whereabouts of Sita and also the capability of his adversary who had abducted Sita. Angad had led the search party accompanied by Hanuman and Jambavant who together gave preliminary inputs about Sita's whereabouts. Hanuman was sent to Lanka to gather more specific information about Sita's exact location and state of mind. Like a good emissary-*cum*-spy, Hanuman took upon himself the mission of assessing the war waging capability of Ravan and looking for any sympathisers in the enemy camp (Vibhishan). Dr. S. Jayashankar while explaining the essence of his book '*The India Way*' during an interview, referred to Hanuman as a very good diplomat. Not only did he gather information about his adversary but also subtly informed Ravan about the capabilities at the disposal of Ramchandra, thus administering caution in Ravan's mind. Later, when Ravan sent spies to Ram's camp to ascertain the facts, the spies were apprehended by the alert sentries in Ram's camp. In spite of advice by Sugreev, to kill the spies, Ram showed good sense in not only treating the spies properly but also letting them go back safely to Lanka. Thus, Ram as the strategist was right, because on returning to Lanka these spies narrated stories of Ram's army's capabilities to Ravan, which further helped insert nervous feeling in the mind of the Ravan, not to take Sri Ram lightly. Wars are first won in the minds of the Generals and then on ground; in spite of Ravan's technological and numerical superiority, the psychological effect of these subtle actions of Ram morally weakened Ravan (even today information warfare is used by armies to have this effect on the adversary).

Just before the war, Rama sent Angad to Ravan's court as a peace messenger to give him one last chance to send Sita back to him and stop the war. The choice of Angad is also interesting, Angad as son of Vali was known to Ravan as the prince of Kishkindha. Ravan would think twice before harming Vali's son. Angad in spite of being son of Vali who was killed by Sugreev and Ram, spoke to Ravan of the wisdom of respecting Ram's wife, and sending her honourably, and thereby avoiding war. Ram's statesmanship and selection of the right person for the right job, is admirable and an example even in today's context. (In UN, Geneva, Pakistan had decided to raise human rights issues about Jammu and Kashmir. The then Prime Minister of India, Sri Narasimha Rao had deployed Sri Atal Bihari Vajpayee, leader of the opposition, to defend India's case.)

Military Strategy

The Military Strategic dimension of the great Indian epic *Ramayana*, has many similarities and lessons for Military Strategists even today. The traditional story of Ramayana as narrated by Valmiki, has many interpretations and versions; *Ramcharitmanas* by Tulsidas, being one of the most famous one. Even in modern times, great thinkers like C. Rajgopalachari have narrated the epic, so as to be understood in the present-day context. However, the military dimension and the strategic insights of the Ramayana deserve a more detailed analysis.

Lord Ram is known as "*Maryada Purushottam*", i.e. he was not only a man of principles, but also practised what was right, irrespective of the consequences, and many a times at the cost of sacrificing his personal comfort and authority. The decision to obey his father's wishes and renouncing the throne to proceed for 14 years of "*Vanwas*" (jungle stay), is the most prominent example of the Ram's righteous behaviour.

For such a principled prince, was waging a war to retrieve his kidnapped wife a just cause? Was he not endangering the lives of hundreds and thousands of soldiers for a personal loss? Does this behaviour get categorized as a 'just war'—*jus ad bellum*?

To get to the details of the justness of the war, and how Lord Ram ensured righteous lessons, were always upheld and followed, one must go into the strategic and military aspects of the epic in detail.

Ravan had kidnapped Sita by using guile and fraud, getting both Ram and Lakshman to leave Sita alone in a jungle cottage, and then dressed as a *sadhu*, he did the heinous act of kidnapping a princess. The 'golden deer act' was also forced upon Mareech who unwillingly performed the act, under the threat of death by Ravan. Mareech knew that this act, would result in his ultimate perishing at the hands of the valiant brothers, Ram and Lakshman, and that too for an unjust cause. Thus, the whole episode of Ravan's deeds, is an example of un-gentlemanly and un-soldierly behaviour.

Despite Ram branded to be an '*avatar*' of Lord Vishnu, he did not have the divine powers as possessed by Lord Krishna of

Mahabharat. Ram had to work on his human talents and instincts. Thus, on returning to his jungle abode, after killing Mareech, and realizing that Sita was missing, his first task was to find the whereabouts of Sita—an 'Intelligence' task.

Ram did not have a classic Intelligence network, since he was not the ruling King, sitting on the throne. He relied on the available sources in jungle. He even set upon a personal reconnaissance to look for his missing wife. The first hint he received was from Jatayu, who had seen Ravan carrying Sita in the flying chariot speeding towards Lanka. Jatayu put up a valiant fight, to rescue Sita, but unfortunately failed to rescue her. Jatayu's input about Sita's kidnapping and likely destination being Lanka, set the stage for the overseas 'search and rescue mission'.

Ram's preparation for the war and the execution of the strategic, operational and tactical battles, is a stunning example of a series of innovations and warfare, which are relevant to this day.

History remembers Ram for the destruction of Ravan, an evil demon king, and in the process, rescuing his wife, and the Queen-consort of Ayodhya kingdom. Hence, the justification—the victory of good over evil.

Once Ram learnt of the enormity of the task—waging a war on the kingdom, across the sea, he decided to raise his Armed Forces (*Sena*). The Armed Forces had all the dimensions, i. e. Army, Air-equivalent-force, since chariots were used in the aerial dimension, more by Ravan's side, and by Ram, only at the last moment. Some of the experts like Sugreev, Hanuman and Angad, could fly over large distances, which was understandably technological innovation. The Force also had expert engineers, who constructed the bridge across the ocean, likened to present day amphibious operations. What needs to be mentioned is that, Ram did not take help from the conventional powerful armies of Ayodhya (his father's kingdom) or from Janak of Videha (Sita's father). Ram chose to befriend another oppressed Prince Sugreev, who too had his kingdom and wife snatched away from him, by his powerful brother Vali. Thus, Ram understood the importance of a 'just war' which would be won, if the cause was justified; and those fighting the war, were convinced that the cause for fighting the war was justified.

Here are the few examples of how the Principles of War were followed.

Principles of War

The Principles of War as followed in contemporary times, by most of the Armed Forces of modern armies, are also evident in Ramayana.

(a) Selection and Maintenance of Aim

Ram always remained focused on his primary aim of rescuing Sita. The thought of abandoning this mission, or re-marrying, never ever crossed his mind. Due to this single-minded focus, in spite of the wily designs of Ravan, Ram emerged as the victor. Ravan had many advantages; a fully trained conventional army, valiant demons with magical powers, the boons which he himself had acquired from the Almighty, in reward of his penances. In spite of all these, Ram's focused, steadfast and patient approach to his mission, proved superior to Ravan's forces.

(b) Maintenance of Morale

Ram's systematic planning of the strategy; his defeat of Vali (who was considered more powerful than Ravan), and Ram's charismatic personality; all helped to maintain his forces with high morale. In spite of adverse situations during the war wherein Ravan's army at times had an upper hand, Ram overcame the minor setbacks easily and sustained a high morale of his army, which is a battle winning factor. Ram also ensured that his admirers in Ravan's camp (like of Bibhishan) also were contacted, and adequate re-assurances given to them, to wait for the opportune moment to switch forces. Such management of the campaign, is proof of Ram's capability as a deft Military Commander.

(c) Offensive Action

Ram maintained the initiative throughout the war. Every action taken by Ram, preparing the right Armed Forces, selection of the local army *vis-à-vis* the conventional armies of Ayodhya or Janak (*Videha*), installing Sugriva on the throne, sending Hanuman and later Angad to Lanka, were all initiatives by Ram which depict a bold and decisive Commander. By seizing initiative, Ram always remained on the offensive, and kept his adversary guessing of his next move.

(d) Surprise

Since Ram was always on the move, his adversary was mostly on the reactive mode. Hanuman's feedback, after his recce, was very useful in maintaining surprise. Ravan learnt of Ram's designs very late, and thereafter his over-confidence and under-estimation of Ram's capabilities, proved to be the main reasons, for his being always caught by surprise. Every action of Ram was reason for Ravan's forces and family members, to react and alter their plans. This reactive mentality has an adverse impact on the forces and causes battle fatigue, which finally resulted in Ravan's debacle.

(e) Concentration of Force

In spite of the fact that Lanka had a huge army, Ram ensured that at the point of decision, Ram's forces always overwhelmed those of Ravan. This was achieved by Ram's deft management of his forces.

(f) Security

Ram's plans of preparing for the campaign, were not known to Ravan's spies, till Hanuman reached Lanka. By then, Ram was more or less ready with his Armed Forces. Ravan had no idea of the preparations in progress; once Ram was ready, he deliberately let Ravan's spies see his prowess, which had a telling effect on the deficient morale of Ravan's army.

(g) Economy of Effort

Ram must have truly appreciated Hanuman's strengths; so he let him go alone to Lanka. Later, knowing fully well, that Ravan would not harm Angad, who he knew to be Vali's son, he again let him go alone. When the bridge was being built across the Ocean, Ram delegated the task to the two expert engineers. All these actions prove his acumen of employing the correct force, for the correct task. Thus, he could easily manage the campaign, in spite of having a smaller and less equipped army *vis-à-vis* Lanka's huge army.

(h) Intelligence

The first task for Ram, was to find out, where and how Sita had disappeared (he was not aware initially that she had been kidnapped); the first input came from Jatayu, who had seen Ravan taking Sita in his flying chariot. As the episode became clear to Ram, about the heinous act of Ravan, it was a foregone conclusion that Ravan was responsible, and he had to be made to pay for his mis-adventure. Ram, the gentleman and a soldier-general, went about his planning very meticulously. The entire campaign was based on hard intelligence gathered from various sources. Intelligence gathering is the key, in the entire preparation for the war.

(i) Cooperation

Ram was a charismatic leader; he was able to win over the confidence of the entire Sugreeva Army, and also had a charismatic influence on the likes of Bibhishan (in the enemy camp), thus managing to get cooperation from all of his admirers. Such cooperation and jointness of effort, plays an instrumental role in winning the wars.

(j) Flexibility

Ram was faced with a number of uncertainties, while in Ayodhya and even after leaving the kingdom. His flexible nature, combined with steadfast path of righteousness, ensured that he remained on the correct (*Dharma*) side of the law and ethics. All these principles are evident in the planning and execution of Ram's just war of good over evil.

Diplomacy to Avoid War

Taking into consideration the military strategy, and the principles of war, which are in vogue, even today. Ram tried the last diplomacy strategy of taking initiative, to avoid war and bloodshed and destruction, involving the civilians. As we know, such diplomacy has been pursued in *Mahabharat* also, to avoid war, by no less a person, but Srikrishna himself volunteering as an emissary of Peace.

Ram thought of making a last attempt to avoid war, bloodshed and destruction, by sending a message to Ravan to honourably release Sita from the custody and return her, with grace and dignity. Who would be the emissary? There was consultation. Bibhishan thought that Crown-Prince Angad would be a good choice. He was a Prince, and known to Ravan since childhood, as Vali's son. He was brave, courageous and could not be bowed down. Ram instructed Angad to go to Lanka as his messenger and deliver this message to King Ravan. Angad went directly to the court of Ravan when the Assembly was in full session. When Angad went to the court of Ravan, as messenger of Ram, he was not offered any seat, as per the protocol. So, Angad extended his tail, coiled it to form a seat, slightly above the height of Ravan's throne and sat on it for delivering the message. He gave Ram's message like this. "Oh, great King of Lanka. I am Angad, son of Vali, whom you knew since my childhood. You were brought to our palace at Kishkindha, when I was a baby in the cradle. Now, I come as the messenger of Sri Ram, the King of Ayodhya. You brought his wife, *Ma*-Sita, by deceit, and has thereby insulted all women, whose curses you are carrying. As you know, our army in battle position is at the gates of Lanka. The war will put an end to your *adharma*. But it will lead to destruction of Lanka and bloodshed, leading to thousands of women becoming widows. We are giving you a last chance, to make peace and avoid war. Apologise to Sita and return Sita honourably. We will withdraw our forces and return to Kishkindha and Ayodhya. You may convey your decision to our messenger, Prince Angad, for further action." As Ravan listened to the message, he was furious. He said, "I am not killing you, since you are a messenger and more so, since you are son of Vali, whom I had seen as a baby in the cradle, and entertained you." Ravan said, "Tell your pitiable human, that he was a wanderer in the forest, thrown out by his own father, King Dashrath. He had no business to put beautiful Sita, daughter of King Janak, to the hardships of forest life, when she deserved all the pleasures, as my consort. I am following *Dharma* by allowing her to take time to accept my solicitations, and the time will expire soon. In the interest of Kishkindha and Ayodhya, they should go back and leave us in peace. Let them not force a war on us leading to their self-destruction. They should be aware that the Trinity gods, Brahma, Vishnu, and Mahesh are afraid of me." Saying this, he instructed guards to throw out Angad. Angad said, "I will go on my own. If your guards have the power, let them move my leg, which I am implanting on the floor. Saying this, he stood firmly on the ground, with his leg implanted on the floor. The guards caught hold of his leg but could not move it or lift it. Many guards followed by warriors and even Indrajit tried, but could not move the leg. Ultimately, Ravan descended from the throne and was bending to catch his leg. Angad said, "Oh, Great king, it is unbecoming of you to touch my leg. It will disgrace your image. Moreover, you had entertained me as a baby. So, you are like my father. I should touch your feet, not the other way round. I will go on my own. Please act on the message fast to save your life and that of your sons, brothers and citizens." Thus saying, Angad returned to the army camp and reported the happenings to the war council, headed by Ram.

War

Ram ordered the army to start the assault on Lanka. Sugreev's army started marching, blowing the trumpets and beating the drums. Ram was hoping that Sita heard the marching of Sugreev army, to the tune of drums and trumpets, which would make her happy with optimism. Sugreev army surrounded the town of Lanka, from all sides and banged at all the four gates. There were gruesome fights among the soldiers of Lankan and Kishkindha armies. Besides, there were duels among the warriors on both sides, such as Angad and Indrajit, Hanuman with Jambumali, Neel with Nikumbha, and Lakshman with Virupaksha and many others. Horses of chariots were killed. Lankan chariots were smashed with boulders used by Sugreev army.

Indrajit shot serpent darts at Ram and Lakshman, thereby the serpents binding their bodies and making them immovable. The snake bites would ultimately poison the blood and kill the persons. Jambavan, the wise old statesman of Sugreev, commissioned Hanuman to search for eagles, the natural enemies of snakes, to undo the binding by snakes and kill them. Hanuman leapt in the space and requested two divine eagles to help. They immediately swooped on the snakes and started biting the snakes. The snakes ran helter-skelter to save themselves, from the sharp beak-bites of eagles. The eagles lifted the snakes high up in the skies. Ram-Lakshman regained consciousness, and healed up completely with the application of herbs, which were known to forest dwelling Kishkindha soldiers.

In the meantime, Indrajit went to his father, King Ravan, and proclaimed that the war was over, since Ram-Lakshman were bound by venomous snakes, who were killing them, with their poisonous bites. Both of them were unconscious beyond recovery. Ravan was quick to spread the news to Ashokvan, that both Ram-Lakshman had been killed and as a proof, arranged to show Sita, from the *Pushpak*, the bodies of Ram-Lakshman, on the battle-field. Trijata was with Sita for aerial survey. As Sita saw Ram-Lakshman lying on the ground, bound by snakes and their bow and arrows on their side, she was certain that they were dead. But Trijata consoled her saying that they were unconscious, and not dead. The faces of the dead could not be radiant, and looking skywards. As Sita was taken back to Ashokvan, she was met with Sarama, wife of Bibhishan, who knew everything, that was going on in the court gossip. She counselled Sita, that the eagles had already rescued both of them, and they were fit to fight the battle. Ravan hearing the renewed battle cries of Sugreev army, got informed that Ram-Lakshman were on their feet, and leading the army. In the battles that ensued, Dhoomraksha and later Akampana, sons of Ravan, were killed by Hanuman, and Vajradamashstra was slain by Angad. With Akampana's death, Ravan was crestfallen and wanted to go to the front himself. But Prahasta, the warrior-chief of Ravan came out of the gate, leading a big army, as identified by Bibhishan. Neel, the foster son of fire-god, *Agni*, smashed the head of Prahasta. Thereupon, Ravan inquired about his giant brother, Kumbhakarna, who was in his proverbial deep slumber. Ravan ordered to wake him up. It was quite a task to wake him up with the use of drums thumping at his ears. As soon as he got up, he needed to have food. He was told about the war, and about senior warriors from Lanka, having been killed. He was summoned urgently by King Ravan for consultations. Kumbhakarna faced Ravan and asked him, "Since you have woken me up from my sleep, something terrible must have happened, when you needed my help. Tell me." Ravan gave him an account of the war and the loss of warriors. Kumbhakarna muttered, that he was warned about these consequences, and was advised to return Sita, since she was not brought as a winning trophy after killing Ram, but by deceit. However, Kumbhakarna assured that he will forthwith destroy the enemy and walked off towards the field. With his big palms and big soles, he started picking up the soldiers of Sugreev army, and smashing them to death. He walked over the attacking soldiers, crushing them under his feet. The attacks by Kishkindha soldiers, with rocks and trees, had no effect on him. King Sugreev, Hanuman, Angad, Neel and even Lakshman's attacks had no effect on him. He was asking for Ram to face him. Ultimately, Ram started shooting darts of arrows to him which caused minor injuries. Bibhishan was also worried, and did not show himself in front of his brother. Ram then severed his arms and legs, but Kumbhakarna did not fall on the ground. Then his head was severed and thrown far, which fell on the streets of Lanka. Thus ended Kumbhakarna. His sons, Kumbh and Nikumbh, had already died in the battle. This was the last straw for Ravan, and he offered to lead the army personally. Son Indrajit sought permission to lead the army, and kill Ram and Lakshman. Ravan knowing that Indrajit was a greater warrior than himself, having defeatd Indra; blessed him and ordered him to lead the army.

Sushen Vaidya saves Lakshman

Indrajit earlier had already made Ram-Lakshman unconscious with his serpent darts. Indrajit called Lakshman for battle, reserving Ram for Ravan himself. Indrajit was very crafty. He would become invisible and show up at several places confusing Lakshman. Arrows darted by Lakshman in different directions of Indrajit's sight, could not hit him. Indrajit taking advantage of the nervousness of Lakshman, injured him severely. Jambavan and Bibhishan told Ram, that only the *Vaidya*—physician of Ravan could save Lakshman. But how to bring *Vaidya* Sushen who was in Lanka? Again Hanuman was commissioned. He got the address from Bibhishan, and went by skywalk to reach Vaidya. He used to live in a hut type structure, in the garden of medicinal plants, created by him for his use. Hanuman told him the problem. He said that although he was Ravan's physician, for him, the *dharma* was to treat a patient, to save his life, irrespective of his social, economic or political status. (Red Cross follows this principle in contemporary times). His problem was how to carry his herbs and equipment during war. Hanuman offered to carry him with his house, which was done. *Vaidya* examined Lakshman's pulse and declared that he was critically injured. Only a herb with the name '*Sanjeevani*', located in the Dronagiri hills in the Himalayan range could save him, if it was procured before sunrise. He also gave some identifying signs to locate the herb. Again Hanuman offered to bring it. He forthwith jumped on the skywalk towards Himalayas. He had to descend at couple of places, since the distance was too much for one jump. He also consulted some persons on the way, about the exact location of Dronagiri, as he reached the Himalayan range. Having reached the place, he was confused about locating the Sanjeevani plant. So he lifted the portion of Dronagiri hills, which was thick with herbs, and brought it to the battlefield. Sushen *Vaidya* treated Lakshman successfully, almost snatching him from the gate of *Yama-Lok*. Lakshman was totally recovered and got up on his feet, ready for the battle. Hanuman restored back the Dronagiri hill, and reached back Sushen *Vaidya*, restoring his house.

Losing War

Knowing Lakshman's recovery, Indrajit went in a cave for meditation, and offer oblations to evil spirits, to acquire more fighting acumen, and newer magical weapons. Bibhishan advised to intercept and obstruct, Indrajit's completion of meditation and prayers. Hanuman, Lakshman, Sugreev and many others went to the cave and disturbed Indrajit, forcing him to come out of the cave. Again the duel of Indrajit and Lakshman resumed. Lakshman wanted to use Brahmastra to kill Indrajit, but Ram advised not to do so, since it would result into wide-scale destruction, may be even affecting Ashokvan. Indra as an enemy of Indrajit, had given a weapon '*Indra-astra*' which Lakshman used, and severed Indrajit's head. Under instructions of Ram, Indrajit's body was taken to the main gate of Lanka. Indrajit's wife Sulochana came out and ascended the funeral pyre of Indrajit, to go with him, to the heavenly abode as *Sati*. Ravan was totally broken with the death of his great warrior son, Indrajit. Now, no worthwhile warrior was left with Ravan. Queen Mandodari and her father again counselled Ravan, to send back Sita, to stop further bloodshed.

Ram killed Ravan, but Sita Defeated Him

Ravan said, that he would rather kill Sita forthwith, who was the cause of death of his brothers and sons, and took out the sword in his hand. He was reminded by Mandodari, that a great invincible king, as he was, could not kill an innocent woman, already under captivity. What kind of bravery he would be exhibiting by this act? So, it was clear that Ravan suffered from a severe nervous breakdown. This has been a clear indication, that Ravan was defeated by Sita, although he got killed by Ram, next day.

Ravan said, "Now there was no going back from the decisive war. Those who have sacrificed their lives for me, including my brothers and sons, would have died in vain, if I call off the war now." Saying that, Ravan with his select forces came out for the battle.

> Mahatama Gandhi writing about the moral strength of women has given the example of Sita. "I have always held that it is physically impossible to violate a woman against her will. The outrage takes place only when she gives way to fear or does not realize her moral strength. If she cannot meet the assailant's physical might, her purity will give her the strength to die before he succeeds in violating her. Take the case of Sita. Physically she was a weakling before Ravan, but her purity was more than a match even for his giant might. He tried to win her with all kind of allurements but could not carnally touch her without her consent. On the other hand, if a woman depends on her own physical strength or upon a weapon she possesses, she is sure to be discomfited whenever her strength is exhausted. (*Harijan*, 14-1-'40)

As Ravan came out of the gate of Lanka, he was attacked by Sugreev. But Sugreev got injured at the hands of Ravan. Ravan was on a royal chariot, while Ram was carried on Hanuman's shoulder. Ram told Ravan, "You are a great and mighty king, but for your misdeeds and *Adharma*, I have no other option but to punish you." Ravan said, "Giving punishment is the duty of the King. But you are a beggar, thrown out of your kingdom, by your father and step-mother. If not for helping Sugreev to kill Vali, by deceit, and get him the kingdom of Kishkindha, you would not have been here. You conspired to take my stupid and coward brother, on your side by fooling him, to make him the King of Lanka. Now face me, the greatest warrior, with whom even Indra dare not challenge face-to-face." Saying this, he showered arrows on Ram. Ram retaliated with equal strength. The soldiers and their generals on both sides halted the battle, and all of them watched the greatest battle among the two. Ravan got injured and his charioteer withdrew the chariot at a side, which was also broken. Since the sun had also started going down, Ram told Ravan, "Go and take rest. We will meet tomorrow."

Next day, Ram was the first to reach the battle-field with Hanuman, who carried him on his broad shoulders, instead of fighting Ravan standing on the ground. As Ravan's chariot was coming out of the gate, a chariot was descending from the skies, and grounded near Ram. The charioteer introduced himself as Maatali and said that Indra had sent his chariot for his use in the battle against Ravan. Ram thanked Maatali and through him, Indra. He circumambulated the chariot thrice and ascended it with his weaponary. Ravan knowing that the Chariot was sent by Indra, made a mockery of Indra, retorting that Indra himself should have come to fight with me, instead of sending a mere chariot. However the fierce battle ensued, whereby Ravan used *tantra* magic and took his chariot to the skies, to attack Ram, without him being visible, as done by Indrajit to attack Lakshman. However, under instructions from Ram, Maatali also took the chariot at the level, to that of Ravan's chariot, and very close to him. Ram's arrow beheaded Ravan, but instantly, it was replaced by another head. This happened atleast ten times. Everybody thought that he was branded as ten-headed, '*Dashanan*', for this reason. Bibhishan ascended to the level of Ram's chariot, and quickly came by the side of Ram. He murmured to Ram, that Ravan's life- force, was located in his navel, and not in his head. Immediately, Ram targeted Ravan's navel to shoot an arrow, which penetrated deep inside. Ravan showed signs of collapsing. His weapons dropped down from his hands, but he did not collapse. Maatali, the experienced Charioteer of Indra told Ram, "My lord, you have the *Brahmastra* with you. This is the time to use it. It will only destroy him and none else." Earlier Ram had prevented Lakshman from using *Brahmastra* for killing Indrajit. But Ram got assured that for an epitome of *Adharma* that Ravan personified, despite his scholarship and knowledge, which he misused for evil designs, *Brahmastra* was an ultimate weapon. With the use of Brahmastra, Ravan immediately collapsed on the ground, saying loudly, "Oh! Sri Ram". At that moment, Ravan realized, that Ram was no ordinary human being, and he saluted him with folded hands, before taking his last breath.

For a moment, people did not believe their eyes; powerful Ravan lying dead on the ground. There was rejoicing in the Sugreev army. Sugreev, Jambavan, Lakshman, Angad were stunned. But Bibhishan was in tears at the death of his brother. He reached at the body of Ravan, and started sobbing and weeping, blaming himself for Ravan's death. Ram looking at Bibhishan went to him, followed by other seniors, and tried to console Bibhishan, with this natural but tragic outcome of the war. Ram said, "Ravan was a great man. He was a scholar. But he had too much ego. He followed with great conviction, what he thought was right. Now with his death, all enmity has ended." He beseeched Bibhishan, to compose himself, and organise the performance of the last rites, befitting Ravan's stature. The war ended with the death of Ravan.

Handing over of Lanka

After some time, Mandodari, accompanied by other queens, and Mandodari's father, arrived on the scene. Mandodari clasped Ravan's body and wept profusely. Her father introduced himself to Ram. He said, "I am the eldest surviving and unfortunate male in the Royal family. My grandchildren whom I used to fondle on my lap, and played with them, are no more, none of them, except Bibhishan, who was thrown out by Ravan and joined you." He had come with the crown of the King of Lanka to be handed over to Ram, and the keys of the Treasury. He addressed Ram thus, "Now I am handing over the kingdom of Lanka to the King of Ayodhya. Lanka would now be a subordinate kingdom, as a colony of Ayodhya Empire. I have brought the crown of the King of Lanka, and the keys of the rich treasury, to be handed over to you. I have only one request to make you. Please love the citizens of Lanka, and govern them with affection, as Ravan did." Ram said, "Sir, I am very sorry for what has happened. But you know the truth. As for Lanka, it is yours, owned by the citizens of Lanka. As you probably know, Bibhishan was already declared as the future King of Lanka. Let his formal coronation as King be ritually performed, as soon as possible. It is for you to guide him, in the governance of Lanka." Mandodari who was listening to this formal dialogue, composed slightly. She said, she had to go with Ravan. "Myself and my father told him several times that he was committing a great, unpardonable sin, by soliciting a chaste woman like Sita, who was so devoted to her husband. I had met Sita. She is an idol for all women. But somehow, when he set his mind on something, he would not leave it, till he acquired it. He has paid the price for it, at the hands of a divine person like you. Sri Ram, you have been so devoted to your wife, Sita. May God bless you both. However, I will go with my husband. I am sure, Bibhishan will be a good king of Lanka."

Ram-Lakshman and others left them, to have their privacy, and requesting King Bibhishan to mange and organize the affairs.

After the befitting funeral rites of Ravan, Bibhishan was formally coronated as the King of Lanka. Lakshman, Sugreev, Angad, Jambavan and others were present for the coronation. Ram was bound by the conditions of 14 years of exile, thereby not to enter any town or city. Hence, he was neither present personally for coronation of Sugreev, nor for Bibhishan's coronation.

Release of Sita

Sita came to know from Trijita, about the death of Ravan. Hanuman went to inform Sita about the end of war, following Ravan's death, at the hands of Ram. Sita expressed desire, to present herself and see Ram immediately. Hanuman told her that Sri Ram was making appropriate arrangements for her presentation, as a free woman. Ram requested King Bibhishan to free Sita from the Lankan captivity, and allow to join her with his family honourably. He said, "She has gone through *Agnidivya*, with fortitude, facing Ravan's immoral fire." Sita was assisted by Bibhishan's wife, in having a proper ritual bath. Discarding the hermit dress, she was given proper royal dress, and bedecked with some ornaments, of a married woman. Bibhishan arranged for her a palanquin, to carry her to the camp of Sugreev army. Everybody was anxious to have '*darshan*' of Sita. Ram requested that no restrictions be imposed on the people who wanted to see Sita. As she came out of the palanquin, outside the geographical boundary of Lanka, she bowed and touched mother earth. Sita was known as '*Bhumi-kanya*'. She expressed the desire to formally thank the God for protecting her in enemy camp, and for victory in the war. As per custom, a small *yag* was performed (*Homa-Havan*). Sita offered the oblations to fire-god, with a resolve to do it properly at Ayodhya. After circumambulating the fire-place three times, she touched the feet of Ram. She offered apologies for her craving for golden deer, which created all the problems, leading to this war. She also bowed down to Lakshman, although Lakshman was to touch her feet, as his elder brother's wife, equivalent to mother. She apologized to Lakshman, for saying bad words to him.

She was formally introduced to King Sugreev, Prince Angad, Jambavan and others, who played a major role in her release by winning the war. Sita said special words of praise for Hanuman, without whom, she could not have survived to see this day. She said, Hanuman was like her son. Everybody was taken over by the divine bliss of Sita. King Bibhishan offered to gift the *Pushpak* aircraft to Sri Ram. However, Ram declined to accept the gift, which was the property of the kingdom of Lanka. He, however, accepted to use it in emergent situations. *Pushpak* had a technology to expand in size, depending upon the number of passengers to board it. *Pushpak* aircraft did not require a pilot. It functioned with the orders from the registerd voice.

Agni Pariksha/Agnidivya

There is considerable feminist hue and cry about Sita reportedly being made to undergo Agnipariksha by Ram, that is, physically entering fire to prove her purity of moral character, after her release from Ravan's custody, after the death of Ravan at the hands of Ram in the war. Sita was led with honour in a palanquin by King Bibhishan outside the gates of Lanka. Actually, nobody from

Ayodhya, except Ram and Lakshman were present there. Nobody except Hanuman had seen her or met her in captivity at the Ashokvan. King Bibhishan saw her when he went to Ashokvan to bring her out of Lanka, with dignity. All other spectators present outside the gates of Lanka were from the Sugreev army, who were anxious to have a glimpse of Sita, who became the cause of downfall of powerful Ravan. Hanuman had witnessed her dialogue with Ravan, rebuking him and prophesying his imminent death at the hands of Ram. Ravan could do nothing but to listen to Sita's rebukes, only repeating that he would be happy to have her as his principal queen. He kept on soliciting her to give up a mere human, that Ram was, who was exiled by his father to forest. In the cultural values of Sugreev army, there was no norm as defilement for a woman, who was forcibly kidnapped by an enemy. So, what is this '*agnipariksha*' which Ram reportedly seems to have inflicted on her?

What is this *Agni* and *Agnipariksha*?

In common linguistic expression, when a person goes through very difficult times, and emerges back successfully, to his normal calling, he is supposed to have gone through *agnipariksha* or *agnidivya*. Fire representing Sun is ritually very important. Domestication of fire led to Man becoming the only animal, cooking food, which led to his biological evolution as *Homo sapien*.

Fire is worshipped in India and the Zoroastrians have also fire temples. No important ritual is performed among the Hindu without fire, and oblations to fire. Marriage is solemnised around fire. Dead bodies among the Hindu are creamated with the use of fire. Homa-Havan is a common ritual in any religious ceremony.

There are references to Yajnya being performed by the Rishis in Ramayana. A successful person has to go through adverse situations, before he earns some reputation or fame. It is commonly expressed that such a person had gone through *agnidivya*.

Sita who had been kidnapped by Ravan and was kept in captivity, trying to persuade her to be his Queen, could not have normally remained pure, untouched by Ravan. It is never believed that a powerful person would not molest a woman in his custody. That has also been reflected in the practice of 'Johar' in Rajasthan. In the event of impending defeat in wars with the muslim invaders, women in royal family would commit suicide by jumping into the well of fire, specially created for such purpose, to protect their fidelity. Nobody would normally believe that Ravan would not have defiled Sita. But Bibhishan knew, as his wife, and possibly his daughter, used to visit her in Ashokvan and boost up her morale. Hanuman who had located Sita in Lanka had an occasion to observe Sita in Ashokvan, surrounded by women guards of Ravan, whose business was to persuade Sita to accept Ravan's proposal of marriage. Hanuman had observed how Sita rebuked Ravan and forewarned him that Ram would surely kill him, for his misdeeds against women. Ravan was a mute listener to such rebukes, but had no courage to touch her.

Purity-Pollution

When Sita was released from the captivity of Ravan and was to be produced before Ram, she was considered ritually impure, coming from the enemy's captivity. Jail could not be considered as ritualy 'pure' and temple as 'impure' or polluting place. Usually purificatory *yajnyas* are performed on such occasions, even in present times, commonly referred as 'Home-Havan'. Before Sita crossed the line of Lanka to cross over to Ram's side, a purificatory make-shift *yajnya* was performed, which was also a thanks giving to the God who protected her, and ensured victory to Ram's forces, and united with him. A promise was made to the fire god that proper thanks giving rituals would be performed after returning back to Ayodhya. Why do people continue to perform *Satyanarayan Pooja*, mostly as a thanks giving ritual for tiding over the difficult times and to seek the divine blessings? Where was the issue of proving to the people of Ayodhya, her morally pure status by proving her character, going physically through the fire, as gold's purity is tested in fire by the goldsmith? Who was present from Ayodhya, when Sita was abducted, and released after the war? None from Ayodhya and Ram's family had any inkling about the whereabouts of Ram, Sita and Lakshman in exile, after they last met at Chitrakoot, about fourteen years ago.

Ritual purity and pollution are the concepts which are significant in Indian culture. *Varna-Caste* hierarchy is based on these concepts. Temple visits without bath, vegetarian *versus* non-vegetarian food, menstrual period of women, bathing in sacred rivers, particularly on certain days such as *Amavasya*, or during *Kumbh Mela* etc. are all issues of ritual purity and pollution. Returning from the cremation site, even from a barber after haircut, requires ritual bath of purification.

In the 19th and early 20th century, visits abroad such as to England, were considered polluting, and purificatory rites had to be performed. Freedom fighter, Barrister V.D. Savarkar was not allowed to sit in the same row as other family members, for taking food, until, some purificatory rites were performed after his return from England. Tilak was criticized for taking tea in porcelain cup-plate, in the house of a Christian nurse, in the city of Pune, as a polluting act. Even tea was polluting, since the leaves came from the British Tea Co. Later, tea was taken, even by old ladies in the house, but in the bronze water cups, not in a porcelain cup. As a protest against the British, several Indians took to coffee, since the coffee estates were reported not owned by the British companies.

Fire worship or rituals around the fire are common even now as purifying acts. Hindus are cremated and not buried, to free the soul from the body for transmigration. So, *agnipariksha* or *agnidivya* does not mean physically entering fire, like the gold processed or tested by goldsmith for purity. It is an allegory to symbolize purity beyond doubt.

Flight Back to Ayodhya

As the fourteen year period of Ram's exile was getting over, and as promised to Bharat, Ram-Lakshman-Sita were ready to go to Ayodhya. They were accompanied by King Bibhishan, King Sugreev, Hanuman, Angad, Jambavan, Nal, Neel and some others.

They all boarded *Pushpak* and took off for the first halt, across the sea, where they had conceived and begun constructing the overseas pathway, *Ramsetu*, for Sugreev army to cross the sea, and reach Lanka. As desired by Hanuman and the Sugreev army, Ram installed a *Shivling* made of sand, in gratitude of the supernatural blessings towards the successful construction of *Ramsetu*. This was also symbolic of laying foundation stone of a new city, Rameshwaram, after the name of Ram. The city was donated to the people, who facilitated the movement of army in the region. It is believed that Lord Shankar/Mahadeo blessed the *Shivling* and symbolized it with his soul, so that people could communicate with him directly, when they visited the temple and prayed. Rameshwaram has thus become an important *Jyotirling*, as one of the most sacred pilgrimage centre in Bharat. Sita was told about the details of construction of *Ramsetu*. *Pushpak* then took off for a destination to meet Agastya Rishi and Lopamudra, on the way to Ayodhya. Ram was showing from the aircraft, and explaining to Sita about Kishkindha, where he could meet Sugreev, Hanuman, Jambavan, Nal and Neel, who had retrieved the ornaments of Sita, which she had dropped from the flying chariott, in which Ravan was forcibly carrying her towards Lanka. *Pushpak* briefly halted to meet sage Agastya and Lopamudra, to pay their respects. Lopamudra had an intimate conversation with Sita about her abduction, her captivity at Ashokvan and subsequent release. Sita conveyed her remorse, about her greed for owning the golden deer, possibly to get a blouse made of golden skin of the deer, which ultimately led to the Lankan war. Next halt of *Pushpak* was scheduled to meet sage Bharadwaj near Prayag, who had directed them to Chitrakoot and subsequently to Panchvati, Nasik. Since the period of 14 years and 14 days of exile was getting over, Ram was concerned about the mental state of Bharat, who had threatened to end his life, failing Ram delaying his arrival to Ayodhya even by a day. Ram directed Hanuman to go and tell Guhak that they would meet him briefly on way to Ayodhya, and to meet Bharat to assure that they were arriving shortly. Guhak was very happy to meet Ram-Sita-Lakshman and Bibhishan, Sugreev, Jambavan and others. Sita had a ritual bath in the sacred river Ganga, and duly worshipped the holy river. Guhak was taken on board of *Pushpak,* to reach the final destination, to land at Nandigram, and join with Bharat. Since Hanuman had told Bharat about the impending arrival of Ram-Sita-Lakshman, Bharat had already sent messages to Ayodhya and gave directions about celebrations on a grand scale on the arrival of Ram.

Diwali at Ayodhya

Sage Vashisth, Shatrughna and Sumant personally monitored the decorations and other proposed celebrations at Ayodhya, to welcome Ram-Sita-Lakshman. Paradoxically, such grand celebrations had been abandoned, which were planned, while Ram was to be coronated as the Crown-Prince, *Yuvraj*, 14 years ago. The Queen-mothers were anxiously waiting, and the citizens of Ayodhya were in the festive mood, to light the lamps and make celebrations, on the occasion. This became the Diwali festival in India, to mark the arrival of Ram-Sita-Lakshman from Lanka, after establishing the eternal values like *Dharma* and *Satya* (Truth). The death of Ravan, Kumbhakarna and Meghnad continue to symbolize the victory of good over evil, on the day of *Dusserah*, across the country, as public display.

Ram-Sita-Lakshman, joined by Bharat at Nandigram, and accompanied by Bibhishan, Sugreev, Hanuman and others reached Ayodhya. There was excitement, enthusiasm and activity, at the residential complex of the King and Queens to receive Ram-Lakshman-Sita, after 14 years. They were received first by Prince Shatrughna and Sumant. Everybody touched the feet of Sage Vashisth. As they entered the palace reception hall, Ram followed by others, touched the feet of Queen-mothers, Kaushalya, Sumitra and Kaikeyi. Kaushalya and Sumitra had tears of joy when Ram-Lakshman touched their feet. They said that Ayodhya had an ambience of an abondoned city for 14 years, although Bharat and Shatrughna made great strides to keep it alive, and promoted peace and prosperity of the citizens. Kaushalya embraced Sita affectionately, stroked her face and said, "You suffered so much for 14 years." Kaushalya presented Sita, with a new diamond ring, as a token of affection. Sumitra blessed Sita with her hand on her head and said, "You suffered so much in the forest." She bedecked her with her own necklace. As Ram touched Kaikayi's feet, she blessed him and wished glorious and long life. She further said, "My life full of grief, has now been redeemed. The citizens of Ayodhya who yearned for Ram would now be happy." When Sita touched Kaikeyi's feet, she said. "You are young, but you have become famous. You enjoyed the opulence of Lanka. Ram had to struggle a lot, in the forest, to get your release by killing the most powerful Ravan, while you were at peace in Lanka. If a dog snatches a plate of food, belonging to somebody else, and although the dog may be punished by the owner; however, the dog-snatched plate remains polluted. Anyway, you have attained fame, causing the destruction of Ravan." Sita felt sad, with such blurting expression, but did not respond. She settled down by the side of Kaushalya and Sumitra, under their benign protection and affection.

They all had ritual bath, anointed with fragrant oils. The hermit apparel by Ram, Lakshman, and Bharat were replaced by princely clothes and ornaments. Sita's *saree* gifted by Anusuya was already replaced after a ritual bath at the residence of King Bibhishan. The hermit hair-do was unlocked and brought back to normal hairstyle. After the quick ritual bath, they visited the palace temple, and the room of the statues of their ancestors, led by Sage Vashisth and Sumant. They felt grieved about the sad demise of their father, King Dashrath, during their absence from Ayodhya. Later they enjoyed the royal banquet, with the guests and *Rishis*, to the tune of music.

Coronation of Ramchandra

Sage Vashisth, minister Sumant, Bharat and Shatrughna rushed for consultation to decide an auspicious day and time, for Ram's coronation as King. Invitations were sent to kings friendly to Ayodhya, and several Rishis. King Janak and Queen Sumedha were specially invited for the big day. They were eagerly waiting to meet the daughters and their husbands. Ram and his brothers, had all married in their family. Proper accommodation was provided to all the guests. Almost, a new city had sprung up to accommodate all the guests and visitors from the countryside of Ayodhya kingdom. Sumant and Shatrughna were monitoring all the details. Vashisth assisted by several priests, performed the coronation rituals. He personally led Sri Ram to the King's throne. Ceremoniously, like a bride, Sita was brought by her cousins, who were also the wives of Lakshman, Bharat and Shatrughna. Sita shared the throne with Ram, while the Vedic rituals were being performed. Bharat placed the '*Paduka*' of Ram in front of his feet, with a sense of satisfaction. For fourteen years, these '*paduka*' were on the throne, at Nandigram, as symbols of Ram as King. Vashisth crowned Ram and Sita, and blessed them. Bharat and Shatrughna were holding the ceremonial, ornate umbrellas (*Chhatra*) over the heads of the King and Queen. All the guest kings led by Bibhishan and Sugreev, offered their respects to the King and Queen, followed by prominent citizens. King Janak and Queen Sumedha blessed Ram and Sita as King and Queen of Ayodhya kingdom. The *rishis* blessed the king and queen.

While these salutations were in progress, Kaikeyi observing Bharat holding the umbrella over Ram's head, expressed to sage Vashisth, her displeasure and grief. She said, "All my past sins have borne this fruit. My son, Bharat, was born as a pauper. For 14 years, he opted to live the life of a hermit at Nandigram. Now he is a slave of the King, holding the umbrella over Ram's head like an attendant. I am so sad." Vashisth retorted, "Atleast, now, keep quiet. You were the cause of Dashrath's death. You sent Ram to forest for 14 years. He has returned back victorious after demolishing the demon kingdom. He has brought new friends to the kingdom. Our advice has been falling on your deaf years. You have antagonized your noble son. He will attain more fame and respect as Bharat, than if he was the King of Ayodhya, as per your evil design. Why don't you focus your mind on the God, and offer prayers to him to get peace of mind?"Saying this, the Sage came out, since Ram also went out, to personally meet the guests, and requesting them to join the ceremonial lunch. Ram and Sita offered appropriate presents to all the guests. Bibhishan and Sugreev were offered special thrones as gifts, to carry back. Ram embraced Hanuman, since he refused any gift. A special pearl necklace offered by *Ma*-Sita to Hanuman was declined by him, saying there was no Ram in the pearls. Sugreev mocked at him in jest, saying where was Ram? Hanuman opened his chest, and showed Ram-Sita at his heart. All people wondered at this miracle of '*Bhakti*', and appreciated, that without Hanuman, it was impossible for Ram to defeat Ravan. The guests took leave of Queen-mothers, Kaushalya and Sumitra, who profusely thanked them for facilitating return of Ram-Lakshman and Sita, after 14 years. The Queen-mothers blessed Bibhishan and Sugreev. While Bibhishan and Sugreev wanted to meet queen Kaikeyi, Bharat dissuaded them from doing so, lest any unkind words bluterred by her could hurt them.

Sri Ram asked Lakshman to be the crown prince, but he declined saying, he would be available for any assistance, as always. He also remarked that Bharat had looked after the kingdom for 14 years. With his experience, he should be the crown prince. Sage Vashisth also endorsed this suggestion of Lakshman. Accordingly, at a simple ceremony, Bharat was anointed as crown prince of Ayodhya. The citizens of Ayodhya greatly appreciated this action, although it did not satisfy Kaikeyi.

King Ram was busy governing the Kingdom, in consultation with Bharat, Shatrughna and Lakshman, while Sumant continued as the Minister heading the entire administration.

Uttarkand: Summary

There is widespread gossip among the citizens of Ayodhya about Ram accepting Sita with full honour as the queen, while she was captured and kept by Ravan for about an year. She was thus considered 'defiled'. Sita also got a tip-off of such gossip through her personal staff of women and felt sad about targeting King Ram, alleging his carnal love for defiled Sita. People waggled their tongues to gossip as to why the King could not remarry while he could have any number of women as queens, or mistresses as per the prevailing practice.

Disapproving the counselling by his brothers and mother Kaushalya, to ignore the gossip, Ram, as King, directs Lakshman to reach Sita near an *ashram* and leave her there. Sita was provided protection by sage Valmiki in his ashram. Twin sons, Luv and Kush were born to her. Sita showed the grit as mother in nurturing her sons with full support of Valmiki. He nurtured and trained them to become warriors to fight the injustice meted to their mother. He told them the story of Ram and Sita, without telling them about their paternity, and trained them to sing it as bards, for its dissemination.

Ram was to conduct *Ashvamedh Yagnya*. Luv-Kush as bards sang the story of Ram-Sita to Ayodhya public, which unfolded the truth, about empowered Sita in Ravan's custody, which resulted in Ravan's nervous breakdown and death. Luv-Kush captured the sacrificial horse which resulted in war with Ram's army. Luv-Kush defeated everybody, forcing Ram to present himself to face the kids. Valmiki intervened and restored Sita and Luv-Kush to Ram.

Uttarkand

After the death of King Dashrath, after about 14 years, Shri Ramchandra, as formally coronated King, started ruling the Ayodhya Kingdom. During the intervening period, the kingdom was being governed efficiently by Bharat, on behalf of Shri Ram, with ground assistance from Shatrughna; the able and experienced administrator, such as Sumant supervising the administration.

Sage Vashisth was always available for wise advice. What Dashrath had desired 14 years ago, to handover the rule to Ram, became a reality after so many tribulations. People of Ayodhya experienced peace and prosperity, with a central authority of the King. They had known Ram as a newly married prince, who was banished due to palace politics, leading to death of heart-broken Dashrath. People had only heard hearsay stories about Sita's abduction by Ravan, and the Ram-Ravan war, in which Ayodhya army was not involved. Nobody had a clear picture of what happened during 14 years of Ram's exile. People could only gossip on the basis of half-baked stories, probably emanating from the attendants, in the palaces of Ram, Sita, Lakshman and Kaikeyi.

After some months, it was reported by Kaushalya to Ram, that Sita was pregnant. After confirmation of pregnancy, after a month, some rituals were performed (*Godbharai*) as a family, in-house function. Ram was very happy, and he took time to take her to the garden, within the palace for short walks, every evening. Since no visible change of behaviour, or food preferences, were noticed, Kaushalya asked Ram, to inquire whether Sita had any particular pregnancy cravings or likings, which needed to be fulfilled, for emotional and physical satiety. When Ram asked Sita, about her cravings or desires, which some women felt during pregnancy, she said, she had wonderful time with him for thirteen years, enjoying nature, during their forest living; visiting *ashrams*, conversing with the sages and their wives, until the mishap happened at Panchvati due to golden deer. She had a desire to live for about a week in such an *ashram*, in a spiritual atmosphere, enjoy nature, listen to the preaching of *Rishi*, and meditate. She thought, it would have a good effect on the overall development of the fetus, including the emotional development. Ram was quite pleased with the proposal. He, however, regretted that he could not accompany her to an *ashram,* due to busy calling of the affairs of the State. It would also lead to gossip that he was so much attached to her, that he would not leave her alone, during pregnancy also.

Patriarchal Gossip about Sita

In the mean time, an incident about a washerman, not accepting his wife back in the home, since she had to live in another man's house for one night, became a hot topic of the town. As we know, washermen and barbers have large clientele, since they provided services to several families. Probably, the woman had gone to one of her kin, across the river, and could not return back, due to flash floods in the river, which she had to cross. So she sought protection in a house of the boatman, near the riverbank. Maybe the boatman was a single person, without a family or maybe, his wife had gone to her parent's house, on an occasional visit. However, this incident led to gossip, since the washerman told his wife, that he was not like Ram, who not only accepted Sita back, but gave an honourable place to her, as Queen, on the throne. Sita was in Ravan's custody for about an year. Ravan was notorious about his soft corner, for beautiful and young women. How could Sita, may have remained pure, in the captivity of the powerful demon king, Ravan? Ram asked his informers, to find out the nature of gossip, about him and Sita. Sita's attendants who hailed from different families in Ayodhya, also reported about such gossip to Sita. Ram personally went incognito, to some localities in the evening, when people usually gathered in their small groups, for a chat. It was very painful for Ram, that although the people were all praise for him, for his extraordinary valour, in punishing Ravan for kidnapping a woman, by deceit, they could not digest, that Sita should have been installed as the Queen, who was considered as mother-figure by the citizens. How could they address her as Mother, when she was tainted? This gossip pained Ram too much, since he knew, how bravely Sita faced the captivity in Lanka and was courageously rejecting the solicitations of Ravan, to be his consort as the Queen. Sita was pained, since inadvertently, she became the cause of stigmatizing the great name of Ayodhya Kingdom and its dynasty. Ram in a tormented state of mind consulted Lakshman, who was with him in the forest for 14 years, and was a witness and participant of every happening, including the war and release of Sita from Ravan's captivity. Lakshman was very annoyed with such non-sense gossip. He counselled Ram that there were always some people, who found faults with good and saintly people. They needed to be ignored. Moreover, Lakshman asked, as to what did people know, about happenings in 14 years of forest life, or about Ravan and about Lanka?

Ram went to meet Sage Vashisth to seek his advice, about his unstable mind, due to some public gossip in Ayodhya, without mentioning the exact subject of gossip. Vashisth did not seek information about the nature of gossip, but discussed the matter philosophically. He said, "If the King feels concerned about a public issue, directed to him, the king has to give up, what is closest to his heart and mind. He has to sacrifice, in the interest of the Kingdom, what is dearest to him." So, Ram took a decision to sacrifice Sita, in public good. He consulted his brothers, Lakshman, Bharat and Shatrughna, about the gossip, originating with the washerman's remarks, about Ram's weakness for Sita. They tried to counsel Ram that they should not go by such cheap gossips. Lakshman as a short tempered person, even gave the example of Ahilya, who was actually defiled by Indra, by impersonating as Sage Gautam. However, Gautam accepted her, having gone through penance, after she met Prince Ram, in the presence of Sage Vishwamitra. Sugreev had accepted his wife, although she was defiled by his elder brother Vali, using his power, against her wishes.

Nothing of that sort had happened in case of Sita. She was carried away by Ravan, using physical force, but he did not use physical force to molest her. Ravan had given time to Sita to accept him, in preference to the 'forest-beggar Ram', who was exiled by his own father; failing which, he threatened that the demoness guards would kill her and devour her. Although Ravan made egoistic claims about his martial power, in his mind, he was afraid of Sita's moral strength and Ram's prowess, who had vanquished his brothers, in *Dandkaranya*, popularly known as '*Janasthan*'.

During reconnaissance tour of Lanka to locate Sita, at Ashokvan, Hanuman was hiding on a tree, camouflaged with the leaves, and listened to, when Sita rebuked and threatened Ravan, that he was ensuring his death at the hands of her husband, Ram, while he was soliciting her to be his principal queen. Sita herself always plucked a blade of grass when Ravan visited to talk to her, with the idea that the blade of grass had the moral strength to become a weapon. Moral strength could become a psychological weapon to weaken the mind of an immoral adversary. Ram and Lakshman knew all these facts, as reported by Hanuman. Ram's inner voice and his intense love for Sita, did not have a shadow of doubt, about her alleged defilement in Ravan's custody. However, he surrendered to the gossip of the people, since Sita was not only his wife, but as the Queen, she was the mother-figure of the citizens. Ram offered to quit as King, so that he could be with Sita in an *ashram*, and requested Bharat and Lakshman, to take up the kingship. However, both of them strongly regretted such a move. Bharat said very emotionally, whether this was meant to be a punishment for his looking after Ayodhya Kingdom for 14 years, as an agent of Sri Ram.

Desertion of Sita

Ram then ordered Lakshman, in his authority, as King, to leave Sita in the vicinity of Valmiki *ashram*. She had anyway desired to spend a week at an *ashram*, during pregnancy, for spiritual meditation and peace. Accordingly, Lakshman left her in close vicinity of Valmiki *ashram*. He lacked courage to face the Sage, and tell him the reason about Sita's visit. He painfully disclosed to *Ma*-Sita that he would not be returning back, to fetch her after a week, telling her the reason for it. Sita was shocked, although she knew about the public gossip. She felt like ending her life, but she did not want to commit the sin of killing the fetus in her womb, who, if male, would be the successor of Raghu Ddynasty. Valmiki was informed by the *Ashram* staff, about a glorious and beautiful woman at the gate, who was wearing dress appropriate for *ashram* life. Valmiki, though not an astrologer, but as a *Maharshi,* could foresee the instability in the palace, due to public gossip, in which tacitly, Kaikeyi fuelled by Manthara, also participated.

Valmiki received her with great affection as a daughter, and provided a distinct hut, as residence for her. She was introduced as Janaki to the *ashramites*, not as Sita, which was her formal name, and told the female inmates to take care of her, particularly, since she was pregnant. Back home, Kaushalya was annoyed with Ram's behaviour about punishing Sita, for no fault of her. However, Ram said that: "This was the decision of the King, and not that of Ram." So, no more discussion was possible in the palace. At a personal level, Ram gave up his Royal bed, and chose to sleep on the ground, on a simple mat. When Janak came to know of this decision of Ram, he visited Ayodhya and seeing the bed-room of Ram, he did not offer any advice to him. He only said, "You are following the *Rajdharma*, which is very painful. You and Sita are being punished for no fault of yours."

The public appreciated the action of King Ram, in response to their wishes, and thought that the king would remarry to have another queen. After all, Dashrath had three queens. The people started gossiping about eligible princesses among the kings, friendly to Ayodhya Kingdom, who would be happy to establish matrimonial kinship connections with Ayodhya. There was possibly no known King, who had only one queen, besides some concubines or mistresses.

There could be another argument about Ram refusing to replace Sita with another woman, howsoever normal, as per prevailing culture pattern. Ram, his brothers and the two mothers, Kaushalya and Sumitra, had witnessed the ill-effects of polygyny in the palace, leading to machinations of Kaikeyi, inflicting punishment to Ram, shared by Sita and Lakshman; for no fault of anybody. There is marked difference between polygyny and serial monogamy, that is, marrying another woman after the death of first wife. Taking another woman after deserting her, alleging defilement, cannot be considered as acceptable moral behaviour. The public mind is reflected in the remark of Kaikeyi, when Sita returned to Ayodhya from Lankan captivity. She had said, if a dog touched a plate full with food, and even if the dog was punished, and not allowed to eat food; the plate got defiled.

There was also a talk about necessity of the queen, in other quarters of priests, since all religious rituals required a wife to participate in the rituals. However, Ram categorically refused even to discuss this issue. He said that, for him, Sita was always with him, in his heart and mind. Sita was as pure as fire-testified gold. Sita was more dear to him than the kingdom, which he had offered to handover to Bharat, Lakshman or Shatrughna. He said that he would be happy to be with Sita and live in some *ashram*. However, Bharat said that he would rather give up his life, than accept kingship. For 14 years, Ram was in the forest to honour the word given by Father-King Dashrath, to queen Kaikeyi. As agreed at Chitrakoot, Ram was the King of Ayodhya, symbolized by his *Paduka*, and Bharat functioned as an agent of the King. Lakshman was visibly annoyed with the behaviour of Ram, since he had expressed his anger, at reacting on the gossip of some foolish citizens, and deserting Sita for no fault of her. He had literally wept in the presence of Sita, when he left her at the Valmiki *ashram*. Ram was apologetic about deserting Sita, in response to the widespread gossip of the citizens. However, he reiterated that he sacrificed Sita, to set an example of the King putting the public wishes, above his personal desires. While the priests sought solution to the issue of having a wife, according to '*Dharmashastra*' for performing religious rituals, Ram said that it was their problem to sort out the issue, if they considered it so important. Marrying again somebody, meant to remove Sita from his heart and mind, was not possible for him. Sage Vashisth endorsed a solution, to symbolize wife, by her golden statue, being a *Kshatriya* and the King.

Abondoning Queen Sita by King Ram, is a classical example, of clash of roles as husband-wife and as King-Queen; that is, between the *Pati-dharma* and *Raj-dharma*. How to educate the masses in patriarchal peasant communities, to change their gender perspective, continues to be a moot question. In Ramayan, this was successfully done by Valmiki, through the child bards, Luv and Kush, by presenting the Ramayan through musical singing. As a result, Ayodhyan public ultimately regretted their gossip, and accepted Sita as *Ma*-Sita or Sita *mai*.

Rajdharma

Common people look upon Sri Ram as an ideal son, ideal brother, ideal husband and ideal king. He treats his *Praja* (citizens) as his extended family, and expresses himself with the pronoun, 'We' not as 'I'. The Monarchy in its classical and ancient form combines the executive, legislative and judicial authority with a single person, designated as King or Emperor. As a King, he follows the *Rajdharma* to the fault and punishes the deviants to protect and promote high ethical values and behaviour. This *Rajdharma* has been upheld as ideal through centuries.

Although there are hardly any nations now, ruled by a King or an Emperor, as the monarch, the heads of states and governments in elected democracies are expected to follow *Rajdharma*, treating all citizens as equals, irrespective of race, religion, caste, class, occupation etc. In the contemporary world also, with democratic and secular governance, the President, Governors, Judges, Ministers, while assuming office, take the oath of secrecy and duty, usually in the name of God, to abide by the Constitution of the country, and not expected to indulge in any kind of discrimination or favouritism.

Ram felt tormented due to conflict between *Dharma*, as husband, to protect Sita from the unfair gossip about her moral character, due to captivity in Lanka, and *Rajdharma*, as King, to respect the wishes of people of Ayodhya to abdicate Sita. He visited Guru Vashisth to seek his counsel about his unstable mind, without announcing the possible cause of it. The sage did not inquire about the cause of his unstable mind, in taking a decision. He only said that in such a situation, the King needed to give up and discard his personal affection or longing (*Moha*). Ram as King, decided to give up his dear wife Sita, whom he loved, howsoever unpleasant was the decision for him as an individual, as the husband. This ethical principle is expressed globally, termed as 'conflict of interest'.

(*Contd.*)

Mahabharat shows the deviation from this eternal value, since the ruling King, Dhritrashtra, who was blind by eyesight, had exhibited blind affection for his son, Duryodhan, who was a Prince, ambitious of becoming the next King, setting aside the rightful claim of his elder cousin, Yudhishthir. King Dhritrashtra thus could not follow *Rajdharma*, as he could not deliver justice, since he neither corrected his erring son, nor could punish him as per Rule of Law. This led to *Mahabharat* war, when almost all the kings and kingdoms perished, with colossal war mortality. Even Bhisma who was a grandfather and great grandfather of the Pandavas and Kauravas could not deliver justice, since, as per his own submission on the death bed, he pledged loyalty to the king, instead of to the kingdom, which would have been more appropriate as per the *Dharma*, to strengthen the solidarity of the nation. Despite Krishna's diplomacy initiatives, personally going as peace-advocate, and Ram's efforts to avoid war with Ravan, by sending Angad, as peace-agent, both the wars in *Mahabharat* and Ramayan took place. The ego and avarice of Prince Duryodhan, refusing to give even needle-point land to Pandavas, not vetoed by his father-King, Dhritrashtra; and ego of Ravan, not to restore Sita to Ram, with dignity, led to both the wars. Truth and *Dharma* over *Adharma* prevailed as per the universal spiritual value, which continues as the reference model to humanity, symbolized by the national Emblem of India, '*Satyamev Jayate*'.

Sita in Valmiki *Ashram*

In Valmiki *ashram*, Sita gave birth to twin sons. Valmiki gave them the names, Luv and Kush. While the babies were less than a month old, Shatrughna who was sent by Ram, to vanquish a demon-king Lavanasur, passed through Valmiki *ashram*, and as instructed by Ram, called on the Sage to seek his blessings. Taking advantage of Shatrughna's presence, Valmiki requested him to perform rituals for the twin babies who were *kshatriya*, born in the *ashram*, without divulging their identity. Shatrughna was happy to follow the request by the sage, to offer royal blessings, without making inquiries about the parentage of the babies.

Luv-Kush were being nurtured by Sita, under the supervision of Valmiki. He personally gave them training in weaponry, in yoga, about Vedas, and other arts. He also oriented them to basics in music, particularly to sing *Ram Katha,* written by him. They were practicing to sing it, as musical composition. Valmiki had updated the lyrics about Sita in the *ashram*, and having two sons. The Sage also performed their Sacred Thread ceremony (*Upnayan*) when they became 8 year old, inviting other *rishis* for the occasion. Sita was rearing the sons like other women, i. e. bringing drinking water from the well, collecting roots, tubers and fruits from the forest, collecting firewood and breaking them to appropriate size, for the hearth made of mud; pounding, de-husking the grains, powdering it on the stone grinding wheel, and cooking food. With babies, she was assisted by *ashram* inmates. As Luv-Kush were growing, they started assisting the mother in daily chores. All this was written by Valmiki in the lyrics.

Ashvamedh Yajnya

There was a drought in Ayodhya, which created a problem for the cattle and farmers. King Ram shared concerns about the cause of drought with Sage Vashisth, who surmised that it could be the divine disapproval of deserting Sita, without her fault. He advised the King to go in for traditional *Ashwamedh Yag* to tide over the difficulties. Other kings could be invited for the final *Yag* whereby, they could also help the kingdom in these difficult times. Accordingly, it was decided to perform the *Yag* at a specially erected township, by the side of river Sarayu. The *yag* was a long drawn affair, divided into two periods of time. First, the rituals were conducted prior to identification of a sacrificial horse, attended by several guests from the kingdoms, and by spiritual heads of *ashrams*. After the horse was selected, he was left to roam about, monitored by armed guards, under the supervision of a member of the royal family, for about a month's time. If anybody prevented the horse from roaming, he had to fight armed struggle with the guards. After the return of the horse to Ayodhya, the sacrificial *Yag* was to be performed again, in the presence of guests and *rishis*. The King performing such *yag* was recognized as sovereign, to rule an empire, with autonomous states ruled by local kings, under his subjugation.

The kings including Bibhishan and Sugreev as special guests, were provided accommodation at the new township. Hanuman, Jambavan and Angad were also present. The *Rishi's* accommodation was in an adjacent locality, specially designed for them. Citizens of Ayodhya also participated in the event. Enternainment was provided by way of music and dance. Food was in abundance.

Luv-Kush Singing *Ram-Katha*, as Bards

Valmiki attended the ceremony with Luv and Kush, and was provided a separate hut. Valmiki instructed Luv and Kush to carry their *Veena* with them and sing *Ram-Katha* loudly, going round the new township, and in the main town of Ayodhya. He also told them to go to the main hall of *Yag*, if invited, to sing in the presence of Sri Ram, and the entire Royal family, including the queen mothers. If asked about the parentage, "You introduce yourself as the students of Valmiki. Do not accept any cash presents, saying that coming from an *ashram* in a forest, they were not used to such gifts and had no use of them." The story of Ramchandra singing in melodious voice attracted the attention of all the guests, particularly, since the people were familiar with some parts of the story, not the details. Melodious singing of Ram-Katha by the children, Luv-Kush, in the town of Ayodhya, became a novelty and talk of the town. Palace staff recommended them to sing in the Court, in the presence of the Royal Family, *Rishis*, ouside guest kings, and prominent citizens. Along with other artists, they were also presented to the King, in the court. They started singing the story of Ramchandra, in his presence, which attracted the attention of everybody. Sri Ram asked them as to how much lengthy were the lyrics written by Valmiki. Luv-Kush said, it might take a week to sing the entire story, singing it everyday for the allotted time. Ram said, they would like to listen to the entire story. As given to other artists, Lakshman offered them the gold coins by way of gift, which they politely declined as per their *Guru's* instructions. The audience was surprised with this gesture by the young boys.

Luv-Kush in their musical composition of the lyrics written by Valmiki, gave the details of forest life of Ram-Sita-Lakshman. It included their interaction with the Rishis in *ashrams*, killing of Khar-Dushan, brothers of Ravan; Panchvati episode of golden deer and kidnapping of Sita by Ravan in deceit; Sugreev, Hanuman seeing Ravan carrying a woman who was shouting for help, finding a pouch of her ornaments, thrown by Sita etc. Audience including the citizens of Ayodhya were greatly fascinated by the details of Hanuman's exploits in Lanka. Hanuman, while searching for Sita in the palaces of Lanka, found her kept in captivity in Ashokvan, under a tree, not in any house, guarded by the *rakshasinis*. Hanuman heard the dialogue of Sita and Ravan, while Sita was fearlessly rebuking Ravan for his deceit, and inviting his death at the hands of Ram. Ravan was fuming, ridiculing Ram as a mere human, and soliciting her to be his queen. But he did not touch her, he maintained a dignified distance, afraid of her spiritual powers and fear of retribution by Ram. Ravan as a highly educated scholar, knew the moral strength of a '*pativrata*' woman. Hanuman also heard Mandodari, telling Ravan to send back Sita to Ram and seek his apologies. Ravan never shouted at Mandodari, but his ego, that he was the greatest of the great in '*Trilok*', having challenged even Shiva and Vishnu; and his son Indrajeet, having defeated Indra, could not bow down to a mere human like Ram. However, he had some doubts about the real identity of Ram, at the back of his mind, since Ram had defeated and killed his brothers, Khar and Dushan with sufficient ease. Hanuman also heard Sulochana, Indrajit's wife criticizing the action of Ravan. For Sita living alone in Ashokvan, with hostile *Rakshashini* guards, was a fire ordeal (*agni-pariksha)* (*agni-divya*)for her. Sita used to remember the blessings showered on her by Sati Anusuya, to remain courageous in difficult times. Only one lady guard, Trijata was sympathetic to her assuring her that some day, Ram would seek her release. On occasions, Sita had a remorse about her desire for the golden deer and the way she said bad words to dear Lakshman, which landed her in this trouble. In the lyrics, it was mentioned that Hanuman had narrated these details to the entire assembly of Ram-Lakshman, Sugreev, Jambvan, Angad, Nal-Neel etc. after his return from Lanka, after burning the golden city of Lanka. Hanuman also reported that he had offered Sita to bring her back to Ram, sitting on his shoulder or back, as he carried Ram-Lakshman several times on his shoulders. But she declined, saying that Ravan needed to be punished for his deceitful behaviour, by Ram, and get her released in a dignified manner. Ravan had given her time to accept his offer of making her Chief Queen, failing which he would allow the *Rakshsini* guards to devour her. When Hanuman met her, two months were left for the time to expire. If Ram could not get her release by that time, she said that, she would end her life. Hanuman had reported all details to the assembly of King Sugreev, with Angad, Jambvan, Nal and Neel, when they met Ram-Lakshman to plan the strategies of war. While Luv-Kush were singing all these details in musical tone, the audience consisting of Ram's family, *Rishis* and citizens of Ayodhya were appreciating the strength of Sita. Bibhishan, Hanuman, Sugreev, Jambvan and others who participated in the Lankan war were present in the royal hall. From their appreciation and body language, it was clear that the lyrics sung musically were nothing but absolute truth. It was also reported in the lyrics, the quote of Mandodari, that Sita was their idol as *Pativrata*. Citizens were regretting their irresponsible and cheap gossip, which led to the King sending Sita out of his life. Kaushalya and Sumitra were weeping and simultaneously appreciating the musical presentation by Luv-Kush. Kaikeyi attended the religious rituals about preliminaries of *Ashwamedh Yag*, but abstained from *Ram Katha*, fearing her role could be mentioned by the singing children. Ram himself occupying the King's throne was sitting like a statue, trying to control his emotions, since he knew everything that Luv-Kush were rendering as musical composition.

After singing the details of war and Sita's return, they presented the details about Ram's coronation and Sita getting the status as Queen. The lyrics then dealt with unholy gossip among the citizens of Ayodhya, triggered by a washerman, refusing to accept his wife back home, since she had to spend night in someone else's house. The gossip started, since he mentioned King Ram, behaving wrongly in giving a place of honour to Sita, who was in Ravan's custody for months together. Ram's mind tormented by the conflict of his roles as husband of Sita, and as the King, putting an end to dirty gossip among the citizens, resulted in deserting pregnant Sita.

The lyrics included the story about King Ramchandra abandoning his wife, Sita, in the forest, near hermitage of a *Rishi*, where she gave birth to two sons. The details of this part of *Ram Katha* are sung as musical composition to tell the following story.

In Ayodhya, there was significant gossip about Sita having gone through *Agni-pariksha,* after her release from Ashokvan captivity, which was like open jail in the present times. There was vicarious pleasure in some quarters, that since the citizens of Ayodhya had not witnessed it, Sita could be made to go through *Agnipariksha* again in the presence of everybody, before she was accepted back again. Actually, after Sita was led out of the gate of Lanka, in a palanquin by the new king of Lanka, Bibhishan, to meet Ram and the entire army of Sugreev, everybody remarked that she had gone through *Agni-divya*, due to her high moral and spiritual stature. As per the custom, a small impromptu *Yaj* was arranged by way of thanksgiving to the Gods for protecting Sita. Sita made offerings to the fire god, as done in a *Yag*, before crossing over to Ram's side, crossing the threshold of Lanka. As Sita crossed over, she touched the feet of her husband Ram and begged apology, for her craving for the golden deer, which led to these tragedies. Although, Lakshman as a younger brother of Ram was treated by Sita like her child, she bowed down and begged apology for saying mouthful of bad words to him, as a result of which Ravan could kidnap her by deceit. All these details, written by Valmiki and sung by Luv-Kush in their melodious musical singing, made a deep impact on the audience. Some people also expressed that Fire-God must have helped Hanuman when he burnt Lanka, using his tail as a weapon, spreading fire all over, except the Ashokvan. The citizens of Ayodhya were in tears, listening to this devotional musical presentation, by sweet looking kids. Luv-Kush also narrated the story whereby Ravan was cursed by his nephew, Nal-kuber, who was the son of Ravan's elder half-brother Kuber, with instant death, if Ravan molested a woman against her consent, as he did to Nal's wife Rambha, on the hills of Kailash. Rambha entreated with Ravan that she was in fact his daughter-in-law, but he was too much intoxicated with liquor to listen to her entreaties. Even Ram-Lakshman did not know this story which Valmiki knew, and he put it in the lyrics. That was another reason why Ravan did not cross the limits of morality while soliciting Sita in the Ashokvan, and maintained significant distance from Sita, who was sitting under a tree, in captivity, guarded by female demonesses.

Sita was abandoned at the gate of an *ashram* by Lakshman, under orders of the King, who over-reacted to the gossip questioning the fidelity of Sita. Sage Valmiki looked after her and her children. Then they presented how Sita, lived the life of a lay woman, doing all daily chores by herself, and bringing up children with dignity. While the daily chores were listed, such as collecting firewood, cutting it into pieces for the hearth; grounding grains on a grinding wheel etc., Kaushalya, Sumitra, King Janak and mother of Sita, were visibly shedding tears, while others had tears in their eyes. Luv-Kush concluded, "We are disciples of our revered *Guru*, Sage Valmiki. We have been fortunate in narrating *Ram Katha* to your Honour, as taught to us by our *Guru*."

After knowing the facts and realizing the truth about the tumultuous journey of Ram-Sita-Lakshman, during 14 years of exile, the citizens of Ayodhya had a feeling of remorse, being the cause of injustice to *Ma*-Sita. There was a discussion that a delegation of prominent citizens could call on the King to seek his pardon, and requesting him to bring back *Ma*-Sita, with honour. So, Luv-Kush by presenting *Ram Katha* in poetic and musical format, established Truth in the minds of Ayodhya masses, replacing the vile gossip. King's administration offered cash gifts to Luv-Kush, as was offered to other singers, but they declined saying that they came from an *ashram* and had no use of it.

Ashvamedh Horse and Skirmishes at Valmiki *Ashram*

The preliminary rituals connected with *Ashwamedh Yag* were performed by King Ram with Sita's golden statue, by his side, representing her. Ram selected a black horse for ritual sacrifice. A notice about *Aswamedh*, that anybody restraining the horse from free roaming would be liable for a war with Ayodhya soldiers, was put up on the forehead of the horse. The horse was set free for roaming in any direction, looked after by some soldiers accompanying him, under the general supervision of prince Shatrughna. One month's time limit was fixed for the horse to return back to Ayodhya to complete the remaining part of the *Yag*. The guests departed to their respective places with a request to be ready to come back after a month. Thus ended the first part of *Ashwamedh* rituals.

The horse went around several places. The chieftains knew about the *Ashwamedh* to be performed at Ayodhya. Even King Dashrath had performed *Ashwamedh Yag* number of times, as was customary for the powerful and well-known kings to do so. Accordingly, no chieftain or king ruling small states, who already had subordinate relationship with Ayodhya, tried to restrain the movement of the horse. On the other hand, they provided hospitality to the soldiers accompanying the horse. Somehow, the horse strayed in the wooded area of Valmiki *ashram*. Sage Valmiki had gone on a long tour for some kind of a conference of the *Rishis*. Even Kush was moving in a wide area in search of lotus flowers, since *Mata* Janki wanted 1000 flowers for some ritual. Luv seeing the beautiful horse, became curious and read the message written on a small metal-sheet put up on the forehead of the horse. When Luv read the message, he felt like challenging King Ram. He felt that the King would be forced to come to seek his ritual horse, which would provide an opportunity to question him, about the injustice meted to *Ma*-Sita. So, he fed the horse, and tied him to a tree, which was in the jurisdiction of the *ashram*. The soldiers who were following the horse did not realize that the horse was captured by the child. For sometime, they were appreciating the natural beauty in the *ashram*. When they found the horse was tied to a tree, and Luv by the side of the horse with bow and arrow, they questioned him and inquired with him, whether he was aware of the implications of capturing the horse. Luv replied that he was a *kshatriya* and he was willing to accept the challenge with King Ram, coming and seeking the release of the horse. The soldiers had a hearty laugh, and replied in jest, that the King would come only if the army was defeated by you. Luv accepted the challenge and raised his bow in a striking position. The elderly leader of the soldiers darted couple of arrows to frighten Luv. Luv's arrows broke the soldier's arrows in mid-air, clearly indicating that the child was an expert and well-trained warrior. The ego of the leader was hurt, being challenged by a child in front of his soldiers, and he challenged Luv for a battle. Luv darted several arrows in succession, injuring several soldiers. Afraid of the prowess of Luv, the soldiers retreated to report back to Ayodhya, that the horse was captured by a child, and they could not set his release, for fear of killing the child. Prince Shatrughna who was to monitor the safe return of the horse in a month's time, personally went to verify the unbelievable story of a child, capturing the horse. By that time, Kush also joined Luv. When Shatrughna arrived, he was surprised to see the same children who sang *Ram Katha* in the Court. He was surprised to realize that this was the *ashram* of sage Valmiki, which he had visited on way to vanquish a demon-king, Lavanasur, at Madhupuri. He inquired about the sage, but was told that he was on a long tour. Shatrughna in a compassionate tone, tried to reason out with the children, to release the horse. But they challenged him to get the horse after defeating them in a battle. Luv-Kush also reiterated that they were interested in meeting Ram and none else. Valmiki had trained them, combining military training with *yogic* powers. As a result, Luv-Kush with their arrows made Shatrughna unconscious. As the news was reported to Ram, Bharat volunteered to go, accompanied by King Sugreev and Hanuman, out of curiosity to see the children. They were shocked to see the bards who sang *Ram Katha*. Knowing the role of Bharat, Sugreev and Hanuman in the whole process of *Ram Katha*, Luv-Kush offered their sincere respects to the three. But they insisted that unfortunately they were facing them in a battle position, since they came on behalf of King Ram, whose horse they had captured. We expected King Ram to come . But he keeps on sending others to capture us. Luv-Kush with their arrows tied Hanuman and made Bharat and Sugreev unconscious. They offered fruits to Hanuman, by way of his role in locating Sita in Lanka, who had addressed Hanuman as son. They untied his ropes with the promise, that Hanuman would use his hands only for eating fruits, and not for attacking them. Hanuman through his spiritual powers, understood that the boys were children of Ram and Sita.

King Ram was shocked to get the news of defeat of all the big warriors at the hands of children. While Lakshman offered to go to the place where horse was captured, Ram said that these could not be mere children. They must be demons taking the form of Luv-Kush. But how could they be in Valmiki ashram? Was it since the Sage was not present there? Lakshman assured Ram that he would take care of all eventualities. Luv-Kush also had great respect for Lakshman, for his Lakshman-*rekha* to protect Sita. But they were annoyed that personally Ram was not coming, with whom they wanted to have a dialogue, about injustice to Sita. Lakshman was in no mood for a real battle, since he had left pregnant Sita at Valmiki *ashram,* against his conscience. So, he could also surmise that Luv-Kush were sons of Ram. In such mental situation, the children made Lakshman also unconscious.

Questioning King Ram

King Ram was not left with any other option, but to go personally. Sita had no inkling as to what was going on at the entry of Valmiki *ashram*, since the Sage had asked the children to guard the *ashram* in his absence. She herself had sent Kush to collect 1000 lotus flowers. Ram was also surprised that the children were actually the bards, who sang *Ram Katha* in the Court, for several days. As Ram was face-to-face with Luv-Kush, they exclaimed satisfaction that ultimately, they met him. They said, all these battle conditions and Hanuman, Sugreev coming was avoidable, if he had personally come to release his horse. At the first instance. Luv-Kush made it very clear, that they were not challenging his authority as the King, nor were they interested in acquiring any kingdom for themselves. But they were annoyed with his behaviour with Sita, and wanted an explanation from him as '*Maryada-Purshottam*' King. Ram requested them to release the horse without which *Ashwamedh Yag* would remain incomplete, with serious consequences like natural calamities affecting the people of Ayodhya. Luv-Kush insisted that the matters could be decided in a battle, as per *kshatriya-dharma*. While both Ram and Luv-Kush raised their bows, Sage Valmiki came on the scene, from his tour, and asked the King as to why was he aiming his arrow towards the children? Ram said, they were not releasing the sacrificial horse, and wanted to settle the matter through battle. Ram said, these beautiful and innocent children, who also sang *Ram Katha* melodiously were very adamant. Valmiki said, it was a natural instinct for children of their age, to be adamant. But the King could not be adamant, with the children. They needed to be ignored. Then Valmiki addressed Luv-Kush. "Lav-Kush, listen. It is very improper to challenge the King. He is father to all the subjects and symbolizes God. So, release the horse and bring all soldiers and warriors to their consciousness, with the knowledge and skill you have learnt during your education. Seek his pardon." Luv-Kush said "As you wish our revered *Guruji*." They sought pardon from the King. They said, "We did all this since we have been annoyed the way you treated Sita and abandoned her, responding to the foolish gossip of the citizens of Ayodhya. So, we wanted you to come here and heal our mental agony. It was not possible for us to meet you at Ayodhya, since it would not have been permitted by your administration. We seek your pardon, but please tell us the reason for bad treatment to Sita. We are keen to know the Truth and your *Dharma*, as King and husband of Sita." Ram said, "I love Sita. She is always in my mind and heart. But that is, as her husband, as a family man. As a King, I had to satisfy the public, who were branding Sita as a defiled woman, not acceptable to them as Mother-Queen, sharing the throne with the King. They thought that as a polluted earthen pitcher was to be discarded, a defiled woman was like an earthen pitcher, not like a copper vessel, which could be cleaned for reuse. The gossip was putting a stigmatized blot on our Ishwaku dynasty, during my regime. For the king, to do a balancing act between the role as King and as a member of a family is a difficult task. Actually, my mothers, my brothers and my *Guru* Sage Vashisth were all unhappy with my decision as the King. I seek the pardon from Maharshi Valmiki for injustice meted out to Sita, due to role of Kingship overriding that of husband. I bow down to you, Maharshi to thank profusely for exposing the injustice meted out to Sita by all of us." Valmiki said, "The whole fault lies with the public, who do not understand the difference between their life, and that of the King. What do people know about Lanka and Ravan, and the moral and spiritual power of Sita to protect herself? They needed to be educated.

I wrote lyrics of *Ram Katha*, as advised and narrated to me by Narad. I set the lyrics to musical composition, and trained Luv-Kush to sing it melodiously, for its dissemination and discussion. Destiny has it, that I myself became a part of it, not just as an author or a poet, since Sita was dropped at my doorstep as a pregnant woman. I do not know whether the musical presentations in the lanes and by-lanes of Ayodhya and later at the Court, by these two young and handsome bards, has made any impact on the public mind, and whether they realised their mistake, whereby they inflicted injustice on women, represented by Sita". King Ram said, "After listening to *Ram Katha*, melodiously rendered by Luv and Kush, the citizens realized the grave mistake they did by their loose, irresponsible gossip, without knowing or verifying the facts. There is now widespread discussion among the citizens to come to me, with a delegation to seek pardon, and to request me to bring back *Ma*-Sita with honour, and give her rightful position on the throne as Queen. I have been told by my informants, that women particularly, were greatly disturbed by the plight of Sita, for no fault of her. "If Sita as daughter of great King Janak, as daughter-in-law of Dashrath, was put to so much trouble, what about us, the women in ordinary households?" Women were all praise for King Ram, for firmly refusing to marry again, after desertion of Sita. Ram, as also his brothers, set an example of having one wife for life, failing which wife was represented by a statue, but not replacing her by another woman. Like Mandodari, Ayodhya women also took Sita as their idol, after listening to *Ram Katha* presented by these young bards."

After listening to King Ram, Luv-Kush sought pardon from the King. Ram said, "You have not committed any crime worth the punishment. Kingdom should be proud of children like you. My gates are always open to you, once your education is complete. *Guru* Valmiki deserve all praise for the development of total personality of Luv-Kush, and for the skills acquired by them in weapon use and in music."

Reunion

The news went to Janaki about these battle affairs, about the defeat of all warriors of Ayodhya. She was very concerned and could not imagine what was going on. It was reported that Sri Ram had personally arrived at the Valmiki *ashram*, and that he was talking to the Sage and to Luv-Kush. In the meanwhile, Luv-Kush brought back to consciousness all soldiers and the warriors. There was a place for reunion with Ram, his brothers, Hanuman and Sugreev.

The sage asked Luv-Kush to bring *Mata*-Janaki to meet the King and the visiting dignitaries. As Luv-Kush reported to Janaki-*Mai* all the happenings, including the battles, and defeat of all warriors of Ram, including Lakshman, Bharat, Shatrughna, and challenging Ram to a battle. Mother Janaki expressed her displeasure at the behaviour of her sons. She blurted out, that they had commited a great sin by challenging their father, Ramchandra, to a battle. When they expressed shock and disbelief to know that

King Ram was their father and the mother Janaki, in Valmiki *Ashram* was Sita, they wanted to know more about the kingdom and the family.

Ultimately Sita told them briefly about Ayodhya kingdom, about Ram and his brothers, about King Dashrath's desire, which he expressed under duress; about the forest life for 14 years, about Ravan and the war. She particularly praised Hanuman for his wisdom, his prowess, his unflinching loyalty to Ram and Sita. Luv-Kush felt very annoyed about Ram deserting Sita. But Sita did not criticize Ram. She said, due to gossiping among the public about the Queen in the custody of a demon-king for considerable period, he as the King, had to abandon her. She also praised Ram, that as husband in love with his wife, Ram did not succumb to public desire for King Ram, to remarry and bring another Queen. Sita told them that the story as written by *Guru* Valmiki in a lyrical form, which they were trained to sing, was her real story, and not just a literary poem.

As she came at the site, with Luv-Kush, in her *ashram* clothes, she was surprised to see the Ram family at one place. Lakshman, Bharat, Shatrughna, King Sugreev and Hanuman, expressed their respect, touching her feet. Sita was overwhelmed with emotions, and again sought apology from Ram, for her craving for the golden deer, and to Lakshman for saying bad words, for not rushing to help Ram in danger. Luv and Kush touched the feet of all of them, and sought their blessings. Ram complimented Sita for the upbringing of two sons, and apologized for not playing his role as father. Luv-Kush in their zest to give justice to Sita had shown great valour, fighting those whom they respected. The children as bards also educated the citizens of Ayodhya, by singing *Ram Katha*. Everybody appreciated Luv-Kush. They thanked Sage Valmiki for looking after Sita and the children, whom he trained as great warriors and developed their total personalities.

Sage Valmiki was very happy about the reunion of the family in his *ashram*. All of them departed for Ayodhya. Kaushalya and Sumitra complimented and blessed Ram for bringing back Sita.

The sacred '*arti*' was performed for Ram-Sita, and specially for Luv-Kush, by *Mata* Kaushalya, Sumitra and Kaikeyi. Luv-Kush who were seen as bards in the Court, were embraced and blessed by the grandmothers. Luv-Kush were introduced to the cousins (children of Lakshman, Bharat and Shatrughna) and to aunties (wives of uncles and cousins of Sita).

Since the month was over for the sacrificial horse to return to Ayodhya, *Aswamedh* rituals were restarted by Ram and Sita, as King and Queen. As Sita shared the throne with the King, the citizens chanted the slogans, "*Sita Mata ki jai, Siyavar Ramchandra ki jai*". This time, Kaikeyi was present for all the rituals. She blessed Ram-Sita, and Luv-Kush, when they touched her feet in salutation. Raja Janak and Queen had specially come to see the reunion of Ram-Sita and to meet the grandchildren, Luv and Kush. King Bibhishan, Sushen Vaidya who cured Lakshman, Sugreev, Hanuman, Jambavan, Chieftain Guhak and other kings and leaders were all present, besides the representatives of citizens, from all parts of Ayodhya. King Ramchandra and Queen Sita thanked all the guests and presented them with appropriate gifts. Thus *Ashwamedh Yag* brought in good luck to Ayodhya. The real *Ramrajya* began and continued under the blessings and supervision of Ram and Sita.

Ram-Sita had a special relationship with Chieftain Guhak, King Bibhishan, King Sugreev and Hanuman. Jambavan as an elderly statesman, and Angad as a young crown-prince of Kishkindha, maintained close contacts with Ayodhya.

Story of Malkasur and Kaikeyi's Visit to Lanka

Kaikeyi maintained cordial relations with Ram-Sita, and with Kaushalya and Sumitra, particularly after Sita's return and participation, at the concluding rituals of *Ashwamedh Yagnya*. She expressed desire to King Ram that she would like to visit Lanka as a tourist, since so much was talked about the golden Lanka. Although Hanuman had burnt down major part of Lanka, Ravan brought it back to its original glory within a short time, commissioning Vishwakarma, the celestial architect to rebuild it. Kaikeyi said that she had a chance to visit the kingdom of Heaven with Dashrath, in the early years of her married life, when Indra sought Dashrath's assistance in some battle with a demon-king. She had a curiosity to see the glory of Lanka in comparison to that of Heaven. Ram sent a word to Bibhishan, requesting him to commission *Pushpak* for Kaikeyi to visit Lanka.

The *Pushpak* aircraft which was originally owned by Kuber, when he was ruling from Lanka, was usurped by Ravan, when he defeated his elder half-brother Kuber and owned Lanka, from where he ruled. Now, *Pushpak* was a property of Lankan Kingdom, under the control of Bibhishan. He had actually offered it to Sri Ram, when Bibhishan became the King of Lanka. However, Ram declined to own it, and had an arrangement that he could use it whenever required.

Kaikeyi went to Lanka in *Pushpak*. She was received by King Bibhishan personally. As desired by her, about the sight-seeing tour of Lanka, one of the ministers was deputed to take her round, to view Lanka from air, and then visiting the palaces of Ravan, Meghnad, Kumbhkarna and Bibhishan, besides taking her to Ashokvan, where Sita was interned as a captive. Kaikeyi appreciated the well planned city of Lanka. The palaces of Ravan, Meghnad were vacant. However, she saw the rooms and bedrooms of Ravan where he used to consort with his several queens. When she entered Kumbhakarna's palace, she was received by Kumbhkarna's wife, who had a bright looking son. On inquiry, she was told by Kumbhakarna's wife that her son, Malkasur, was born on an inauspicious planetary constellation, i. e. *'Mul Nakshtra'*, which could have evil effect for his father's life. So, he was abandoned by the father, at birth. The mother brought him up surreptitiously, in some other house, with some other family. After Kumbhakarna's death in Ram-Ravan war, he was brought back in the house, after due rituals were performed to propitiate the evil effects of *Mul Nakshatra*. The mother complained to Kaikeyi that Bibhishan alone was owning Lanka, while Malkasur should have his share in it. Kaikeyi advised her, that let Malkasur go in for penance in the

Himalayas, surrendering himself to Lord Shiva, and getting special powers to challenge Bibhishan. Then Kaikeyi visited the palace of King Bibhishan, who had spiritual training and leanings. She received due hospitality. Bibhishan accompanied her personally, to visit the Ashokvan, which was a beautiful place, meant for the exclusive visits of Ravan's queens. Kaikeyi was shown the Ashoka tree under which Sita was kept on a raised platform, which surrounded the trunk of the tree. She was guarded by *Rakshashinis* round the clock. Hanuman had met Sita here. After this, the tour of Kaikeyi ended, and she bade farewell to Bibhishan, and returned back to Ayodhya.

As per advice of Kaikeyi, Malkasur did go to Himalayas, and went for hard penance, which attracted the attention of Lord Shiva. Shiva asked him for a boon. Malkasur sought a boon to become immortal. Shiva said, nobody could become immortal. Then, Malkasur requested that, let him not die at the hands of Dev or Danav, or some animal like monkey or bear, and man. Shiva smiled and delivered the boon. Shiva also gave him some special weapon for use in war.

After returning to Lanka, Malkasur challenged King Bibhishan to hand over Lankan Kingdom to him, since Kumbhakarna was elder brother of Bibhishan. The King Bibhishan called him to meet. However, armed with Shiva's boons, he declared a war against the King. The Chief-General of Lankan army fought with Malkasur, but he was killed by Malkasur. Then Bibhishan led the army. Bibhishan was badly injured in the chest. He was advised to seek the help of Sri Ram. Accordingly, he rushed to Ayodhya, and apprised King Ramchandra about the happenings. Sage Vashisth interpreted the boons by Lord Shiva to Malkasur, saying that he could be killed by a woman, if not by a man. Ram and Sita both decided to go with some army personnel, deputed by King Sugreev. Sita was dressed in man's uniform riding on a horse. Along with the horse, Ram-Sita went in *Pushpak* to face Malkasur, who was sure, that he could not be killed by Ram, who was a man. Sita took the position slightly behind Ram. By invoking the powers of Janak, Dashrath and her loyalty to Ram, she hit the arrow which beheaded Malkasur. They returned back to Ayodhya immediately.

***Bhumi-kanya* rejoining *Bhumata* (Mother Earth)**

After some days, there was a Court reception in honour of Sita, having killed Malkasur, who was the last vestige of Ravan-*Raj* in Lanka. Everybody, including the Sage Vashisth, Queen mothers, Kaushalya, Sumitra and Kaikeyi were present. The events leading to death of Malkasur, due to challenging King Bibhishan to hand over Lankan Kingdom to him, as elder Kumbhakarna's son, were presented by some minister. King Bibhishan was also present. He thanked King Ramchandra and Queen Sita for terminating the 'kingdom of cruelty and passion'. He felt very sorry, that he hailed from the same demon family, but was blessed by his sage-father, to be spiritual in nature. He thanked as representative of the people of Lanka, the Kingdom of Ayodhya, for continuing the sovereignty and autonomy of the Kingdom of Lanka.

Kaikeyi blurted out suddenly, that she had been to Lanka as a tourist, while she was looked after by King Bibhishan. She thanked King Bibhishan for the hospitality. She said that she was greatly impressed by the opulence and beauty of Lanka. Continuing, she said, "Sita who had a craving for golden dear, was spotted by the powerful demon—King Ravan, and he kidnapped her. Sita did not follow the advice of Lakshman, not to cross the safety line. She was all by herself in the beautiful Ashokvan, which was exclusively reserved for the visits of Ravan's queens. Ravan had promised to make her the chief Queen and visited Ashokvan, occasionally, to solicit her favours. It was a great wonder, that a young beautiful woman, was not attracted by the opulence and power of Lanka; that she could protect her character, in body and mind, all by herself, without any assistance. There appeared no hope of getting located and rescued by Ram and Lakshman, who were in Panchvati. Sita needed to be complimented for this wonderful disposition."

Everybody was stunned by these sudden, unprovoked remarks, which appeared complimentary in words, but had a sarcastic tone, with double meaning, coming from a mother-in-law, who had a penchant for such talk. Sita was almost in tears. All other people, including Bharat, knowing Kaikeyi's unstable personality, ignored this babbling, but their facial expressions indicated strong disapproval of these gossiping remarks, at the largely attended formal Court gathering.

The deciding moment was, while the King's formal Court, *Darbar,* was in session to honour Sita for killing Malkasur, son of Kumbhakarna, who challenged and defeated his uncle-king, Bibhishan, Kaikeyi expressed 'wonder' as to how could young and beautiful Sita protect her fidelity and spurn the offers of mighty and rich Ravan to his offers, while she was totally unprotected in his custody. One would feel inclined to support the presentation of *Sant* Eknath in '*Bhavartha Ramayan*' about Kaikeyi's capricious behaviour, which has been consistent with her unstable personality, cornering King Dashrath, to seek cruel demand of boons which led to his death, and destroyed the reputation of Ayodhya Kingdom. At no point, Kaikeyi showed any remorse for her behaviour, which inflicted unimaginable miseries to Ram and Sita. There could be no worse punishment for a woman, as mother, whereby her son, Bharat, literaly disowned his mother, for her cruelty inflicted on the husband, becoming the immediate cause of his death. He consistently maintained a distance from her and avoided visitors meeting her, lest she would embarrass them and hurt them, with her incoherent comments. The two Queen-mothers, Kaushalya and Sumitra also maintained social distance from her.

Sita reflected that despite her best of intentions and suffering, despite her unflinching loyalty to Sri Ram and his family, which he knew and appreciated, the people were not willing to sympathise with her, or accept her. She felt, that was the time for her to quit and go back to her mother, now that Luv-Kush had been properly rehabilitated in the family, and she had no specific role to play in her life. So, in a meditative mood, she invoked and prayed to the mother earth, to take her back in her womb, from where she had come, and was found and adopted by King Janak. Instantly, the open space in the centre of the hall of the Court opened up, as if by earthquake, with a loud sound. A man appeared rising from the opening, with an ornamental bench, appearing like a throne. Mother earth appeared in person and called Sita affectionately. Sita walked down from the throne. She saluted all, King Ram, Queen mothers, Ram's brothers and their wives, her cousins, the *Rishis*, and representatives of the citizens of Ayodhya and said, "My time has come to go, from where I came. Please forgive me." Luv-Kush started crying. She told them, that they had been honourably restored to their father, King Ram, and would be looked after well. She blessed them for their bright future. Then Sita went to her mother, seated on the bench with her, and went down the earth. The opening in the hall closed to its previous, normal surface. The whole event unexpectedly happened so fast, like lightening, that nobody could grasp the sequence, and completion of the happening. They were all flabbergasted. Sita disappeard instantly. Sita left, of her choice of time and space, in full view of everybody. There was a shock on every face, since she had bravely and openly rejected the patriarchal world, which kept on inflicting emotional harassment to women of high moral and spiritual character, despite unflinching loyalty to the families of their husbands.

King Ram woke up from the shock to say that Sita's disappearance like this, was unacceptable. "If Sita could be recovered from beyond the ocean, from the custody of powerful demon-king Ravan, she could be brought back from mother earth."

Sage Vashisth counselled the King, and he remarked about the comments by queen-mother Kaikeyi. He said, "Queen mother seems to have forgotten that Janak-*kanya* Sita, as a devoted wife, had opted to go to the forest with Ram, and live a difficult life, giving up her experience of living in the palace of her father, and later at Ayodhya. So, the opulence of Lanka had no meaning in her life. Sita had the blessings of Sati Anusuya, that due to her total devotion to her husband Ram, women would feel blessed, whenever they thought about Sita. Actualy, Sita had defeated Ravan, before he was killed by Ram. He was afraid of Sita's spiritual powers, and had to gulp the harsh words and warnings given by Sita in Ashokvan, several times, whenever he went to meet her, and solicit her assent to be his queen. Ravan already had a nervous breakdown when he took out his sword and threatened to kill Sita, after the death of brother Kumbhkaran and warrior son Meghnad. Queen Mandodari reminded him that as a great King, he could not afford to kill a woman in his custody, tarnishing his image for all times to come." Sage Vashisth further said that, most of the spiritually strong people, including the great sages, departed to their heavenly abode, of their choice, after their role in life ended, as destined. Sita, as *Bhumi-kanya*, had chosen to go to mother earth, from where she came, instead of going to heaven. Sita was destined to live the life of adversities. She had discharged all her responsibilities in life, as a devoted wife, as an able mother, without losing her balance of mind. She set a role model to the women as to how to deal with difficult situations in adversity. By rejecting the patriarchal values, whereby women were subjected to ridicule, Sita showed a way for women's empowerment, by choosing the time, when she would depart from all of us. "Sita has become immortal and people would remember Ram as Siya-Ram, as Sita-Ram". This destiny need not be challenged, since all of us mortals have to depart some day.

Ramayan: The End

During the next few years, the Queen mothers died a natural death. King Ramchandra made arrangements about the distribution of Ayodhya empire. Shatrughna who had killed the demon Lavanasur, as directed by King Ram, was given his kingdom of Madhupuri. Bharat was called by his mother's brothers to defeat the *Gandharvas* who had evil eyes on the kingdom of Kaykey. He established the city of Takshashila, where subsequently, the first University in the world, Takshashila University, was located. Lakshman's sons, and Luv and Kush were also given respective kingdoms such as in Kaushal region.

Ram had reached the stage to give up, having discharged all the responsibilities. Lakshman had some altercation with the ever angry Sage Durvasa. So, he was the first to release his soul from the body, in Sarayu river. Later, Ram and his brothers decided to withdraw from their destined duties, and surrendered their bodies to Sarayu river. Ram, Bharat and Shatrughna went together for heavenly abode through the medium of Sarayu river, as they were also born together, after *Putra-Kameshti Yag* was performed, which resulted in their birth. The *Ram Katha* as was documented in a lyrical form by Sage Valmiki ends here.

How do we sum up Ramayan for the common people? In the words of Aruna Deshpande, presenting "India—A Divine Destination".

"Ramayana is a mirror of the highest ideals of the Hindu tradition, culture and civilisation portrayed through the vehicle of an interesting story.... Ramayan instructs humanity on how to lead a fruitful life and attain the *purusharthas*... Herein is described Rama, the ideal hero, brother, king, son, husband, warrior, an embodiment of *dharma*.... In Bharat and Lakshmana, we have the ideal brother, and to Sita, the noblest flower of Indian womanhood devoted to her Lord in thought, word and deed." (2005, 75-76)

4

Concepts

Soul, Dharma, Culture and Civilisation

In all human communities, there is philosophical discussion about life, death and soul. In Indian philosophy, there is the concept of continuum of life and death, also expressed in ancestor worship, or the personal names being repeated in a family. The universal value about life and death that He gives life and He alone shall take it away or end it, is accepted as a religious or moral principle. When an old person, having discharged all familial and social responsibilities dies a natural death, without languishing in bed, the person is complimented being rewarded by God for his good moral character, as a pious person. The individual life cycle is meant to equip a person and the families to the aging process leading to death. In the epics of *Ramayan* and *Mahabharat*, the ruling kings in their old age embraced death by entering the forest fire, going to the Himalayas or entering the river water. Sita opted to go from where she came, that is to mother earth.

Those who die for the country, defending the country or to protect the dignity of women, are called as martyrs, or as *Hutamta.* Killing an enemy during war or a terrorist is not branded as murder, since the act of killing is to defend the moral cause of protecting the innocent people or protecting the citizens of your country.

What happens after death? There is the concept of Soul discussed in all human communities and in religious orders. The words Soul and Spirit are commonly used as synonyms. In common usage, when a person dies, people pay their condolences with an expression, "Let the soul rest in peace". Concept of Soul appears to be universal among all the human communities, including the tribal communities and in all religious doctrines. Concept of rebirth may be the Hindu phenomenon, closely linked to the concept of *Moksha*. When the human soul—*Atma* merges with the supreme spirit of the God—*Parmatma,* one attains *Moksha,* that is freedom from the cycle of birth and re-birth, meaning the soul resting in eternal peace. It is an obvious argument that the two elements to merge would necessitate high degree of similarity. This might appear to be difficult, that is, *Jivatma* may not become congruous with the divine, spiritual qualities of *Parmatma*, to facilitate merger, in one birth. So, there is provision of rebirth, to provide opportunities, to upgrade the quality of *Jivatma* on the spiritual scale, by performing the deeds, and conduct in a truthful way, with honesty, as per requirement of the expected role, to be played on the occasion. Correct and truthful behaviour is referred as performance of *Karma* as per *Dharma*, which would be rewarding, to rise up the scale or ladder, in each birth, to attain *Moksha*.

There does not appear to be discussion about the concept of Soul in Ramayan. In *Mahabharat*, the concept of Soul is discussed on the battlefield of Kurukshetra, while the armies of Pandavas and Kauravas, were in battle positions, awaiting the formal conch-shell—*shankhanad* signal from the eldest warrior, Bhishma, to start the war. As requested by Arjun, Sri Krishna, the charioteer stationed his chariot at the centre of the battlefield, and sought Arjun to have a look at the expanse of Kaurav army led by the great warriors, like General-in- Chief (*Senapati*) Bhishma and *Guru* Dronacharya, with whom he had to wage the war. Arjun observing the warriors on both sides, could see that the close kin like grandfathers, uncles, *Gurus*, brothers, cousins, sons, and friends were the warriors on both the sides, and they would vanquish in the war. He had a remorse, that in the process to regain the rightful portion of the kingdom denied to them, there would be mass destruction and killing of the close kin, such as grandfather Bhishma, teacher-Guru, Dronacharya and the cousins, Duryodhan and his brothers. He muttered soliloquy, "Why should I commit the great sin of killing my elders, who reared me since childhood, and other kin, to get the kingdom? It is better to get killed than killing these elders. It is better to beg, than destroy the entire lineage of kin, for enjoying the pleasures of kingdom." Arjun said to Sri Krishna, "I do not want to kill these grandfathers, *Gurus*, cousins and destroy the *Kul*, for getting to enjoy the kingdom." Saying thus, he lets down the bow and arrow in the chariot, and almost collapsed to sit down, with depression and nervous breakdown. Sri Krishna, as the mentor of Pandavas, was shocked and grieved by Arjun's remarks, and tried to console him. He said, "From where have you got these remorse, while warriors are afraid of your valour and bravery? Why are you suffering from cynicism and skepticism, out of the blue? How are you suddenly talking like an imbecile and impotent person? You are no more Brihanada" Arjun said, "Oh! Keshava, I am totally confused. Please guide me". The continuing questions or the doubts expressed by Arjun, were addressed by Krishna in 18 discourses, presented as 18 chapters of *Gita*.

Briefly, Sri Krishna tells Arjun "Oh! Partha, knowledgeable and wise persons do not condole the death of a body. Body is perishable. Nobody is immortal. One who is living will have to die. Those who die have to take rebirth. The body disappears, but the soul never dies. It takes another body. As we change our clothes which are worn out, and get new ones, the soul discards a body and takes another. Soul is indestructible."

नैनंछिन्दन्तिशस्त्राणिनैनंदहतिपावकः ।
न चैनं क्लेदयन्त्यापो न शोषयति मारुतः ।।

The characteristics of Soul is also expressed thus:

"… soul is the spirit,—Him the sword cannot pierce—Him the water cannot melt—Him the air cannot dry… In its very essence it is free, unbounded, holy, pure and perfect." (Deshpande, Aruna: 2005, 32).

Sri Krishna further counsels Arjuna

> "You have to perform your duty to punish those who indulged in criminal and immoral activities, or were witness to it; did not correct it, despite having the position and authority to do so. This is your duty—*Dharma*, as a *Kshatriya*, trained to be a warrior, to bring justice to the aggrieved. Your teachers and elders who are on the other side in the army also taught you this. But they tolerated injustice—*Adharma* and did not punish or reprimand the wrong doers, including the King, who was not only physically blind but also blind to the principles of justice. As a king, following the *Rajdharma,* he was expected to punish his errant sons. Every living being has to keep on doing the work—*Karma*, commensurate to his *Dharma.* If you do not perform your duty, as a warrior from the princely family, you will be disgraced, as shirker of duties, and tacitly siding with *Adharma.* Your reputation as the greatest warrior on earth will be tarnished, for all times to come. So, rise Partha, and fight the war, as your destined duty."

The concept of body and its identity is expressed commonly, at the crematorium. When the kin of a dead person carry the body to crematorium, the record keeper asks a question, "What is the name of the body?" He does not say, 'what is the name of the person?" Usually, we refer a person by his name, or ask the name to address a person. So, a dead body loses its personal and social identity. When an adversary is killed in a fight, the winner declares that now there was no enmity. Let the body be treated with respect, as per custom of the group or community. When Sri Ram killed Ravan, he paid his respects and directed Bibhishan to perform cremation appropriate to his status and prestige. When Chhatrapati Shivaji killed Afzalkhan, who had actually come to kill him, Shivaji arranged for his burial properly, the place—*dargah* continuing to be looked after with dignity. The message has been; the body was dead, the soul was living, without any blemish.

Basham in his classic book, "*The Wonder That Was India*" has summarized the concept of Soul and its characteristics thus:

> "In whatever way the doctrine of transmigration was developed, it involved belief in the repeated passage of the soul from life to life, either for all eternity or for an inestimably long time. It linked all forms of life into a single system......Animals, insects, and even, according to some sects, plants, all lived under the same law... that even water, dust and air were filled with minute animalcule, and that these too had souls which were the same, in essence, as those of men" (1954: 242-43).
> "The Self, who is free from evil, free from old age, free from death, free from grief, free from hunger, free from thirst, whose desire is the Real, whose intention is the Real, he should be sought after, he should be desired to be comprehended.... The wind is bodiless; cloud, lightning, thunder—these are bodiless. ...There are eight virtues of the soul—compassion for all beings, patience, contentedness, purity, earnest endeavour, good thoughts, freedom from greed, and freedom from envy.... All Hindu texts teach mercy, compassion and friendliness, ... among the lists of virtues we find "desire for the welfare of all beings" (338- 339).

There is story of Nachiketa in Kathopanishad about Yama, the lord of death, who had to yield to educate a young boy, Nachiketa, about what was life after death, and blessed him granting *Moksha.*

Nachiketa's father, Vajasravas, also known as Uddalaka, organised a *Yajnya* for peace and prosperity. He decided to gift cows to the Brahmins, as a part of the ritual. Nachiketa, a boy of 8-10 years saw that the cows to be gifted were old and emaciated. He asked his father about this anomaly, and thought his father would not gain peace and prosperity by such an act. He said, "To whom would you offer me?" Father was already annoyed by his son's questioning him. He bluttered, "To Yama". Immediately, he regretted his words, but Nachiketa insisted to go to Yama. When he reached Yama's abode, he found it closed. He waited there for three days, without food and water. When Yama returned and saw this young boy waiting for him, he regretted a young guest kept starving instead of getting hospitality. Yama offered him to seek three boons from him.

The Dialogue of Nachiketa and Yama

The first boon, Nachiketa said, "I seek the welfare of my father as my first boon." Yama granted him happily.

The second boon. "Sir I desire to know how one could reach heaven where there is no sorrow, old age or death." Nachiketa did not ask this second boon for himself but for the sake of the people. He wanted everyone to learn this secret knowledge and free themselves from the sufferings.

Yama was pleased with the unselfishness of Nachiketa. Yama gave all the details of a particular sacrifice, the performance of which would take one to heaven.

As Nachiketa was an intelligent and a sincere boy with a spiritual knowledge, he could understand all that was taught. Yama was pleased with him and in appreciation, named that particular sacrifice after Nachiketa himself.

The third boon . . .

Nachiketa asked to learn the mystery of what comes after death.

Yama was reluctant on this question. He said that this had been a mystery even to the gods. He asked Nachiketa to ask for some other boon, and offered many material gains.

But Nachiketa argues that all worldly treasures and heavenly pleasures come to an end sooner or later. If not day after, after hundred years. These are not permanent means of enjoyment. He insists to get the ultimate knowledge of Self, "O Lord of Death, you have promised me the third boon".

Yama was pleased with such a young truth-seeker who had rejected the path of enjoyment and chose the path of goodness. Then Yama taught him the knowledge of the *Atman*, realizing which man attains immortality. Know the Self as lord of the chariot, The body as the chariot itself, The discriminating intellect as charioteer, And the mind as reins.

The senses, say the wise, are the horses; Selfish desires are the roads they travel. When the Self is confused with the body, mind, and senses, they point out, he seems to enjoy pleasure and suffer sorrow.

The all-knowing Self was never born, nor will it die. Beyond cause and effect, This Self is eternal.

When the body dies, the Self does not die.

One must discriminate the Soul from the body, which is the seat of desire. After death, it is the Soul that remains; the Soul is immortal.

Thus, having learned the wisdom of the Brahman from Yama, Nachiketa was freed from the cycle of births.

Nachiketa has been one of the most influential characters in Hinduism. Indian monk Swami Vivekananda said: "If I get ten or twelve boys with the faith of Nachiketa, I can turn the thoughts and pursuits of this country in a new channel. "

This forms the subject matter of one of the Upanishads called *Katha Upanishad* (google:speaking tree)+https:/www. speaking tree. in)

Jawaharlal Nehru in his book, '*The Discovery of India*' has given his idea of soul and spirit. 'What is the soul'? "He who sees the one spirit in all, and all in the one spirit, . . . must have affected life and produced that atmosphere of tolerance and reasonableness, that acceptance of free thought in matters of faith, that desire and capacity to live and let live, which are dominant features of Indian culture." (1946, 11th impression 1991, 91)

The Greek philosopher, Socrates in his dialogues with his disciples, reported by Plato, discussed the concepts of truth, virtue, and soul.

"The principle of Socrates' reform may be stated in a single sentence. It was 'to reconstruct human opinion on a basis of "reasoned truth". Conduct which proceeded from emotion, enthusiasm, impulse, habit, and not from reason, he would not allow to be virtuous. His whole teaching rested on the paradox that 'virtue is knowledge'... And conversely, if Virtue is Knowledge, Vice is Ignorance, and consequently involuntary". "Further than that, an Idea will not only not admit its opposite; it will not admit that which is inseparable from its opposite.... So life is the opposite of death, and life is inseparable from the soul. Therefore, the soul will not admit death. She is immortal, and therefore indestructible: and when a man dies his soul goes away safe and unharmed." ("*The Trial And Death of Socrates*". Translated into English by F.J. Church: Macmillan and Co. 1923, First Edition 1880, xlvi-vii-lxxxiv-xv)

Dharma: Ramayan-Mahabharat-Gita

The essence of Ramayan as truth and *dharma* has been expressed thus:

"The Ramayan first and foremost, expounds *dharma*, the Universal Law, which for every individual, translates into conquering the enemies—lust, anger and greed. In Sundar Kand, a *brahmastra*—bound Hanuman advises Ravan to return Sita or face ruin at the hands of Sri Ram. He tells Ravan that although the power to do good or evil equally stem from *dharma*, he who commits evil strikes at the root of his freedom of choice, inviting upon himself sure death—the truth which Ravan realises only too late."

"The Ramayan is as much a guide to right living for the commoner as it is for the rulers. The epic emphasises *Rajdharma,* that, rulers can never be above the law but must for ever sacrifice their personal interests, their paramount consideration being only the welfare of the state and all its citizens.... Indeed, Sri Ram is an exemplar, the *Maryada Purshottam* and his thoughts, acts and deeds are a guide to human beings effectively realising the four *Purusharths—dharma, artha, kama* and *moksha* (true faith, economic well-being, sensual enjoyment and spiritual salvation)."

(S. Ragi Simhan: Role Models, Prince of Ayodhya, Prophet of Peace; The Best of Speaking Tree, Vol. 4, 2007, 3rd, reprint, 2013: 62; Times Group Books, New Delhi)

Ramayan and *Mahabharat* are the two great Epics, which probably depict the spirit of Indian Civilisation. Ramayan covers the wide geographical area, co-terminus with the Nation-State of India. *Mahabharat* covers all the Kingdoms, north of Narmada river, who participated in the great war, amounting to widespread destruction of all the Kingdoms. *Mahabharat*, as a story or *Itihas* depicting the greed for authority and property, among the near kin, transgressing all values of morality, leading to war and violence is still prevalent. *Mahabharat* is discussed and referred in day-to-day communication by the lay people, to analyse their mundane problems and concerns. It is not uncommon that *Mahabharat* is referred in Indian Parliament to advocate the arguments. They try to find solutions by referring to *Gita*, which summarises the essence of Hindu philosophy.

According to Jawaharlal Nehru in his book '*Discovery of India*': "The *Mahabharat* contains . . . the famous poem, the *Bhagwad Gita*. . . it lays stress on ethical and moral principles in statecraft and in life generally. Without the foundation of *Dharma* there is no true happiness and society cannot hold together. The aim is social welfare, not the welfare of a particular group only but of the whole world, 'for the entire world of mortals is a self- dependent organism' .... "Innumerable commentaries on the *Gita* have appeared in the past and continue to come out . . . by Tilak, Aurobindo Ghose, Gandhi. . . . The *Gita* deals essentially with the spiritual background of human existence. . . but always keeping in view the spiritual background and the larger purpose of the universe. Inaction is condemned, and action and life have to be in accordance with the highest ideals of the age.".... "The message of the *Gita* is not sectarian or addressed to any particular school of thought. It is universal in its approach for everyone. . . it has found favour with all classes and schools." (1946, Elevanth Impression, 1991: 107-109)

Minister for External Affairs, S. Jaishankar in his book, "*The India Way: Strategies for an Uncertain World*", has advocated Indian way about diplomatic relations in the world in an ethical way.

"The *Mahabharat* is as much a tale of ethics as of power . . . . As Indians prepare for greater contributions, they must rely on their own traditions to equip them in facing a tumultuous world. . . . . Being an ethical power is one aspect of the India Way." (2020, 67)

Abid Hussain in his book '*The National Culture of India*' has commented on *Bhagwad Gita*: "The *Bhagwad Gita* is not only a commentary on but a supplement to the Upanishads. In the Upanishads the emphasis is on the theoretical aspect of religion, ... in the *Gita* on the practical approach." "Strictly speaking the *Ramayan* is not a religious poem but may be regarded as the first specimen of secular poetry. But it presents the lofty characters of Ram, Lakshman and Sita in such an attractive way that the readers are inspired with the deepest religious sentiments of love and devotion, and to them it is no less sacred than the holy books of the Hindu religion,"

> ". . . we have to look at the various aspects of the culture of an age in which religion was not merely a part of life but dominated the whole of it, social and political organizations, the sciences, fine arts, mode of living, food and dress—everything was cast in the mould of religion." (1978, Sixth Reprint, 1994: 48-49)

Currently, we find that even secular rituals like unfurling National Flag and singing National Anthem are performed ceremoniously. The traditional new year days in different linguistic regions of India are heralded ceremoniously with special foods, dances, music and colourful art work.

The great politician-philosopher-mathematician of India, Lokmanya Bal Gangadhar Tilak, has written 850 pages commentary on *Gita*, in Marathi, "*Sri Bhagwad Gita-rahasya* or *Karmayog-*

shastra", while in Mandalay Jail for six years, published in 1915. He was sentenced on charges of sedition to say in the court of law, "*Swaraj* is my birth right and I shall have it". He has discussed *Gita* as "The Hindu Philosophy of Life, Ethics and Religion." The discussion constitutes about in 588 pages, which includes the review of writings of Western social scientists like August Comte, Kant, Hegel, and Greek philosophers, Socrates and Plato. Tilak has also made comparisons with Buddhist and Christian philosophy. If Arjun was confused about fighting to kill his elders and kin, so was Hamlet in Shakespear's drama, "Hamlet" according to Tilak, about punishing his uncle-king, who usurped the kingdom after killing his father, and established relationship with his mother. Hamlet had a dilemma, as to whether to kill the uncle, who was a ruling King and a life-partner of his mother, or not. Sri Krishna has counselled Arjun, according to Tilak, to take him out of his Hamlet-psyche of "To be or not to be: that is the question," and fight the war to punish the wrong-doers. Tilak has further provided the original Sanskrit *Shlokas* of *Gita* with explanatory meanings in Marathi, which have additionally been published in a small book format, being referred by thousands of people. (1927)

As mentioned by Tilak, the first commentary on *Gita* was written by *Adya* Shankaracharya. In Marathi, the most popular commentary on *Gita* was written by *Sant* Dnyaneshwar in the 13th century. *Sant* Dnyaneshwar is addressed and referred as *'Mauli'*, that is Mother, by all the people in Maharashtra, as a tribute as an author of Dnyaneshwari, written for the lay people, in Marathi language, which they could understand. Earlier all such books of philosophy were written in Sanskrit, which required the services of Brahmin priests to interpret and explain to the common people. Knowledge of Sanskrit language became the vested interest of the Brahmins which became a source of their livelihood. Recently, Mahatma Gandhi's distinguished spiritual disciple, Vinoba Bhave has written *Gita*, with the title, "*Gitai*", in simple Marathi, as lyric poetry.

Ramayan and *Mahabharat*, both great epics, meant to punish the immoral, evil forces, by the God in their incarnated forms, such as Sri Ram and Sri Krishna, to re-establish *Dharma,* that is ideal, moral code of conduct, are different. In *Ramayan*, kin were not involved, although the step-mother, Kaikeyi was instrumental in successfully playing palace-politics for her son, without his consent. In *Mahabharat*, power game was played by the cousins, leading to great war. Sri Krishna also a distant kin of Kunti, Pandava's mother, made attempts to avoid war. Krishna's biography is entertaining, being born in a jail, brought up by foster parents. As a child, his pranks entertained mothers and grandmothers, and as a young man, as an expert fluit player, young women were attracted to him romantically. Sri Krishna is respected for his philosophy, expressed as *Gita*, for his advocacy of *Karmayoga*. Since it was advocated on the battlefield, *Karma,* in the context of the occasion, rationalised the extermination of evil forces, howsoever close kin they may be, by following the principles of justice, known as *Dharma*, or *Rajdharma* since no personal interests were at stake. Krishna rationalised war by convincing that mere killing of evil bodies did not mean committing sin, since the souls residing in the bodies were immortal, aiming ultimately to join the soul of the God. "So, perform *Karma* according to *Dharma*, without bothering about the results or fruits of *Karma.*" This philosophy serves as the practical guide to all living beings. Everybody should be involved in focused activity, commensurate with the duty expected of him. In Social Sciences, concepts of Status and Role, provide guidelines about the plural responsibilities, associated with ascribed and achieved statuses and roles.

कर्मण येवाधिकारस्ते मा फलेषु कदाचन।
मा कर्मफलहेतुर्भूर्मा ते सङ्गोऽस्त्वकर्मणि।।

This is all discussion about Soul of a body, of a living organism. When we talk about human groups, communities or nation-states, do these have a body and a soul? In the history of humanity, of nation-states, of empires, so many dynasties of kings have disappeared, and new once established. Is there any continuity amongst them? Almost all over the world, electoral democratic governance has been established, although at some places, symbolic feudal lords, are heads of Nation-states as Kings.

New religious thoughts are floated by great spiritual leaders, and people follow them over large geographical areas, across the national boundaries. What sustains these ideas and religious organizations? Within these religions, sects and cults appear, providing different interpretations to the main religious or philosophical thought. Usually, the religious groups, and sects and cults, follow endogamous marital relations. What is the meaning of Soul in the contexts of such groups? What constitutes the body of human groups and communities? What is *Dharma* and *Karma* in the context of such groups? Can Nation or a cultural-linguistic geographical entity, called as State or Province be a body-politic with a distinct personality, which could have a Soul?

Meaning of *Dharma*: Status and Role

What exactly is *Dharma*? Is it variable ? What are the parameters of variability? In *Ramayan*, conflict of *Pati-dharma* and *Rajdharma* has been portrayed. In *Gita*, Arjun is being reminded of his *Kshatriya dharma*. What does it mean?

Dharma is not religion, which may have a philosophical foundation. Many religions have founders such as Jesus, Prophet Mohammad, Buddha, Mahavir, Guru Nanak etc. What is commonly referred as Hindu religion does not have a founder, like other religions. There are philosophical foundations like Vedas and Upanishads. There are Puranas, Mythologies like *Ramayan* and *Mahabharat*. At the common man's level, this is followed in some rituals, connected with life cycle events, or with the various ceremonies and festivals.

Dharma is associated with the duties, as per one's role. *Rajdharma* is the duty of the King or those who discharge the duties of governance. What is role? Role is associated with status. Status means a position in a particular culture pattern. Certain statuses like that of father, mother, brother, husband, wife and other kinship categories are culturally defined, and continue for centuries as ideal behaviour. These statuses could be universal across humanity, according to patriarchal or matriarchal pattern of society. Continuity of human species biologically is ensured by an institution of marriage which forms the primary kin-group as family. Different families are bound in extending wider kinship relations through marriages. We find these in *Ramayan* and *Mahabharat*. In Ramayan, the families of Dashrath and that of Janak are closely knit through brothers marrying sisters in two princely families.

The statuses which one gets at birth and subsequently without any special efforts are called as ascribed status. All these statuses are assigned some roles defined by cultural traditions or patterns. A female is a daughter in her parental family, also referred as family of orientation, while daughter-in-law in her marital family, referred as family of procreation, performing different roles. There could be some occupational statuses and roles, such as a carpenter or washerman, goldsmith etc. in a village. In traditional cultures, the occupations become hereditary, that means the ascribed statuses and roles become co-terminus. Eldest son becoming the next King is an ascribed status. He may be specially trained to perform the role as a King when he would be coronated. So in ascribed status, the status comes first and the person is subsequently trained to perform the commensurate role.

In contemporary societies, when there is freedom to attain a status, such as that of Doctor, Engineer, Lawyer, Plumber, Lagislator, Judge etc., a person has to master the expected role commensurate with the acquired status. One acquires the status by way of designation, only after the proof having been given about the acquired competence of the designated role to be performed, as per the status.

Dharma refers, therefore, to the performance of ascribed roles as well as to acquired roles, to an optimum efficiency. In *Gita*, Lord Krishna is telling Arjun to perform his role as a *Kshatriya* to fight a war in the name of justice, and defeat the forces of *Adharma*. When Ram abdicated pregnant Sita, he was not performing his *dharma* as a husband but performing his role of *Rajdharma*, subordinating his personal affection for Sita, to the wishes of the people. This is a classical example of the conflict of roles. Ram was willing to surrender the role of *Rajdharma*, by surrendering his kingship. The soul is believed to ascend towards divinity in subsequent births depending upon the truthful performance of *dharma* in the present life. So, *Gita's* message to keep on performing your destined duties, that is, *dharma*, as per the assigned role, is nothing Hindu about it. It is a universal principle of truthful behaviour.

Indian Social organisation is summarised as *Varnashram Dharma.* Social structure is organised into four broad groups and have been assigned the socialy relevant duties. Brahmin *varna* traditionally have been in the occupation of teaching and priesthood. Kings have been belonging to the *kshatriya varna,* governing the kingdom and defending against foreign invasion. *Vaishya varna* looks after commerce and trade. *Shudra varna* refers to services such as carpenter, ironsmith, potter etc. It is argued that originally these *varnas* were open categories, gradually developing into sub-groups as endogamous caste groups. Agriculture remained an open category not limited to any *varna.* Such occupational division of labour ensured stability in the society. So the *dharma* of each *varna* was different as per their duties, which became hereditary. There is a classical example of *kshatriya* king, Vishwamitra, becoming a Brahmin, a Brhmarishi, by performing penance and austerities . Both Buddha and Mahavir were *kshatriya* kings.

Individual life cycle is organized according to *Ashram* system into four stages: *Brahmacharya, Grihasthashram, Vanaprasthashram* and *Sanyas,* each having associated with the duties, responsibilities and privileges. *Grihasthashram* has the longest period of life, begetting children and earning a livelihood, and looking after the persons in other three *ashramas.*

Basham has summarized about *Varnashram Dharma* in these words:

> "Often and in many contexts we read of the 'the *Dharma* of class and stage of life' (*Varnashram-Dharma*)." The

> implication of this phrase is that *Dharma* is not the same for all. There is indeed a common *Dharma*, a general norm of conduct which all must follow equally, but there is also a *dharma* appropriate to each class and to each stage in the life of the individual." (1954:137) ... The *Arthshastra*... puts the kingly duty in simple and forceful language, setting an ideal such as few ancient civilisations can boast of comparing the king and the ascetic it says . . . "The king's pious vow is readiness in action, his sacrifice, the discharge of his duty"... "In the happiness of his subjects lies the king's happiness, in the welfare of his subjects, his welfare. The king's good is not that which pleases him, but that which pleases his subjects." (1954: 89)

Culture

Different terms like Culture and Civilisation are used, sometimes as synonyms. Common people use the word Tradition—*Parampara,* discussing it at different levels, that is, traditions of a family, lineage, caste group, *varna*, or nation. *Raghukul parampara* as dynastic tradition was repeatedly invoked by Kaikeyi to blackmail Dashrath to agree to her demands and conditions.

Concept of Culture has emerged as the basic theory in Anthropology, based on the field studies of isolated communities, generally referred as tribal communities. Culture refers to 'way of life' which includes the material and non-material aspects of life, the rational, non-rational and even irrational aspects, which guide the people in their day-to-day behaviour. Culture is also understood in terms of 'hard' and 'soft' aspects. Material aspects, such as housing, dress patterns, and all kinds of technology and products, including medicinal drugs which are amenable to change easily are in the 'soft' domain. The religious beliefs, rituals, deities, concepts of morality and sin, which are referred as 'Faith' fall in the category of 'hard' aspects of culture, not easily amenable to change. People could use most modern technology continuing to have faith in their symbolic rituals, willing to sacrifice their lives to protect the faith. The universal use of mobile phones in India, in all age groups and even among the illiterate and pre-literate people does not develop scientific or rational attitudes towards aspects of life. They could continue to be superstitious.

Culture is an integrated whole, shared by a community. Culture is learnt through language, during child-rearing. Culture and Language are considered two sides of a coin. Human baby probably takes the longest period to become physically independent. Although lying in horizontal position for more than six months, the baby listens to the communication around and absorbs the ideas, which moulds the basic personality as per norms of culture. The story of Abhimanyu, son of Arjun, in *Mahabharat*, refers to Abhimanyu listening and understanding the war techniques, entering *Chakravyuha,* in the fetal stage. It could be an issue to discuss as to how is the age of life counted, from the day of conception, or the time of baby coming out of the uterus. What happens in cases of Caesarean delivery? What do the astrologers take as time of birth to prepare an astrological chart of a person?

A community is ethnocentric and proud about its culture, and tries to protect its identity. Spirit of tolerance and compassion is expressed in respecting the cultural identity of communities, which is conceptualized in Anthropological theory as Cultural Relativism. This is also expressed in Declaration of Human Rights of the United Nations. Sri Ram respected the autonomy of the Kingdom of Lanka, ruled by Bibhishan, Kishkindha by Sugreev and the area ruled by Guhak.

David Bidney has discussed the issue of cultural relativism and human rights in his paper on "The Concept of Value in Modern Anthropology":

> "Cultural Relativism" is used as a value-charged term denoting a positive, praiseworthy attitude, while "ethnocentrism" denotes a negative value incompatible with an unbiased, objective approach. . . ." The absolute

> value of truth, goodness, and beauty which men profess are thought to have only a limited, relative, historical validity for a given society and culture. Truth is God and God is beautiful and everlasting. (*Satyam, Shivam, Sundaram)*. (Kroeber, Ed., "*Anthropology Today*", 1953. 693)

Gandhi has said, "And there is no religion other than truth. Truth is Rama, Narayana, Iswar, Khuda, Allah, God…". "God is Truth and Truth is God" (*What is Hinduism*? Mahatma Gandhi, National Book Trust, India, 1994: 14, 65)

Thus, values are ideal aspects of culture, the qualities and attitudes of individuals inspired by these values are subjective aspect, physical objects such as buildings, pictures etc. in which these values are embodied would be its material aspects. Temples are physical or visual aspects, as symbols of values, like the national flag or national emblem.

Abid Hussain in the book "*The National Culture of India*" has extensively discussed about culture and values. "Culture is a sense of ultimate values possessed by a particular society as expressed in its collective institutions, by its individual members in their dispositions, feelings, attitudes and manners as well as significant forms which they give to material objects." "Culture resides in a group of human beings called society. If a certain society has or wants to have political as well as cultural unity, it is called a nation, …we have to define a nation as a group of people living of their own free will or striving to live under the same political order in the same state." (1994, 3-9)

We have the example of the newly formed nation of Bangla Desh, since people of their own free will decided to be a separate nation, not to continue as part of Pakistan.

Civilisation

In Anthropology, there is more discussion about Culture than about Civilisation, since the concept of culture developed from the field studies of isolated and pre-literate communities. However

Archaeology and Linguistics, considered to be sub-disciplines of classical holistic anthropology are dealing with the past and linked to texts, as also visible monuments of ancient origin. Western scholars thought about extinct civilisations, such as Inca, Aztec or Egyptian, Mesopotamian civilisations. They turned to study the living Indian and Chinese civilisations of ancient past having written texts.

Mandelbaum having done anthropological field studies in India has reiterated that the study of civilisation has been the natural agenda in Anthropology.

"The study of civilisation and civilized societies was part of the birth-right of anthropology and has never been relinquished. For reasons both internal and external to the discipline, anthropologists concentrated on non-literate cultures and tribal peoples. In recent years, the impetus of anthropological research in such areas as Japan and India, and on problems of civilisation and complex societies, has brought a freshet of new data and concepts into teaching."

He has made these remarks in his co-edited volume about "The Transmission of Anthropological Culture", in "The Teaching of Anthropology" for American Anthropological Association, Memoir 94, 1963, . 9). The book discusses the content of Anthropology curricula for the undergraduate and post-graduate courses, in American Universities.

David G. Mandelbaum in his paper on 'The Study of Complex Civilisations' has said thus:

> "The term "civilisation" generally means a culture which includes the use of writing, the presence of cities, and the development of occupational specialization. . . the civilisations of China, of Japan, of India, of the Arab world, of Western Europe, come to mind as examples of such complex civilisations."

Mandelbaum has quoted Kroeber—"To the student of culture, civilisations are segregated or delimited from one another by no single criterion: partly by geography, partly by period, partly by speech, religion. Government, less by technology; most of all, probably, by those activities of civilisation that are especially concerned with values and the manifest qualities of style." (Thomas William, ed., "*Current Anthropology*", 203-205)

These quotes provide initiatives to shift the central focus from anthropological studies of Cultures of pre-literate communities to the studies of 'complex civilisations', as that of India.

The politician-scholar like C. Rajagopalachari has made his own distinction between Culture and Civilisation, in the booklet "Our Culture". According to him, "Culture has more to do with behaviour and way of living than with character. . . Civilisation in the true sense of the word is the development of restraint. . . to overdo the use of his senses. . . Humility is an essential part of true culture. . . If there is any honesty in India today, any hospitality, any chastity, any philanthropy, any tenderness to the dumb creatures, any aversion to evil, any love to do good, it is due to the old faith and the old culture. . . . The Ramayan and the *Mahabharat* . . . enter into the pattern of thought, speech and action which prevail in India, Indian mythology, Indian religious rites, and Indian philosophy—these are all intertwined—can be recognised in every part of our culture. . . Our music is, practically all of it, religion, philosophy and prayer. . . . So also our dances. Our beggars go begging singing religious songs and deep philosophy, telling the people how to live. Nothing illustrates our culture so well as the songs of our vagrants and beggars." (2005:1-35). In the same booklet, the politician-scholar, K.M. Munshi has explained civilisation in the following words: "We seek the dignity of man, which necessarily implies the creation of social conditions which would allow him freedom to evolve along the lines of his own temperament and capacities: we seek the harmony of individual efforts and social relations, not in any makeshift way, but within the framework of Moral Order; we seek the creative art of life, by the alchemy of which human limitations are progressively transmuted, so that man may become the instrument of God, and is able to see him in all and all in Him." (2005: vi)

There has been discussion about the development of technology and its impact on the values which sustain cultures and civilisations. David Bidney has reported Boas's ideas differentiating the material or technological progress, making a direct and immediate impact on such absolute values as morality and religious faith. "Cultural progress was dependent upon man's rational efforts to perfect himself and his institutions. Culture or civilisation was recognised as the instrument evolved by man, under divine providence, for the perfecting of humanity. . . . Boas admitted that there had been progress in technological achievements, as well as refinement and clarification in conceptual thought, but he denied that there had been linear progress in the sphere of arts, religion, and morality" (Bidney in Kroeber, Ed., 1953: 682-688)

Ramayan has been called as mythology. It has to be conceded that the myths and mythology sustain the values and faith on which the cultural values and civilisation sustains. The myths have a positive function. "The function of myth was to validate the cultural institutions, customs, and rites of a culture, not to explain them intellectually, and to provide a common bond of social solidarity through a common faith. Thus myth was evaluated positively as having a functional, pragmatic value for a given society in facing the crises of life. . . . The function exercised by myth in primitive societies continues to be exercised by religion in contemporary civilised societies." (Kroeber, Ed. 1953: 695-96)

Rajgopalachari has reinforced this idea with reference to epics like Ramayan and *Mahabharat*, in his book on "Ramayan". "The Ramayana is not history or biography. It is a part of Hindu mythology. . . . Mythology is an integral part of religion. It is as necessary for religion and national culture as the skin and the skeleton that preserve a fruit with its juice and its taste. . . . Mythology and holy figures are necessary for any great culture to rest on its stable spiritual foundation and function as a life-giving inspiration and guide" (1996, 29th Edition: 9-10).

This provides us the evidence as to how the civilisations or basic values sustain over centuries, irrespective of technological advancement. What is true of Ramayan is also true of *Bible*, Quran or the mythical stories in Buddhist or Jain literature or scriptures. Myths develop about the heroes in contemporary times also, as about Shivaji. Rana Pratap or even about Nehru and Gandhi and Ambedkar. Such mythical stories are more prevalent about spiritual leaders like Saibaba of Shirdi or about several local shrines and *dargahs* which sustain the basic moral values.

The legend about Panna Dai in Chittorgadh, Mewar who sacrificed her baby son getting killed in front of her eyes, to save the life of baby-prince is too famous, setting an example of the ideal value of sacrifice. Now several educational institutions have been named after Panna making her immortal. The principle and value of 'Sacrifice before Self' continues to live eternally through such legends, when they get institutionalised. The legend of a Bhil tribal youth, Eklavya, from *Mahabharat*, who sacrificed his thumb, and gave as *Gurudakshina* to Dronacharya, who was actually only a mythical *Guru,* has bestowed Eklavya the identity of a noble soul. The legend lives eternally as a civilisational value, due to acknowledgement by institutionalising Eklaya schools. However, Dronacharya, an expert *Guru* in military training of the Kauravas and Pandavas, sided with *Adharma*, as a paid employee of the King, and had to be killed by his most dear student Arjun in *Mahabharat* war. Similar is the legend of Shabari, a tribal woman, in Ramayan. Shabari also has been institutionalised as public sector undertakings and schemes of welfare and development for the marginalised communities. Raising statues of heroes and leaders and constructing temples, also serve the similar function of reinforcing the moral and spiritual values, on the plinth of which civilisations sustain. Statues of Mahatma Gandhi symbolise non-violence as a value to address the issues; importance of means, not ends; as against the muscle power of war. Sri Ram's bow and arrow is a symbol protecting and defending the peace-loving people, not for attacking the innocent people and usurping their dignity and human comforts.

These legends which have become live examples for the people, become reference models for desirable and undesirable patterns of behaviour. The values get idealised and contribute to sustenance of civilisation.

Margaret Mead as an anthropologist has summarised the issue: "When studying complex societies, the historically given model, the biography of a single individual, the role played by a family. . . the study of a single community or institution—all may function in the same way." The use of living models have an advantage . . . increasing the probabilities that the derivations which are made will be "true to life." ("National Character" in Kroeber, ed., *Anthropology Today*, 1953: 653)

Irving Hallowell in his paper on "Culture, Personality and Society" has reiterated the concept of moral values thus: "A human social order, for example, is always a moral order. . . If I cannot assume moral responsibility for my conduct, how can guilt or shame arise. What conflict can there be between impulse and standards if I am unaware of values or sanctions? (in Kroeber, ed., *Anthropology Today*, 1953: 615)

Kroeber in his paper "History of Anthropological Thought" has quoted Kluckhohn. "Kluckhohn defines values as conceptions of desirables. The desirables influence selection from available modes, means, and ends of action. . . They are consistently connected with approvals and disapprovals. . . Finally Kluckhohn reviews the relation of values to attitudes, motivation, cathexis, needs, goals, acquired drives, utility, functions, sanctions, ideals, belief, and ideology". (Thomas, William ed. "*Current Anthropology*", 301)

To briefly summarise, the discussion about Values in Anthropology is central to the concept of Civilisation. These quotes from reputed anthropologists published in "*Anthropology Today—An Encyclopaedic Inventory*" edited by Kroeber (1953) clearly provides that Civilisation based on absolute Values, has to be an agenda of Anthropological studies, and not merely the studies of Cultures of Pre-literate communities. Indian Civilisation has evolved through ancient textual wisdom, passing through history, providing observable experiences of plurality and diversity, with tolerance and compassion. This is the agenda of Indian Anthropology to show the 'Indian Way' to the world.

5

Indian Civilisation

History of India

Indian Civilisation has been a subject of academic study by scholars, branded as Indologists, and who essentially had good knowledge of Sanskrit language. Prof. A.L. Basham's book "*The Wonder that was India*' emerged as a classic discussing all aspects of Indian Civilisation. He has complimented ancient India in the following statement:

> "Our overall impression is that in no other part of the ancient world were the relations of man and man, and of man and the state, so fair and humane. In no other early civilisation were slaves so few in number, and in no other ancient law book are their rights so well protected as in the *Arthasastra*. No other ancient lawgiver proclaimed such noble ideals of fair play in battle as did Manu. In all her history of warfare Hindu India has few tales to tell of cities put to the sword or of the massacre of non-combatants. To us the most striking feature of ancient Indian civilisation is its humanity." (Basham, A.L., 1954: 8-9)

Ancient Indian Civilisation has been understood by the philosophy, mythology, scriptures, astronomy, mathematics, architecture, social and religious organisation, art and music and by sacred geography including trees, hills, rivers, places of spiritual importance and systems of medicine. There is plurality and diversity, philosophy of tolerance and absorption of foreign rulers who settled here. Besides Hindu faith which is inherited by the majority of people, certain faiths like Jainism, Buddhism, Sikhism originated in India. Christianity and Islam came from outside but people following those faiths, largely follow the framework of Indian social organisation.

While this cultural idiom has been successfully used in Indian literature, visualised in films, it has not been an agenda in Indian Anthropology. The novels and stories by Sharatchandra Chatterji, Bankimchandra Chattopadhyay, Ravindranath Tagore in Bengali and such writings in Marathi or other Indian regional languages have been portrayed as films. Film directors like Bimal Roy, Satyajit Ray, V. Shantaram, Shyam Benegal, to name the few have immortalised the novels by portraying them as films. *Mahabharat* personalities continue to be portrayed in films. Visual ethnography, showing the struggles of common people, their family life, their houses, their concerns and the way they find solutions within the cultural framework is very effective and have become successful commercially. Special films have been made focusing the lives of Indian Diaspora. Life histories of hero-warriors, freedom fighters and now the biopic of living legends are also being portrayed as films. Although anthropology does not have good ethnographic monographs of socially marginalised communities like the so-called denotified or *vimukta* jatis, the autobiographies from these communities provide the ethnographic material as life histories. The British authors compiled crime ethnography by interviewing the elderly persons from the communities branded by them as 'criminal tribes'.

Swami Vivekananda has eulogized India with the following words:

> Immortal India: "If there is any land on this earth that can lay claim to be blessed *Punya Bhumi*, to be the land to which souls on this earth must come to account for *Karma*, the land to which every soul that is wending its way Godward must come to attain its last home, the land where humanity has attained its highest towards gentleness, towards generosity, towards purity, towards calmness, above all, the land of introspection and of spirituality—it is India." . . . "The little toleration that is in the world, the little sympathy that is yet in the world, for religious thought, is practically here. . . . It is here that Indians build temples for Mohammedans and Christians: nowhere else. . . . You must see that every worship is given into Him, whatever may be the name of the form; that all knees bending towards the Kaaba, or kneeling in a Christian church, or in a Buddhist temple, are kneeling to Him. . . . Differentiation, infinitely contradictory, must remain, but it is not necessary that we should hate each other; it is not necessary therefore that we should fight each other.". . . . "O India! Forget not that the ideal of thy womanhood is Sita, Savitri, Damayanti; —forget not that the lower classes, the ignorant, the poor, the illiterate, the cobbler, the sweeper, are thy flesh and blood, thy brothers. . . . I am an Indian, every Indian is my brother." (Swami Vivekananda: "*Our Motherland*": Bhartiya Vidya Bhavan, 1963; 1, 14, 57-58)

Swami Ranganathananda, in his book "*The Essence of Indian Culture*": Indian Culture: A Historic Panorama has quoted Will Durant, "Nothing should more shame the modern student than the recency and the inadequacy of his acquaintance with India. Here is a vast penninsula, one-fifth population of the earth; an impressive continuity of development and civilisation from Mohenjo-daro, 2900 B.C. or earlier, to Gandhi, Raman and Tagore. . . spiritual pantheism from the Upanishads, eight centuries before Christ, to

Sankara, eight centuries after him; scientist developing astronomy three thousand years ago. . . . wise and beneficent rulers like Asoka and Akbar. . . . minstrels singing great epics. . . . artists raising gigantic temples for Hindu gods from Tibet to Ceylon and from Cambodia to Java, or carving perfect palaces. . . —this is the India. ("*The Story of Civilisation*," Vol I: Our Oriental Heritage, 391). It has further been argued, "One of the important fruits of Indian philosophical thought was the broadening of the Indian religious outlook. The discovery of the spiritual unity of all existence, and the emphasis on spiritual realization as the goal of religion, fostered inter-religious harmony. . . . . One of the most glorious aspects of India's cultural history relates to the treatment that her states and peoples gave to the religious and racial groups which came to India as refugees.... Jews of Palestine and Zoroastrians of Iran sought shelter in India." Swami Vivekananda referred to this glorious chapter in Indian history: "I am proud to belong to a nation which has sheltered the persecuted and the refugees of all religions and all nations on the earth". . . . Romain Rolland has said, "Vivekananda's constructive genius may be summed up. He embraced all the paths of the spirit: the four *yogas* in their entirety, renunciation and service, art and science, religion and action from the most spiritual to the most practical". . . . "India's gift to the world is the light spiritual . . . Slow and silent, as the gentle dew that falls in the morning, unseen and unheard yet producing a most tremendous result." (Advaita Ashram, Ramakrishna Mission, 1965, First reprint, 2015: 5-6, 41-48)

Shashi Tharoor in his book, "*India: From Midnight to the Millennium*" has reiterated these happenings:

"Jews persecuted in the Babylonian conquest of Judea in the sixth century B. C. and Zoroastrians fleeing Islamic rule in Persia in the eighth century A. D. found refuge and established flourishing communities." . . . . "What makes so many people one people? One answer is the physical realities of the subcontinent. . . which have carved out a distinct geographical space for Indians to inhabit. A second, equally revealing answer may be found in the attitude of generations of foreigners, . . . who consistently saw the people of the land beyond the Indus,—"Hindustan—as one. Divided, variegated, richly differentiated, but one." (1997, 2000:12-13)

The great statesman-scholar of modern India, C. Rajagopalachari has expressed his ideas about Indian Culture and Civilisation, in his booklet, "*Our Culture*": "Culture has more to do with behaviour and way of living than with character. . . . Civilisation in the true sense of the word is the development of restraint . . . to overdo the use of his senses. . . Humility is an essential part of true culture . . . . If there is any honesty in India today, any hospitality, any chastity, any philanthropy, any tenderness to the dumb creatures, any aversion to evil, any love to do good, it is due to the old faith and the old culture. . . . The Ramayan and the *Mahabharat* . . . enter into the pattern of thought, speech and action which prevail in India, Indian mythology, Indian religious rites, and Indian philosophy—these are all intertwined—can be recognised in every part of our culture. . . . Our music is, practically all of it, religion, philosophy and prayer. . . . So also our dances. Our beggars go begging singing religious songs and deep philosophy, telling the people how to live. Nothing illustrates our culture so well as the songs of our vagrants and beggars." (1963: 1-35)

Another great leader and sister of Jawaharlal Nehru, Smt. Vijaylakshmi Pandit, in writing the 'Foreword' to Rajagopalachari's booklet has commented about the colonial mindset developed as a result of British rule in India.

"The word culture has been much misused and abused. . . I have not quite forgotten how some of us reached out to grasp the shadow allowing the roots which had sustained and nourished us for centuries to dry up for no better reason than to appear the "equal" of the foreigner. This period has, mercifully, passed and India is awake, alert and anxious to find her Soul again. . . . The principal values that have been the moorings of our culture have been eroded through the vicissitudes of centuries. But they have persisted and will continue to do so. . . . our culture is the one silver thread that gleams unbroken all through that has sustained our nation in its many hours of travail." (1963, ix-x)

Vivekanada has talked about the connection of past with present and future. "Ay, when a man has begun to hate himself, then the last blow has come. When a man has begun to be ashamed of his ancestors, the end has come. . . . So long as they forgot the past, the Hindu nation remained in a state of stupor, and as soon as they have begun to look into their past, there is on every side a fresh manifestation of life. It is out of the past that the future has to be moulded, this past will become the future" (Swami Harshananda: "*An Introduction to Hindu Culture: Ancient and Medieval*", Advaita Ashrama, Fifth reprint 2018—Ramakrishna Math, Banglore)

Is Indian Civilisation a Hindu Civilisation, since the ancient knowledge or philosophical treatise have been textualised in Sanskrit language? What has language, which is a medium of communication to do with religion? Is English language or even Greek and Latin languages connected to Christianity? Is Hinduism a religion? Who established Hindu religion?

Concept of Hindu

Several national leaders, scholars and philosophers have clarified on this point that the word Hindu comes from a geographical past and is a matter of semantics or pronunciation.

Jawaharlal Nehru has said: "The word 'Hindu' is clearly derived from Sindhu, the old, as well as the present, Indian name for the Indus. From this Sindhu came the words Hindu and Hindustan, as well as Indus and India". Mahatma Gandhi has attempted to define it (Hinduism): "If I were asked to define the Hindu creed, I should simply say: Search after truth through non-violent means. . . Hinduism is a relentless pursuit after truth. . . Hinduism is the religion of truth. Truth is God." . . . "Whatever the word we may use . . . for our cultural tradition, we see in the past that some inner urge towards synthesis, derived essentially from the Indian philosophic outlook, was the dominant feature of Indian cultural, and even racial, development." . . . . "The central idea of old Indian civilisation

. . . was that of *Dharma*. . . it was a conception of obligations, of the discharge of one's duties to oneself and others.". . . "in a spirit of detachment." (1991: 74-76, 87, 90)

Swami Vivekanada has reiterated the same connotation of the word 'Hindu' coming from the river 'Sindhu', which has been the entry point to reach out to river valley fertile basin. "The word Hindu. . . merely meant those who lived on the other side of the river Indus (Sindhu) . . . The word. . . covers not only Hindu proper, but Mohamaddans, Christians, Jains, and other people who live in India. . . . This mass of writing, the Vedas, is divided principally into two parts—the work portion and the knowledge portion, the ceremonial and the spiritual. . . . What is the soul?. . souls are without beginning and without end, and immortal. . . . In every man and in every animal, . . . resides the same omnipresent, omniscient soul. . . . the difference is only in manifestation. . . . That is why in India there have been such merciful ideas about the poor, about animals, about everybody and everything else"…. . "The word Hindu, by which it is the fashion now-a-days to style ourselves, has lost all its meaning, for this word merely meant those who lived on the other side of the river Indus (in Sanskrit, Sindhu) (Swami Vivekanada;"*Essentials of Hinduism*": Advaita Ashrama, 2004, 3-7)

S. Radhakrishnan, the great scholar-philosopher, who rose to become the President of India, and whose birthday on 5th September, is celebrated as the 'Teacher's Day' in India has also written about these issues.

"The people on the Indian side of the Sindhu were called Hindu by the Persian and the later Western invaders. . . . As the civilisation extended over the whole of India, it suffered many changes, but it kept up its continuity with the old Vedic type developed on the banks of the Sindhu. Mr. Vincent Smith observes, "India beyond all doubt possesses a deep underlying fundamental unity. . . that unity transcends the innumerable diversities of blood, colour, language, dress, manners, and sect" . . . "Those who tried to bring together different races in India are worshipped as the makers of the Hindu society. Rama used the aboriginal tribes in the work of civilising the South. He brought together the Aryans and the non-Aryans, and so did Kṛsna and Buddha."

While commenting about the Epic of Ramayan, Radhakrishnan has talked about the inclusiveness in Ramayan and about the ideal of monogamy practised by Sri Ram.

"The Epics relate the acceptance of new tribes and their gods into the old family circle. . . . Many tribes and races had mystic animals, and when the tribes entered the Hindu society the animals which followed them were made vehicles and companions of gods. One of them is mounted on the peacock, another on the swan, a third is carried by the bull, and a fourth by the goat. The enlistment of Hanuman in the service of Rama signifies the meeting point of early nature worship and later theism". (Radhakrishnan: *The Hindu View of Life*, Allen and Unwin. 1927-54, ninth impression, 39, 97)

From these quotes taken from the leaders and scholars of contemporary India, whose ideas continue to guide the march of India, after breaking the shackles of colonialism and colonial mindset, linking the ancient and modern India, the Soul of India taking rebirths; it is quite clear that what is termed as Hindu religion or philosophy is the Indian mind. There is no godman who established Hindu religion. The term 'Sanatan Dharma' could not gain currency in India. So, majority of Indian people who follow certain life cycle rituals, worship the deities, such as Vishnu in the form of Sri Ram and Sri Krishna, or the formless Shankar or Mahadev, symbolised as *Pindi* and mother goddess with names as Durga, Laxmi, Saraswati, are referred as Hindu. There are national level pilgrimage centres, such as Badrinth-Kedarnath, Jagannath Puri, Rameshwaram, Dwarka. Now the Tirupati Balaji, or Shirdi for Sai, have attained national importance. There are Gurdwaras, such as at Amritsar, Nanded; Churches and Mosques—*Masjids,* located in different parts of India, which are visited by the devotees, as sacred pilgrimage centres. There are sacred Shiva temples called as *Jyotirlingas* or special temples of Ganesh, called as *Ashtavinayak*, which are considered very sacred. There are pilgrimage centres of the Jains and Buddhists. Bodh-Gaya, Sarnath or Sanchi are international pilgrimage centres of the Buddhists. There are several smaller shrines or local names of deities, such as Vithoba or Khandoba, as variants, mainly of Shiva or mother goddess, which are worshipped by the Hindus. Many Muslim *Dargahs* are visited more in large numbers by Hindus than Muslims. Indians worship stars and planets, trees, rivers, hills and mountains, and lakes. There are sacred cities like Ayodhya, Haridwar, Kashi-Varanasi, Ujjain, Ajmer, Nashik, Mathura, Kanchipuram, Madurai, Tiruvantpuram, Kanyakumari, in all parts of India. Besides there are several religious and social festivals of the all India level and regional levels.

These practices have been analysed in Anthropological literature by scholars like M. N. Srinivas, L. P. Vidyarti, Milton Singer and others. Robert Redfield has conceptualised the relationship of all India practices and local practices, as the textual Great tradition-Little tradition interaction which sustains the civilisation. It needs to be mentioned frequently that during Mughal Rule in India, the name of India continued to be Hindustan, pronounced as Hindostan. The ruling king was designated as Emperor (*Badshah*) of Hindostan. The famous Muslim poet, Allama Iqbal, has called Sri Ramchandra as Imam-e-Hind.

The artificial divide between Hindu and Muslim has been fosterd by the 'divide and rule' policy of the British rule, dividing the country into India and Pakistan. It becomes a part of military strategy to foster Hindu-Muslim identities, to hamper the development of India. The division of Pakistan in the birth of Bangla Desh, as separate nation, with its distinct cultural-linguistic identity is a testimony that the religious rituals or prayers and practices cannot be the identity of a nation. People belonging to different faiths, worshipping and following their religious or cultural practices, respecting the pluralities and diversities share a common civilisation.

Abid Hussain has addressed this issue: "It must be mentioned here that when the book was first written in Urdu, India had not yet been split into two separate sovereign states and my scope of discussion comprehended the whole of undivided India.... But I must emphasise that I regard the whole subcontinent as one cultural unit. . . not merely by common history and geography, but by a thousand inner bonds, that their total severance in the present form cannot last long and the day is not far when they will have to form at least a virtual confederation like the United States and Canada." ("*The National Culture of India*", 1956, x, Reprint 1994)

India: Civilisation

In a country like India, people across the country follow a similar yearly calendar; the new year in different linguistic regions, separated by few days in a month, celebrated with gaity, with dance, music and special foods. In Punjab, it is Baisakhi, Puthandu in Tamil Nadu, Pohela Boishakh in Bengal, Bohag Bihu in Assam, Vishu in Kerala, Pana Sankranti in Odisha, Gudipadwa in Maharashtra and Ugadi in Andhra Pradesh, Telangana and Karnataka. Some of the bigger festivals among the Hindu like Diwali, Holi, Ganeshchaturthi, Navratri in honour of goddess Durga, preceding Dusserah; *Makarsankranti* and several others are celebrated all over India, with regional nomenclatures. Similarly, the Muslims, Christians, Jains celebrate their religious festivals participated by friends and families from other religious groups. Besides, in each locality and among the group of villages, there are smaller shrines, *dargahs*, around which yearly *yatras* or *urs* are celebrated, participated by thousands of people. Major tourism in India has always been pilgrimage tourism. It is remarked that India is a land of 'Unity in Diversity', or with plural cultures.

India may be a country with maximum ancient heritage sights approved by UNESCO. There are thousands of forts, abandoned habitation sites, with remarkable architecture, huge houses owned and used in the past, by noble lords, each having its history. The variety of cuisine in India continues to be enjoyed in the homes and also available in the restaurants. The cuisines are also linked to life-cycle rituals and ceremonies, and festivals, and are different on different occasions. There are different dance forms, which are termed as classical, as also the folk varieties, enjoyed during religious festivals and ceremonies, such as at marriages. Are we talking of these pluralities and diversities in terms of a political Nation-State of India, that is, Bharat, sharing a common history and geography? Or, are we comprehending these pluralities continuing over the centuries in terms of common Culture and Civilisation?

How has Indian Civilisation developed, since when, and through what process of history?

Romila Thapar in her book on '*History of India*' has started with the legend about the origin of Earth, *Prithvi.*

There is legend about the origin of *Prithvi*, the earth ruled by king Prithu, one of the Manus, the first one directly born of the god Brahma, who was a hermaphrodite. "Prithu cleared the forests, cultivated the land, and introduced cattle-breeding, commerce, and other activities associated with a settled life."From the great floods occurring at the time of tenth Manu, God Vishnu as fish saved him, his family and seven sages of antiquity. "The human race sprang from Manu and his family . . . . The eldest of his nine sons was a hermaphrodite . . . known by a dual name . . . . . There arose the two main lines of royal descent, the Solar dynasty (*Suryavansha*) and the Lunar dynasty (*Chandravansha*)." "The Puranas trace the descent of Manu's progeny to the kings of the epic period—the royal heroes of the two epics, the Ramayana and *Mahabharat*a—and then continue to chronicle the dynasties of the historical period." (1966, reprint 1972, Penguin Books. 28)

According to Irawati Karve "Manu had two sons, Ila and Ikshvaku. Ila through Yayati, Puru, Dushyant, Bharat, had Kauravas and Pandavas of Hastinapur dynasty as the descendants. Ikshvaku as founder of Ayodhya dynasty through the descendant line had Dashrath and Ram brothers. The younger son Nimi founded the kingdom of Videha of the king Janak, whose daughter Sita was married to Ram. That is, both Ram and Sita were Ikshvaku." (*Kinship Organisation in India*, 1953. 30)

Basham has hypothesized character of the Indian people being influenced by the natural phenomena. "Many other ancient civilisations, such as those of the Greeks, Romans and Chinese, had to content with hard winters, which encouraged sturdiness and resource. India, on the other hand, was blessed by a bounteous Nature, who demanded little of man in nature sustenance, but in her terrible anger ('major disasters, such as flood, famine and plague or total dependence on monsoon') could not be appeased by human effort. Hence, it has been suggested, the Indian character has tended to fatalism and quietism, accepting fortune and misfortune alike without complaint." Basham has referred to the "kingdoms of Kosala, to the east of the Doab, and in Kasi, the region of Banares. The former, which grew up in importance with time, was the realm of Rama, the hero of the . . . great Indian epic, the Ramayan.... Another important kingdom was Videha, to the east of river Gandak and north of the Ganges.... Janak, king of Videha ...was a great patron of the hermits and wandering philosophers who propagated the new mystical doctrines of the Upanishads, and himself took part in their discussions." (1954: 3, 39-40)

It is believed that what we know of the past about India was through the texts of Vedas, Upanishads or the epics. How has Indian civilisation evolved? We have the excerpts from the following book by Gyan Swaroop Gupta: "*INDIA—From Indus Valley Civilisation to Mauryas*".

S.S. Gupta in his Foreword to the book has said, "It is an admitted fact that our rulers, both Mughals and specially British, made original efforts to distort and colour Indian history with ulterior motives and make "Indian Intellectuals"mentally slave, incapable of collecting facts impartially, arrange them in a natural order and interprete them correctly...these scholars repeat, like a parrot, that India was never one country, or one nation with one culture; it was British who tried to unite India and make it a country..... But when excavations at Mohenjodaro and Harappa stare them at face, they look bewildered.... Their condition becomes miserable when excavations have revealed that a Dwarka exists under the sea." (1999: 7)

"The contribution of the Indus Valley Civilisation to the growth and enrichment of Indian culture and society is only one of its myriad achievements.... Indus Valley Civilisation had given birth to Indian culture and religion and nurtured it. It had also influenced the whole of the surrounding world, giving life and sustenance to the people of the old world." (1999: 25)

Man has always tried to understand himself in relation to the Universe, as he could perceive and observe. To the Man, nature is God, which one could observe and experience. The theory of *Panchmahabhuta* has evolved out of this understanding of the Universe. *Panchmahabhuta* is a philosophical and spiritual concept which is also practiced in Indian systems of Medicine.

Man being the only cooking animal which has drastically impacted his biological and cultural evolution, the fire, "Agni, the god of fire is considered very important and there are hymns in honour of Agni. Holi festival probably is linked with igniting new fire, ceremoniously rubbing the two sticks together at a public place and taking a stick to ignite the domestic fire in each house in the neighbourhood. In our house, in the city of Gwalior, in our childhood in 1940s, the fire in the hearth with firewood was always kept alive, covered with ash, the two or three sticks joined together, to be ignited every morning, with the start of cooking activity, including for making tea for the family, or hot water for bath.... "when they discover fire, the system of seasonal rain and realize the power of the Sun. They feel that the Fire, Sun and the one who gives rain are divine and they must propitiate them.... So these totems must be identified with these divine beings.... Bull, goat, bird, horse etc. must be identified with Fire, Sun, Rain god Indra, Wind god etc... or in close association with them as either their mounts or yolked to their chariots". In the Vedas, "A very large number of hymns are either addressed to animals and birds or to trees or plants or references to them." These are the totems in tribal society. The totems get associated with supernatural powers and elevated to the status of divinity." Trees like Pipal and Banyan are considered holy among the Hindu, Jains and Buddhists.

Among the archaeological remains found in Mohenjodaro and Harappa: "There are 3455 seals found so far. . 1159 contain the figure of Unicorn, a curious animal horse-like but having a single horn on his head, 156 contain the picture of a bull, 14 of a buffalo, 56 of an elephant, 21 of a tiger, 40 of a rhinoceros, 36 of a goat antelope, 10 of a hare, 49 of a gharial, 14 of an animal in the shape of fish, 1 of a tortoise, 1 of a frog, 10 of a serpant, 4 of birds in flight, 34 of a tree generally within a railing or on a platform." Were these totems subsequently associated with supernatural beings, such as Sun-god, Fire, Rain-god, Wind-god etc.? (1999: 39-42)

It is a matter of great revelation, that the concept of *Panchmahabhuta* has found evidence from the laboratory based modern sciences. Irving Hallowell in a paper 'Culture, Personality, and Society' (*Anthropology Today,* ed., A.L. Kroeber, 1953. The University of Chicago Press) has given a quote from Shapley (1950), "Considered in purely material terms, man's constitution contains no chemical elements that are not found in other animals, rocks, and even distant nebulae biologically, man is also continuous with other living things in nature. . ...We are chemically, made of nothing unusual or exotic", Shapley (1930) . "Our studies of the universe, show the uniformity of its chemical structure and generally of its physical laws. We are colloids. Our very bodies consist of the same chemical elements found in the most distant nebulae and our activities are guided by the same universal rules. The recent analyses of the chemical constitution of man, beast, rock and star have brought to light the remarkable uniformity of all chemical compositions... . We are chemically, made of nothing unusual or exotic." (Shapley, Harlow: 1930, 'Flights from Chaos', New York, McGraw Hill Book Co.) (Kroeber, Ed. 1953: 601)

These observations are commensurate with the theory of *Panchmahabhuta* on the basis of which Indian philosophical ideas of tolerance, as also the system of Medicine like Ayurveda are based. The theory is also used in Yoga and Naturopathy. Accordingly, all living and non-living objects in the universe are made of five basic elements. It means human being also is made up of the same elements as other living beings and inanimate objects like hills and rocks. No wonder, in India, natural objects such as trees, rivers, hills, rivers, and the natural phenomena such as sunlight, moon, stars and planets, wind, lightening, rain are revered and considered divine. According to one legend, in Ramayan, Ahilya defiled by Indra, was cursed by her husband, Sage Gautama, to become an inanimate rock, till Sri Ramchandra would instill life in her and purify her by touching her.

Expression and Sustenance of Civilisation

While looking into the scriptures of all religions, we find there is priestly class amongst all. "They were scholars, learned in scriptures, had knowledge of everything from medicine to crafts, even the use of arms in times of wars.... . They gave advice to kings either as priests or as *mantris*-Minister." (Gupta: 1999: 173)

Civilisation is visible through the architecture. The temples particularly in the South are marvels in architecture which has also been copied in the South-East Asian countries, such as Cambodia, Thailand, Vietnam etc.

Swami Harshananda in a book, "*An Introduction to Hindu Culture: Ancient and Medieval*" has briefly described the characteristics and contributions of ancient Indian Culture. The areas covered are philosophy, society, education, political institutions, economics, judicial system, science, fine arts and music, including dance-drama, and the Hindu culture in Asian countries. (2018, Fifth reprint: pp. 125)

"The word 'Vastushilpa' used to indicate that this science is comprehensive in scope and includes all types of building construction.... Megasthenes (300 B. C.) has given an interesting account of Candragupta's palace, fort and other structures. The stupas and pillars of Asoka. . . cave architecture, temples of Bhubaneshwar and Puri, Konark; the huge temples in the south built by Pallavas, Colas, Vijaynagar kings, Gomateshwar and several others as the exquisite carvings in stone." (2018: 63)

Similar is the case of system of medicine such as Ayurveda —even *Vriksh, Gaja or Ashva Ayurveda* . . . the process of melting or purifying metals, metallurgy in general . . . mathematica and Astronomy with names like Aryabhata, Brahmagupta, Ramanujam and even Bal Gangadhar Tilak are but few names. The fine arts, music and dance connected with spirituality and temples had attained excellence. Some of the well-known dance traditions; Bharat-natya, Kathak, Kathakkali, Kuchipudi, Manipuri, Odisi-natya, Sattriya-natya. Yakshgana, (2018: 87)

Besides, there are several folk dance traditions in various geographical regions, besides the folk dances of the tribal groups; Bhangra—Punjab; Garba—Gujarat, Ghamar—Rajasthan, Holi—Manipur, Kolata—Karnatak, Ludi—Punjab, Pangi—Himachal Pradesh; Suggi-kunita—Karnatak; Lavni—Maharashtra etc. There are Naga dances, Varli dance and art; Bhil Holi dances etc. There is Natyashastra of Bharat. Drama as known from Kalidas and Bhavbhuti are well-known. Ramayan presented in a drama format as Ramlila is very popular.

Arts: "Nearly all the artistic remains of ancient India are of religious nature, or were made for religious purposes" (Basham, 1954:346): Temples, particularly in the south, promoted by Pallava and Chalukya kings, such as at Mamallapuram and Kanchi. Under Chola dynasty, the great Siva temple at Tanjore, the Pandyan style is evident at Madurai and at Srirangam; the temples at Konark and Jagannath at Puri, Khajuraho, the Jain temples at Mount Abu, Stupas; Cave temples: carvings and sculpture. Another art is about paintings, such as the cave paintings at Ajanta, or in the palaces and homes of the rich; the music and dance, linked to religion and to festivals, including folk music and dances. The literature, besides the epics, Ramayan and *Mahabharat*, had such classics from Kalidas and Bhavbhuti.

Abid Hussain in his book, "*The National Cultue of India*" (1994), has continued with such illustrations.

"India's cultural history of several thousand years shows that the subtle but strong thread of unity which runs through the infinite multiplicity of her life, was not woven by stress or pressure of power groups but the vision of seers, the vigil of saints, the speculation of philosophers and the imagination of poets and artists, and that these are the only means which can be used to make this national unity wider, stronger and more lasting."…. "The great scholars…. occupy a high place in the history of science not only of India but of the whole world. The researches of Aryabhatta, Varahmihira and Brahmgupta in mathematics and astronomy, of Charak and Susruta in medicine, guided scientists in other lands for centuries and exercised a direct influence on scientific thought of Arab and other Islamic countries, and, indirectly, on Europe."

"The Rajput courts became centres of art, literature, poetry and drama. Raja Bhoj of Malwa, Raja Lakshman Sen of Bengal—patron of Jaydeva—author of *Geet Govinda*. The kings were the patrons of such art. We have examples of classic literature such as from Kalidas—*Shakuntala, Raghuvansa, Kumarsambhava, Meghduta*; Bhavbhuti—three plays *Maltimadhava, Mahavircharita,* and *Uttarramcharita*; poet Bhartihari.

Despite Muslim rule, "One of the most powerful factors which contributed to the reconciliation (between the Hindus and Muslims) was the historic mediating role played by the Muslim Sufis and Hindu saints of the Bhakti school". Examples: Ramanuja-Ramananda, Kabir, Guru Nanak Chaitanya; Namdeo, Tukaram, Thyagraj, Mirabai and several others.

About the patronage to be offered by the king, Abul-Fazl, Akbar's friend, philosopher and guide writes in Ain-I-Akbari: "The king should be above all religious differences and should see that religious considerations do not come in the way of the duty which he owes to every class and community. Under his all-embracing care everyone should find peace and happiness so that the benefits conferred by the shadow of God are universal"…. "The Atharva-Ved and Ramayan were translated into Persian by Mulla Abdul Kadir Badaoni in cooperation with a Hindu *pundit*. Later several translations of the Ramayana were made in Persian prose and poetry by Hindus."

"In eastern India, the state of religion is entirely different. In the beginning of the 6th century B. C. the area produced two great world teachers, the Mahavir and the Buddha and two world religions, Jainism and Buddhism." The information about Ashoka who spread Buddhism in south-east Asia, is available through 14 rock Edicts engraved on the rocks in various parts of the country and pillar inscriptions.

The contributions of Ramayan and *Mahabharat* have been acknowledged: "these two epics are the most precious gifts of Sanskrit and of the age which continues to mould the thinking of Hindus in India and of the people of South-East Asia including Indonesia, Thailand, Cambodia and Malaysia where despite the people not remaining Hindus, these still continue to be their epics."

Personality as Symbol of Civilisation

In Anthropology, there is considerable discussion about common personality type, emerging from common culture, termed as Basic Personality Configuration, as a result of common child rearing practices, celebration of ceremonies, ritual and festivals in a similar pattern. There may be a difference in Culture-Personality interaction in pre-literate simple societies and the complex societies with urban centres. Margaret Mead, in her paper on "National Character" has said. "When studying complex societies, the historically given model, the biography of a single individual, the role played by a single family in the industrial development of region, the study of a single community or an institution—all may function in the same way." (Kroeber, ed., *'Anthropology Today'*: 1953, 653)

Swami Harshanand has echoed similar opinion: "That an ideal civilisation-*cum*-culture can throw up an ideal person has been proved by the sage Valmiki in his celebrated work, the Ramayana. Apart from Sri Ram, the principal hero, we come across a galaxy of great persons such as Laksmana, Bharata, Hanuman, Vibhisana, Sita, Sumitra and Mandodari, as also the sages like Vashisth, Agastya and Atri." (2018: 18-19)

Following Irawati Karve's model of studying and presenting *Mahabharat* through the personalities, like Draupadi, Kunti, Karna, Bhishma, Vidur, and Krishna and some others, Ramayan could also be presented through the personalities, who continue to be ideal role models in India. It may not be judicious to think of *Maryada Purshottam* Sri Ram only. The Ram temples meaningfully and invariably have the idols of Sita, Lakshman and Hanuman. Personality of Bharat, as a role model of renunciation is exemplary. He did not mind disowning his mother, socially, for causing the death of father and heaps of grief, to Sita and Ramchandra.

Education

Nehru has written about the great educational centres in ancient India, which produced great scholars in all academic disciplines are being recognised now.

"Varanasi or Kasi and Taksasila were well-known as great centres of learning even from the 8th century B.C. Some cities like Patliputra, Vidisa and Kancipuram were called . . . as centres capable of measuring the scholarship of the savants." "The universities of Taksasila (400 B.C.), Vikramsila and Nalanda had attained phenomenal growth and fame. . . . In Nalanda university alone there were 8500 students taught by 1500 teachers with at least 100 lectures delivered per day. . . . a large number of students from foreign countries like China, Japan, Korea, Turkestan, Burma, Gandhara (Afganistan), Sumatra and Persia were attracted to Nalanda.

"A few important literary works in these languages composed during the early and medieval periods may now be cited":

Assamese: Hemasaraswati, Harihara Vip and Sankara Deva

Bengali: Mangala and the Vijaya literature

Gujarati: Narsi Mehta and Ramananda

Hindi: Tulsidas, Mira, Vidyapati and Kabir

Kannada: Kesiraj, Pampa, Ranna and Harihara, Sivasaranas and Haridasa

Marathi: Jnanesvar, Eknath, Tukaram and others

Oriya: Pancasakhas
Punjabi: Guru-Granth Sahib
Tamil: Kural of Tiruvalluvar, Tevarams and Divya-Prabandhams
Telugu: Srinatha, Potana, Vemana and Annamacarya, p. 41.

According to Nehru:

"One book of inestimable value is Kautilya's '*Arthshastra*' of the fourth century B.C., which gives details of the political, social, economic, and military organisation of the Maurya Empire.". . . In the 'Arthashastra' we are given the weights and measures which were in use in North India." The book deals with all aspects of the theory and practice of government. "The king at the time of his coronation had to take the oath of service to the people. 'May I be deprived of heaven, of life, and of offspring if I oppress you." (1991, 11th Impression:110-126)

"In the epic period we have frequent mention of some kind of forest universities, situated not far from a town or city. . . . . Banares has always been a centre of learning, and even in Buddha's day it was old and known as such. . . . In the north-west, near modern Peshawar, there was an ancient and famous university at Takshshila or Taxila. This was particularly noted for science, especially medicine, and the arts, and people went to it from different parts of India" (1991: 115). Panini, Chanakya and may be Charak were students. The Jatak stories provide accounts of sons of nobles and Brahmins travelling to Taxila. It was considered an honour to have graduated from Taxila.

According to Romila Thapar, "Apart from the university at Kanchi, which acquired fame equal to that of Nalanda, there were a number of Sanskrit colleges. In the eighth century, the *maths* (Hermitages) became popular. This was a combination of a rest house, a feeding centre, and an education centre, which indirectly brought publicity to the particular sect with which it was associated."…. "The temple was the bank, the landowner, the employer of innumerable artisans and servants, the school, the discussion centre, the administrative centre for the village, and the place for major entertainments in the form of festivals." (1972: 181,

271). Even now, the village temples perform such functions. During our anthropological field investigation, several of our community meetings are convened in the temple premises.

Bhakti

One of the important landmarks in the march and refinement of Indian Civilisation has been the Bhakti movement, the saint poets drawn from all Indian religious groups and from all levels of social hierarchy. Majority of them were actively seen during the medieval period during the Moghul rule.

Among the 'Sources of Indian Tradition', songs of Medieval Hindu Devotion, generally referred as Bhakti tradition are significant from the perspective of sustenance of Indian Civilisation.

"Besides the great intellectual and artistic achievements of Indian culture... bhakti, the devotional religion that spread throughout India and expressed itself in the regional languages... began perhaps as early as the fourth century B.C. in Tamil Nadu, in South India, but flourished from the twelfth to the eighteenth century in all regions and languages." "One fairly certain social function of the *bhakti* tradition as it developed in the different geographical regions of India was the providing of an outlet for economic and social discontent as well as for religious aspirations."... "The contributions of saints, those who adored Shiva (Nayanars) and those who sang of Vishnu, form the bedrock of Tamil culture and a most appealing part of Tamil literature... From the Tamil country bhakti singing spread to the Karnnada-speaking area, whence the spark was ignited in Maharashtra; then the Hindi-speaking areas took it up, and North India was aflame with this fervent faith." The saint-musicians and their *bhajan* halls still continue in force all over the country even in modern cities like New Delhi, Bombay, Calcutta, and Madras.... "The stories of the great hero Rama had been enshrined in the Sanskrit epic, the Ramayan, which under the inflence of *bhakti*, had been retold in regional languages, most notably by Kamban in Tamil and Tulsidas in Hindi.".... "Next to Tulsidas, Kabir is the best known of all the Hindi poets of North India.... He was a member of a low caste of weavers from near Banares, Julaha, a Muslim... Hindus and Muslims both claim him and revere his poetry for its intense devotionalism .... he has been hailed in modern India by leaders like Tagore and Mahatma Gandhi as the authentic voice of the Indian people". There are several other names like blind Surdas, Mirabai, Ravidas, Tukaram, Basavanna, in different regions of India. (1988: 342-373).

Islam in Medieval India

'Muslim mysticism in India... three great Sufi orders had migrated from Iraq and Persia into northern India: The Chishti, the Suharawardi, and the Firdausi. The tombs of the mystic-saints are still honoured by both Hindus and Muslims. The saints like Nizam ud-din Auliya and Nasir ud-din Muhammad Chiragh of Delhi besides the cultural hero like Amir Khusrau. "Akbar ordered the translation of the Atharva-Veda, the Ramayan and the Mahabharat... prohibited the killing of cows, refrained from eating meat on certain days and celebrated non-Islamic festivals."..."Dara Shikoh addressed himself to the study of Hindu philosophy and mystical practices... It was from his translations of Upanishads first that Upnishadas became known to the West, when a French version was made of Dara Shikoh's work." (1988: 465-473)

According to Romila Thapar:

> "The Sufis in India dissociated themselves from the established centres of orthodoxy often as a protest against what they believed to be misinterpretation of the Quran by the Ulema . . . the Sufi *pirs* were as much revered by the Hindus as were the Hindu *gurus* and ascetics, all of them being regarded by the Hindus in general as being of the same mould." . . . "The Islamic stress on equality was respected by the Sufis far more than by the Ulema and this brought the mystic orders into contact with the artisans and cultivators." . . . . Sufi and Bhakti thought and practice coalesced at various points. The essential

> belief in the need to unite with God was common to both.... . From the historical point of view the most significant contribution of the Bhakti movement during the period came from Kabir and Nanak. (1972: 308)

The Bhakti Movement proved to be an important landmark in the cultural history of the medieval India and ushered in the silent revolution in society brought about by a galaxy of socio-religious reformers About the time Islam made its appearance in India, a religious upheaval was in the offing. The leader of this Hindu revivalist movement was Shankaracharya, a great thinker and a distinguished philosopher. But his preaching of the doctrine of pure monoism (*Advaitwad*) being beyond the intelligence of the common people, it was left to Ramanujam in the twelfth century to revive Hinduism (*Vaishnavism*) by preaching "Bhakit"as a means of salvation.

The terms Sufi, Wali, Davesh and Faqir are used for Muslim saints who attempted to achieve development of their intuitive faculties through ascetic exercises, contemplation, renunciation and self-denial. By the 12th century AD, Sufism had become a universal aspect of Islamic social life as its influence extended over almost the entire Muslim community. Sufism represents the inward or esoteric side of Islam or the mystical dimension of Muslim religion. However, the Sufi saints, transcending all religious and communal distinctions, worked for promoting the interest of humanity at large. Sufism is the philosophy of oneness of all goodwill and religion of love of God. Sufis regarded God as the Supreme Beauty. To achieve the Beauty, one must admire it, take delight in his thought and concentrate his attention on Him only.

Religious Groups in India

Sikhism was founded by Guru Nanak Dev, the first Guru of the Sikhs, a leading personage of the Bhakti Movement during the latter medieval period. Guru Nanak Dev was born at Talwandi, now called Nankana Sahib, in 1469. Even as a child, he was given to deep thinking with no interest in worldly pleasure. At the age of thirty, he got enlightenment. Thereafter he travelled almost the whole of the country and went over to Mecca and Baghdad, preaching his message. Guru Nanak Dev believed in the Unity of God and brotherhood of man. He rejected the caste system, idol worship, blind superstitions and the Brahminic hold over the religion.

Jainism, Buddhism and Sikhism as religious and cultural systems are indigenous as developed in India. Mahavir and Buddha identified as founders of Jain and Buddhist religion were the Kshatriya kings. The Christianity, Islam, and Zorostrianism were implanted from outside, but became wholly Indian, culturally and socially. All external religious groups in daily life, function as caste groups, having been identified with occupational specializations. The Muslims are considered to be good artisans. The Jains are good in trade and commerce. Considerable Hindu mythology and influence of saint poets like Namdeo from Maharashtra find place in the religious texts of the Sikhs. Within these religious groups, there are groups and sub groups functioning like endogamous castes and sub-castes. Actually several social reform movements launched against social discrimination in Hindu Social Organisation, becoming religious cults, ended up functioning as endogamous groups. While Christianity and Islam had the support of imperial powers in India for proselytizing, the Parsis, sharing the concept of fire worship, with the Hindus, and the way they were given refuge in Gujarat by the king, have completely merged as the native Indians. The contribution of Parsis in the industrial development of India and in humanitarian work such as establishing the hospitals and educational institutions has been remarkable. The Jews having been rehabilitated in India have been good in trade and commerce and established several educational institutions and hospitals. It is surmised that Jainism and Buddhism as non-violent philosophies sprang up as reaction to large scale violence that happened in *Mahabharat* war. Emperor Ashoka took to Buddhism after the bloody Kalinga war. Akbar settled down trying to integrate the Hindu-Muslim religious doctrines, after winning the wars to establish his empire.

Buddhism although of Indian origin flourished more in South-East Asia, believed through the efforts of Ashok. Buddhism almost disappeared from India, despite the important Buddhist pilgrimage centres in India. After B.R. Ambedkar, the chief architect of the drafting of the Constitution of India, embraced Buddhism, and Dalai Lama settled in India, there is resurgence of Buddhist influence in India. The pilgrimage centres such as at Bodh Gaya, Sarnath and Sanchi-Vidisha are again flourishing.

Accrding to Basham: "India'a ancient culture did not perish before the onslaughts of the Moslims, as did that of Persia. Under the rule of some of the Delhi sultans of the Middle Ages, there were persecution, and we read of temples being razed to the ground... and at all times Hindu chiefs continued to rule in outlying parts of India, paying tribute to their Muslim overlords..... Akbar fully realized that the Empire could only stand on a basis of complete toleration.... Rajput princes and other Hindus were given high offices of state, without conversion to Islam, and inter-communal marriages were encouraged by the example of Emperor himself. (1954: 479-80)

Muslim Invasion of India

The Muslim invasions in India changed the course of Indian history. Muhanmad-bin-Qasim invaded India in 711 AD and captured Sind and Multan, but his career came to a sudden end. It was after about three hundred years that Sultan Mahmud of Ghazni, carried out as many as seventeen raids on India during the years 1000-1026 AD, mostly against Kanauj in 1018 and plundered Somnath temple in Gujarat several times.

When Muslim rule was established in India, and Muslims spread over even in rural areas, performing their traditional occupations, they became other caste groups like the Hindu occupational castes. '... the treatment of Muslims by Hindus as merely another caste; the interpenetration of Hindu customary law among Muslims in the villages; the creation of Hindu-Muslim ruling class by the Mughal emperors with a system of rank in the imperial service...

common modes of dress, the development of a *lingua franca*, Urdu, combining Hindi grammar with a largely Arabic and Persian vocabulary; the study of Hindu thought by Muslims like al-Biruni or Abul-Fazal...the syncretic religions by Kabir and Guru Nanak ...could be interpreted as 'cultural coexistence as a prelude to cultural assimilation' (Embree, Ed., "*Sources of Indian Tradition*", 1988: 382). Abul-Fazal advocated royalty as a representative and symbol of God and thought of five qualities such as—'A paternal love towards the subjects; A large heart; A daily increasing trust in God and Prayer and devotion.' (1988:426)

History *(Based on the book: The Great India by Dhirawit Pinyonatthagarn, www. ebooks. in. th/DiamondBooks)*

India has been regarded as the cradle of world civilisations and motherland of several great leaders like Lord Buddha, Mahavira, Shankaracharya, Guru Nanak, Chanakya, King Ashoka, Chhatrapati Shivaji, Vivekananda, Mahatma Gandhi, Rabindranath Tagore, B.G. Tilak, C. Rajagopalachari, S. Radhakrishnan, Jawaharlal Nehru and several others in the field of knowledge, spirituality and science.

Origin of Hinduism cannot be traced to the preaching of any particular Prophet, Saint, *Guru* or *Avatar*. It is in fact a philosophy developed over ages, Vedas and Upanishads have discussed the universal principles of Truth and *Dharma*. For the common people, it is projected through Ramayan and *Mahabharat*, including *Gita*, which has a great bearing on the Indian values and way of life.

Bhagwad Gita is among the holiest books of Hindu religion. But the discussion about concept of Soul or duty as per *Dharma* without the allurement of success as per our desire, is nothing Hindu about it. It is an ideal principle or guide for good behaviour and following our ordained duties as per our multiple roles in life. That is how, *Gita* received universal acceptance as a basic treatise on philosophy of life.

History of India as common people know, probably begins with Alexander's invasion of India, followed by Chandragupta Maurya establishing an empire. Mohenjodaro and Harappa excavations and their analysis are of recent time in the 20th century.

With its capital at Pataliputra, now called Patna in Bihar, India, Chandragupta, for the first time, unified into one strong central power. According to the accounts of Megasthnese. Chanakya/ Kautiya's '*Arthashastra*' and Vishakhadatta's '*Mudra Rakshas*' give a vivid description about the system of Mauryan administration founded by Chandragupta. The King looked earnestly to the welfare of his subjects. Kautilya lays down, "The happiness of his subjects is the happiness of the King, the good of the subjects his good. What pleases him is not good for the King."

Chandragupta's grandson, Ashoka, conquered Kalinga after a bloody war in which, as recorded in Rock Edict XIII, "one hundred and fifty thousand people were slain and much many times that number died of disease, privation and pestilence." The sight of this massive bloodshed and slaughter so deeply affected Ashoka that he vowed not to wage a war any more. He accepted Buddhism and used his vast resources for the spread of this religion both at home and aboard, in Sri Lanka and in south-east Asian countries. It was through his efforts that Buddhism became a worldwide religion. He evolved a paternalistic concept of kingship and declared: "All men are my children, and just as I desire for my children, that they may enjoy every kind of prosperity and happiness, in both his world and the next, so also I desire the same for all men." He thus founded the first welfare state of the world and took effective measures for both the moral and material welfare of his subjects. He built roads and planted tree over them, made hospitals for both men and animals, engraved principles of good conduct and religion on the rocks and pillars, and exhorted the people to lead a simple and pure life. Ashoka died in 232 BC after having ruled the country for 40 years, a period which is called the golden years without any parallel in world history.

The next important king, Chandragupta II (380 AD-413 AD), also known as Vikramaditya. He conquered the extensive territories of Malwa, Gujarat and Kathiawar and transferred his capital to Ujjain. It was most probably during his reign that Kalidas, the greatest Sanskrit poet and dramatist, as well as many other scientists and scholars flourished. The famous Iron Pillar, standing near Qutab Minar in Delhi, was erected during his reign. In fact his was the golden age of art and literature. Fa-hien, a Chinese traveller who visited India during his reign, speaks highly about prosperity and good administration of the country. Vikramaditya's son, Kumar Gupta and grandson, Skanda Gupta maintained the noble traditions established by their ancestors and upheld the principle of *Dharma*.

In the sphere of education, the well-known universities of Nalanda, Takshila, Sarnath and Ujjain attracted students from foreign countries, particularly from China. Hinduism and Jainism flourished side by side under liberal policy adopted by Gupta kings. Between the eighth and tenth century AD, a number of powerful Empires emerged in India. While the Palas dominated over the eastern and northern parts of India, the Pratihara Empire extended over the western and parts of northern India. In the south, the Rashtrakuta Empire which dominated the Deccan, had also under its control some territories of north India. Of these three, the Rashtrakuta Empire lasted the longest.

The Palas, The Pratiharas, The Rashtrakutas, The Chola Empire of the South, covered a large part of Indian peninsula as well as parts of Sri Lanka and the Maldive Islands. It was founded by a Pallava feudatory, Vijayalata, who captured Tanjore in 850 AD. The greatest among the Chola rulers were Rajaraja (985-1014 AD) and his son Rajendra I (1012-1044 AD). Under Rajaraja, the Chola kingdom grew into an extensive and well knit Empire. Rajaraja, in his career of aggression and conquest, defeated the Pandyas of Madurai, the Chera ruler of Kerala, and also invaded Sri Lanka and annexed its northern part of his Empire.

South Indian Kingdoms

South was ruled by the Cholas, Cheras, Pandyas and Pallavas. Kanchipuram and Mahabalipuram were impressive cities that the

Pallavas adorned with large Hindu temples. The Vijayanagaram and The Bahmani Kingdoms emerged during the later years of the reign of Muhammad Tughlaq and dominated southern India for more than two hundred years. The kings built beautiful capitals, magnificent buildings, promoted art and culture, maintained law and order and encouraged trade and commerce. In brief, while the northern part of India was overrun by the forces of disintegration, the southern India was witnessing an era of peace and prosperity.

The most famous king of Vijayanagara Empire was Krishnadeva Raya (1509-1529). A learned man, an enlightened ruler, and as a great builder, he built magnificent temples, constructed irrigation projects, beautified the capital and the other cities and promoted the welfare of his people.

Landmarks in Indian History

Medieval India: The Palas, The Pratiharas, The Rashtrkutas, The Chola Empire of the South.

Islam: The invasions. Moguls settled in India. (1526-1707): Babur, Akbar, Jehangir, Shahajehan etc. Bollywood films. Aurangjeb (1658-1707).

Sikh power: GuruNank Deo, 10 Gurus, Maharaja Ranjit Singh.

Marathas: Shivaji the Great, Peshwas extending Maratha Empire.

British Rule by East India Company; 1857: Mutiny, Queen's Proclamation; Empress of India.

Struggle for *Swaraj*: Social Reform movements; Tilak, Gandhi, Subhaschandra Bose, Rammohun Roy, Jyotiba Phule.

Great Indians: Categories: Enterpreneurs, Leaders, Musicians, Dancers, Painters, Film Personalities, Writers, Scientists, Doctors, Social Reformers.

Gautam Buddha, Mahavir, Nanak, Ashok, Shankaracharya, Kabir, Vivekananda, Rabindranath Tagore, J. Krishnmurty, B. R. Ambedkar.

Brief History of India

India was subjected to military conquests through north-west or through west coast trade voyages. The Moghals settled down as rulers and citizens of 'Hindostan', the Portuguese and French occupying some territories as small colonies. The East India Company took possession of the whole country of India with extended adjacent territories such as Burma (Mynmar) and Ceylone (Sri Lanka). With the process of transculturation among Hindu and Muslim, Indian culture developed in new integrated forms visible in art and architecture, music, cuisine, apparel etc. Overwhelmed by British technological, administrative and management supremacy, British education impressed the Indian intellectual class through which the concepts of democracy, equality, welfare state became the cherished goals. Freedom struggle for self rule was required to reach these goals by controlling the resources of the country owned and exploited by the British. This goal of self-rule or Independence was achieved through the sacrifices of freedom-fighters, through the combination of militant and non-violent freedom struggles. India became a Secular, Sovereign Republic, continuing to cherish the absolute values of ancient Indian Civilisation.

Indian Civilisation in South East Asia

Indian culture diffused to South-East regions not through military conquests but through poetic narrations of mythology and history as non-violent processes. It is believed that Ashok made a great contribution in the spread of Indian Civilisation to south-east Asian countries, through the medium of Buddhism. However, we find so much of Hindu architecture and art in these countries. Sanjeev Sanyal in his book "*The Incredible History of the Indian Ocean*" has discussed about the maritime trade between Tamil Nadu, Odisha with south-east Asian countries. Trade from Odisha and Tamil Nadu, Andhra, Puduchery, Bengalto South-East: Cambodia, Thailand, Vietnam, Indonesia-Bali.

"Trade links with South-East Asia led to cultural exchange. . . evidence of the adoption of the Buddhist and Hindu religions, the presence of the epics *Mahabharat* and *Ramayan*, and use of the Sanskrit language, scripts and styles of architecture." This led to rule by kings with Indian names such as Suryavarman, Yashovarman, Jayavarman, Indravarman. It is believed that Suryavarman II built Angkor Wat, the largest religious building in the world.

"Angkor Wat was originally a temple dedicated to the Hindu God Vishnu. When it was adopted to Buddhist use in later times, the main idol of Vishnu was moved out of the sanctum to a corridor near the main entrance. Visitors will find that it is still lovingly worshipped by the locals."

There are several Hindu temples in all south-east Asian countries with south Indian architectural style. The local names may have changed as also the Buddhist influence is visible. However, the extension of Indian Civilisation promoted by Ashok and south Indian kings, and promoted by close trade links, as presented by Sanyal is visible. Such links no doubt would have meaningful implications for India's foreign policy. (Sanjeev Sanyal: 2020, 76, 127. Penguin Random House, Gurgaon, Haryana, India)

There are several observable signs of the historical and living connections in south-east countries with India. "Geographical place names ...were adopted, e.g. Ayuthia the ancient capital of Thailand was named after Ayodhya, the capital of the kingdom of Rama...." "The Indian impact is understandable in terms of a more advanced civilisation meeting a less advanced one, with the elite of the latter moulding themselves on the pattern of the former.... but the local culture was visible in all aspects of life in these countries, whether it was the Javanese version of the Ramayana, where only the bare bones of Indian story have been retained, the rest being the incorporation of traditional Javanese legends. (Thapar, Romila, 1972: 165)

The current trend of several Hindu cults and temples flourishing in the West, needs analysis of the Indian civilisational values, spreading in the West. The number of Indians and persons of Indian origin are increasing in the West who are occupying important positions in industry, technology and politics. The

Western anthropologists studied Indian villages, Indian Caste System and wrote several monographs about tribal communities. The Diaspora studies were initiated but there is great potential for Indian Anthropologists to study the extension of Indian Civilisation in the West.

6

Destination

Satyamev Jayate

In the book, we have tried to address a single and simple question: Why do the people of India dote upon the story of Ramayan—*Ram Katha*, through the centuries? Despite several standard versions of Ramayan in different languages, the main story reveals to the masses, through the idols of Ram, Sita, Lakshman and Hanuman, seen in a temple. Ramayan continues to be expressed through all kinds of mainstream and folk communication media. It is not that only common people in the villages, towns and cities express their faith in Ramayan. We have Mahatma Gandhi who was greatly influenced by the values practised by Ram, and has written extensively about it. Enough to give one quote "My life is His, in Him I live. I see Him in all men, and therefore look on everyone as father, mother or son, according to his age. In the *Bhangi* (sweeper-untouchable) and the *Brahmin,* I see the same Ram and to them both I bow." (Navajivan, 1924). For Gandhi, Ram is Truth, and 'Truth is God'. Gandhiji's popular *Bhajan*, "*Vaishnav Jan To*" by Narsi Mehta from the 15th Century, asking people to 'understand the grief and sorrow of others and be compassionate to help them' is very popular. Similarly, his prayers in the evening, with the lyrics,

'*Raghupati Raghav Raja Ram, Patit Pavan Sita-Ram*', is also very popular.

Another great leader of modern India, Rabindranath Tagore, who as nature lover, took a clue from the forest schools—*Ashramas* to establish Vishwabharati University, at Shantiniketan, has said this about Rama: "In the Ramayana, a God has not cut himself down to the size of a man: a man has become God by the virtue of his many qualities" (Chandrika, "*Rama—The Human Expression of the Divine*", Vakils, Feffer & Simons Pvt. Ltd., 2017). Actually the ultimate aim of Humanity is to march towards Divinity, which is termed as *Moksha*. Rabindranath Tagore's play, 'Chandalika' about an untouchable girl giving water to Anand, a Buddhist monk, disciple of Buddha, and falling in love with him; with a desire to hold him, is very touching about human feelings and behaviour. Sri Ram's special relationship with Bibhishan, Sugreev, and Guhak, and respecting Shabari as mother, are in the same inclusive category, irrespective of socio-religious hierarchy. As seen earlier, Swami Vivekanand talking about Indian ideal values, narrated the story of Ramayan to American audience in Shakespeare Club, in California on 31 January, 1900.

Barack Obama, the former American President, was exposed to *Ramayan* and *Mahabharat*, due to his childhood in Indonesia, and he had great fascination for Mahatma Gandhi.

Swami Ramdas, contemporary of Chhatrapati Shivaji, was a devotee of Sri Ram and Hanuman. He established several Hanuman temples, to encourage valour and self-confidence. One of the saints in Bhakti movement, he has written widely advising people about the correct behaviour to be followed as a householder. In a lighter vein, he has given the contrasting characteristics of a wise person and that of a stupid person. He has advocated the aim of life: 'to be respected, with good reputation, after death'. There is a legend, that his token gift of a piece of cloth, to King Shivaji was turned into the saffron flag, of Maratha kingdom. Rabindranath Tagore has written about this event in his poem 'Pratinidhi' about Shivaji. Another poem was meant for Shivji Festival in Calcutta (Kolkata), the festival having been inspired by Lokmanya Bal Gangadhar Tilak, initiating Shivaji *Jayanti* festival in Maharashtra, to promote the patriotic spirit among the people. Shivaji's son's name was Rajaram, who ruled from Kolhapur, and the descendants continue to be respected accordingly.

Sri Ram in the people's mind is the ethnomorphic symbol of Indian Civilisation. Ram is the cultural symbol of India. Ramayan refers to the 'Journey of Virtue to annihilate Vice'. In the *Raghuvansha-Raghukul* dynasty, there has been King Harishchandra, who was tested for his honesty and truth, which amounted to his torture. His wife Taramati who had to suffer, has been listed as one of the *Panchkanya*. The first feature film in India made by the film-production pioneer, Dadasaheb Phalke, in 1913, was titled 'Raja Harishchandra'. The film was remade in 1917 with the title '*Satyawadi Raja*'. The first Marathi talkie film was made in 1932, by Master Vinayak, titled as '*Ayodhyecha Raja*', not about Ramchandra, but again about King Harishchandra. The film was later dubbed in Hindi, becoming the first double language film. So, the concept of Truth in Indian civilisation has not been portrayed beginning with Ramchandra, but with his earlier ancestors. That is how, Kaikeyi kept on blackmailing Dashrath, to act on his promises to her, lest he would be violating the honour and reputation of 'keeping the word at any cost', of his ancestral dynasty. Ram keeping his promise to go to forest for 14 years, has become a proverb, "The death shall not deter from honouring the given promise." (*Pran Jaay per Vachan na Jaay*). Another remarkable ancestor has been King Bhagirath whose untiring efforts and doggedness brought the celestial and sacred river Ganga to the Indian soil, with assistance by Lord Shiva. Ganga river is considered the most sacred river in India and is invariably referred as Mother Ganga. 'Bhagirath effort', like the term, 'war footing' has become an adjective or an indicator, to qualify the extent and intensity of effort. There are references to Ganga in *Mahabharat* also, Bhishma being the son of Ganga and King Shantanu. Thousands of girls in India have their personal name as Ganga. Sita on return trip from Lanka, during the stopover, had a purificatory bath in Ganga river. Millions of Indians yearn to take a holy dip in the Ganga river on certain religious ceremonies and festivals. As mentioned earlier, Shehnai Maestro Bismilla Khan from Varanasi, *Bharat Ratna*, declined offers to shift to Mumbai, with the remark that there was no Ganga river in Mumbai. So, the absolute values of Truth, *Dharma* and Sacrifice, are the identity of *Raghukul*. Bharat and Lakshman have also given evidence of it, while their wives suffered silently.

Having established the gold standard of moral behaviour, and pursuit of Truth and *Dharma-Rajdharma*, there have been several emperors in India, such as Chandragupta, Ashok, Vikramaditya, Rajaraja Chola, Prithviraj Chauhan, Maharana Pratap, Shivaji, Ranjitsingh, Krisnadevraya, Ahom kings, and Akbar, and several others, who having established their rule, even through wars, like Ashoka; followed the moral principles of governance. Bhakti movement has been another moral yardstick of encouraging people to follow the right, spiritual path of livelihood, in times of crises and occasional cruelty.

What rebirths have the soul of Ramayan taken?, How have the basic values of Truth and *Dharma* transmitted through centuries, with what obstacles? How do we keep Ramayan living—through temples, Music, Art, Lectures, films, personal names, place names, recreating Ramayan in parts, recreating sacred geography as tourist spots, folk music, folk art, folk tales linking to Ramayan; by remembering the kings, saints, poets, great personalities, who imbibed the spirit of Ramayan in their expressions and deeds?

Now we are visualizing the linking of the absolute values of Indian civilisation, with the emblem of the Nation, with the motto, *Satyamev Jayate*. This becomes obvious when we delve into the debates and resolutions in the Constituent Assembly, particularly about the adoption of national symbol, the National Flag.

Resolution about National Flag : In the Constituent Assembly by Jawaharlal Nehru on July 22, 1947:

> "I should like you to think that the Asokan period in Indian history was essentially an international period

> of Indian History . . . It was a period when India's ambassadors went abroad to far countries and went abroad not in the way of an Empire and imperialism but as ambassadors of peace and culture and goodwill."

Dr. S. Radhakrishnan supporting the resolution said:

> "The Asoka's wheel represents to us the wheel of the law, the wheel of the *Dharma*. Truth can be pursued only by pursuing the path of *Dharma*, by the practice of virtue. Truth-*Satya*, *Dharma*-Virtue, these ought to be the controlling principles of those who work under this Flag.... All forms of renunciation are to be embodied in *Rajdharma*. Philosophers must be Kings. Our leaders must be disinterested. They must be dedicated spirits."

S. Radhakrishnan in his 'Foreword' to the book "*The National Culture of India*" by S. Abid Hussain has again reiterated the basic value of Indian civilisation (20th April, 1955).

"Asoka in Rock Edict XII proclaims: "One who reverences one's own religion and disparages that of another from devotion to one's own religion and to glorify it over all other religions, does injure one's own religion most certainly. It is verily, concord of religions that is meritorious"—*Samavaya eva sadhuh*. Centuries later Akbar affirms : "The various religious communities are divine treasures entrusted to us by God. We must love them as such. It should be our firm faith that every religion is blessed by Him. The eternal King showers His favours on all men without distinction. This very principle is incorporated in our Constitution which gives full freedom to all to profess and practice their religious beliefs and rites so long as they are not repugnant to our ethical sense. We recognize the common ground on which different religious traditions rest." (1978, National Book Trust edition, viii)

Greek philosophers, Socrates and Plato in their dialogues about the utopian state, titled 'Republic', with their other disciples have discussed the issues of Truth and Justice.

Republic: "The nominal purpose of The Republic is to answer the question—What is Justice? The Greek word for justice also includes much more than our concept of legal or political equality; it also means righteousness, in the sense of the exercise of virtues rather than mere absence from vice, Plato's search for justice is the search for the good life, for some principle or mode of conduct by which both men and States may exploit their best natures to the fullest . . . Wisdom in the rulers, courage in the warriors, and temperance in the common citizens are to be the virtues of the State. This Utopia, Plato asserts, will not come into being "until philosophers are kings, or the kings of this world have the spirit and power of philosophy". (*Dialogues of Plato*, Pocket book, 1950: 236-37)

Continuing with the spirit of Radhakrishnan's deposition, we understand the change in governance pattern in an electoral democracy. Now, the values which were to be protected by a single person, King, with support from the wise, sage-teachers, are now replaced by division of functions of legislature, executive and judiciary, by balancing the authority and functions, to uphold the universal values of Truth and *Dharma*. Media or mass communication has emerged as the fourth pillar of democracy, as conscience keepers. Educating the public about truth is the duty of the media. But now, occasionally, the social media is functioning like spreading gossip as washerman's gossip in Ramayan, without knowing the truth about the empowered Sita in Ashokvan. In Ramayan, Valmiki educated and corrected the gossip mongering public through the musical compositions presented by the young bards, Luv-Kush.

Mahatma Gandhi undertook self-suffering fasts to curb the communal violence. Ramchandra Guha in his book, "Gandhi—the years that changed the world, 1914-1948" (2018) has given the vivid account of his fast in Calcutta (Kolkata), in the first week of September 1947. "The return of peace to Calcutta prompted Mountbatten to write to Gandhi that 'in the Punjab we have 55 thousand soldiers and large scale rioting on our hands. In Bengal our force consists of one man, and there is no rioting" (2018: 849).

The basic values of *Rajdharma* are perpetuated through oath taking by the persons occupying high public office, such as the President, Ministers, members of the Judiciary, or even witnesses in the court of law. In several countries, oath of office, is administered by the religious clergy, raising the moral value of oath, to the level of divinity. In common parlance, within a small group or family, people reinforce the truth by taking vows in the name of father, mother or child, whom one loves intensely.

In Indian history, the Moghuls settled down as rulers and as citizens of Hindutan/Hindostan, and got merged in the Varna-Caste social organisation. The British, however, captured the political and economic power in India with ease. Basham has commented about the phenomena.

"The comparative ease with which the British established their supremacy is a measure of political decadence of India at the time . . . By the end of 19th century, . . . A new generation began to realize that Hindu culture had much of permanent value, and that the slavish imitation of the West could not solve India's problems." (1954:482)

The freedom struggle, systematically launched by the educated Indians, mainly in Maharashtra and Bengal was a two pronged attack, (a) directed to oust the British rule and establish political self rule, (b) rectify the social rot of social hierarchy practicing untouchability, and exploitative treatment to women, particularly to widows, based on superstitions. Tilak started relentless fight against the British rule, through journalism, exposing their exploitation. Jyotiba Phule, Agarkar, Ram Mohun Roy, Ishwarchandra Vidyasagar, D.K. Karve and several others, in different regions in India, launched social reform movements, against social discrimination based on caste, and to empower women.

If aspersions were cast on the militant activities by the freedom fighters, for ousting the foreign rule, which was established through economic and military power, the British judicial action to punish persons like Barrister V. D. Savarkar for 50 years in life imprisonment, at Port Blair; to Tilak for six years in Mandaley, or Nehru, Gandhi and other political leaders in various jails, could not be certified, based on moral justice. Jallianwala Bagh episode killing hundreds of innocent people and brazenly justifying it, was the height of immoral and criminal act. Looting the resources of the country and inflicting famine deaths cannot be justified by any ethical principle.

Mahatma Gandhi with his South Africa experience, after returning to India and having observed the socio-political reality as guided by the liberal like Gopal Krishna Gokhale, combined the freedom struggle with his constructive programmes for social reforms. Through non-violent, ethical approach, he was successful in involving the masses in these movements.

According to Basham:

> "Mahatma Gandhi was looked by many, both Indian and European, as the epitome of Hindu tradition.... Gandhi believed in the fundamentals of his ancient culture, but his passionate love of the underdog and his antipathy to caste...championing of women's rights is the result of Western influence." Basham further ascertains, " Hindu civilisation will, we believe, retain its continuity. The *Bhagvad Gita* will not cease to inspire men of action, and the Upanishads men of thought.... In fact the whole face of India is altering, but the cultural tradition continues, and it will never be lost." (1954:483-484)

Dr. B.R. Ambedkar according to Shashi Tharoor has something similar to say about our ancient heritage. "As far back as 1949, during the debates on the draft Constitution of India, its principal draftsman, Dr. B.R. Ambedkar, had pointed out that Indian democracy was as old as its ancient village republics. India had political assemblies with elaborate parliamentary procedures at a time when most of the rest of the world suffered under despotism or anarchy.".... "The Indian adventure is that of human beings of different ethnicities and religions, customs and costumes, cuisines and colours, languages and accents, working together under the same roof, sharing the same dreams."..."That Indian mind has been shaped by remarkably diverse forces : ancient Hindu tradition, myth, and scripture; the impact of Islam and Christianity; and two centuries of British colonial rule. The result is unique, not just because of the variety of contemporary influences available in India, but because of the diversity of its heritage." (Shashi Tharoor: "*India: From Midnight to the Millennium*", Penguin Books, India 2000, 5-9)

To repeat the quote given in chapter 4: Minister for External Affairs, Sri S. Jaishankar in his book, "*The India Way: Strategies for an Uncertain World*", has advocated Indian way about diplomatic relations in the world in an ethical way.

"The *Mahabharat* is as much a tale of ethics as of power. . . As Indians prepare for greater contributions, they must rely on their own traditions to equip them in facing a tumultuous world. . . . Being an ethical power is one aspect of the India Way." (2020, 67) (Harper Collins, Noida, U.P, India, 2020)

The mind of India as it has emerged after Independence on 15th August, 1947, reflects the basic values of Indian civilisation. The Preamble to the Constitution of India, reflects the 'Objectives Resolution' moved by Nehru on December 13, 1946 in the Constituent Assembly and adopted on January 22, 1947.

Durga Das Basu in the book, "*Introduction to the Constitution of India*", (22 edition. 2015, 31, Lexis Nexis) has quoted Mahatma Gandhi's vision about "India of My Dreams" ". . . an India, in which the poorest shall feel that it is their country in whose making they have an effective voice . . . an India in which all communities shall live in perfect harmony. There can be no room in such an India for the curse of untouchability or the curse of intoxicating drinks and drugs. Women will enjoy the same rights as men." Abid Husain has also lauded Mahatma Gandhi's real mission about professing and practicing moral values in public life. "Mahatma Gandhi's political activity was only an off-shoot of his larger mission—the spiritual and moral regeneration of humanity.... He began by putting this great ideal—the realization of truth through non-violence—the pursuit of truth was to him the ultimate moral value—by achieving good ends through means which are equally good and pure . . . in every field of life—political, social or economic." (1994: 140)

McKim Marriott, an American Anthropologist with extensive experience of field research in Indian villages, participated in a series of symposia to discuss the issues about teaching of Anthropology in the American Universities. His contribution about a course on Indian Civilisation has been briefly presented here.

How does anthropology as a 'generalizing and historical science' looks at the study of Indian civilisation? According to him, a course on Indian Civilisation would require inputs from 'such disciplines as art, history, comparative religions, economics, education, geography, medicine, philosophy, social thought, and sociology'... To understand 'India's culture history', 'views of experts in the fine arts, drama, architecture, sciences and technology' are required. Being an old civilisation with wide peripheries and large internal refuge areas, India displays not only urbanites and peasants but also indigenous tribal cultures of many sorts, some of them resembling the ancestors of today's intelligentsia... because Indian civilisation is a living civilisation, portions of its complex reality can be recreated' through 'movies, performances, art exhibits, feasts, lectures by persons experienced in the culture, and much more.' So, study of Indian civilisation would require analysis from multidisciplinary perspectives. (Mandelbaum, *et al.*, 1963: 203-216)

To conclude: We had set our goal, to understand the rebirths and march of the soul of Indian civilisation based on absolute values of humanity. Understanding and appreciating the faith of Indian people, we felt people referred to Ramayan as role model, for pursuing the values of *Satya Dharma* and *Tyaga,* that is, Truth, Righteous Conduct and Sacrifice.

While people of India had first taken the historic pledge for Independence on January 26, 1930, in public meetings held all over India; on January 26, 1950, India became a Sovereign Republic, named as Republic Of India, guided by the Constitution of India. The National Emblem, representing the Lion Capital of Buddhist Asoka from Sarnath, with the motto *Satyamev Jayate*, meaning 'Truth Alone Triumphs' from *Mundaka Upanishad*, symbolizes the destination of the Soul which has been embodied in the *Ramayan*.

> **Where The Mind Is Without Fear** (A poem from *Gitanjali*)
> Where the mind is without fear and the head is held high;
> Where knowledge is free;
> Where the world has not been broken up
> into fragments by narrow domestic walls;
> Where words come out from the depth of truth;
> Where tireless striving stretches its arms towards perfection;
> Where the clear stream of reason. . .
> Into that heaven of freedom, my Father, let my country awake.

References

Basham, A.L. (1954). *The Wonder that was India*, New York, The Macmillan Co.

Basu, Durga Das (2015). *Introduction to the Constitution of India*, Lexis Nexis.

Bidney, David (1953). "The Concept of Value in Modern Anthropology", in Kroeber, Ed., *Anthropology Today*, University of Chicago.

Chaturvedi, Dwarkaprasad Sharma (1927). *Valmiki Ramayan* (Sanskrit with Hindi translation), Allahabad, Ramnarayanlal Publication.

Church, F.J. (1923). "The Trial and Death of Socrates", London, Macmillan and Co. Ltd.

Childe, Gordon (1953), "Old World Prehistory: Neolithic" in Kroeber, Ed., *Anthropology Today*, University of Chicago.

Debroy, Bibek (2017). (Translation). *The Valmiki Ramayan* (3 Vols.), Gurugram, Haryana, Penguin Random House India Pvt. Ltd.

Deshpande, Aruna (2005). *India: a divine destination*, New Delhi, Crest Publishing House.

Eknath, Sri, *Bhavartha Ramayan* (Sanskrit–Marathi), Pune-Mumbai, Saraswati Book Distributers.

Embree, Ainslie T. (1992). *Sources of Indian Tradition*, New Delhi, Penguin Books (P) Ltd.

Gandhi, Mahatma (1994). *What is Hinduism?* New Delhi, National Book Trust, India.

Guha, Ramchandra (2018). *Gandhi: The years that changed the world, 1914-1948*, Gurgaon, Haryana, India, Penguin Random House India Pvt. Ltd.

Gupta, Gyan Swaroop (1999). *INDIA–From Indus Valley Civilisation to Mauryas*, New Delhi, Concept Publishing Co.

Hallowell, Irving (1953). "Culture, Personality and Society" in Kroeber, Ed., *Anthropology Today,* University of Chicago.

Hussain, S. Abid (1978). *The National Culture of India*, New Delhi, National Book Trust of India.

Harshananda, Swami (2018). *An Introduction to Hindu Culture: Ancient and Medieval*, Banglore, Advaita Ashrama (Ramkrishna Math).

Jaishankar, S. (2020). *The India Way: Strategies for an Uncertain World*, Noida, U. P. India, Harper Collins.

Karve, I. (1953). *Kinship Organisation in India*, Pune, Deccan College Postgraduate Research Institute.

Manavalan, A.A. (Translation by Indra C.T. & Jagannathan Prema) (2021). *Ramayan: A Comparative Study of Ram Kathas*, New Delhi, Vitasta Publishing Pvt. Ltd.

Mandelbaum, David G. (1963). The Transmission of Anthropological Culture" in Mandelbaum, David G., *et al. The Teaching of Anthropology*, American Anthropological Association, Memoir 94.

Mandelbaum, David G. (1956). "The Study of Complex Civilisation" in *Current Anthropology*, University of Chicago.

Marriott, Mckim (1963). "An Indian Civilisation Course" in Mandelbaum, David G. *et al.* , *The Teaching of Anthropology*, American Anthropological Association, Memoir 94.

Mead, Margaret (1953), "National Character" in Kroeber, Ed., *Anthropology Today,* University of Chicago.

Munshi, K.M. (1951). "Kulpati's Preface" in C. Rajagopalchari, *Our Culture* (2005), Mumbai, Bhartiya Vidya Bhavan.

Mutatkar, R.K. (2020). *Anthropological Paradigm for Policy and Practice*, New Delhi, Concept Publishing Co. Pvt. Ltd.

Nehru, Jawaharlal (1991), *The Discovery of India*, New Delhi, Oxford University Press.

Pandit, Vijaylaxmi (1963). "Foreword" in C. Rajagopalchari, *Our Culture* (2005), Mumbai, Bhartiya Vidya Bhavan.

Pinyonatthagarn Dhirawit (Compiled & Edited). *The Great India*, www. ebooks. in. th/Diamond Books)

Ramakrishna, Lalita (2014). *Ancient Indian Greats*, Chennai, Sri Ramkrishna Math.

Rajagopalchari, C. (2005). *Our Culture*, Mumbai, Bhartiya Vidya Bhavan.

Rajagopalchari, C. (1996). *Ramayana*, Bombay, Bhartiya Vidya Bhavan.

Radhakrishnan, S. (1954). *The Hindu View of Life*, London, George Allen & Unwin Ltd.

Radhakrishnan, S. (1955). "Foreword" in Hussain S. Abid (1978), *The National Culture of India*, New Delhi, National Book Trust, India.

Ranganathanada, Swami (2015). *The Essence of Indian Culture*, Kolkata, Advaita Ashram, Ramkrishna Mission.

Redfield, Robert (2018). *The Little Community & Peasant Society and Culture*, Jaipur, Rawat Publications. (Indian Reprint)

Sanyal, Sanjeev (2020). *The Incredible History of the Indian Oceon*, Gurgaon, Haryana, India Penguin Random House.

Tharoor, Shashi (2000). *India From Midnight to the Millenium*, New Delhi, Penguin Books, India.

Thapar Romila (1972). *A History of India*, Vol. I, Penguin Books Ltd., England.

Vivekanada, Swami (2004). *Essentials of Hinduism*, Kolkata, Advaita Ashram.

Vivekanada, Swami (1963). *Our Motherland*, Bombay, Bhartiya Vidya Bhavan.

Index